# 汉英语言
## 对比与翻译策略

Chinese-English
Translation:
Contrastive Studies

张 云 / 著

四川大学出版社
SICHUAN UNIVERSITY PRESS

# 图书在版编目（CIP）数据

汉英语言对比与翻译策略 / 张云著. — 成都：四川大学出版社，2023.12

（西南政法大学外语学院成立25周年纪念 / 曹志建主编. 外国语言文学丛书）

ISBN 978-7-5690-3485-1

Ⅰ．①汉… Ⅱ．①张… Ⅲ．①英语—翻译—研究 Ⅳ．① H315.9

中国版本图书馆 CIP 数据核字（2020）第 015514 号

| | |
|---|---|
| 书　　名： | 汉英语言对比与翻译策略 |
| | Han-Ying Yuyan Duibi yu Fanyi Celüe |
| 著　　者： | 张　云 |
| 丛 书 名： | 西南政法大学外语学院成立25周年纪念-外国语言文学丛书 |
| 丛书主编： | 曹志建 |

---

| | |
|---|---|
| 选题策划： | 曾　鑫 |
| 责任编辑： | 曾　鑫 |
| 责任校对： | 孙滨蓉 |
| 装帧设计： | 墨创文化 |
| 责任印制： | 王　炜 |

---

| | |
|---|---|
| 出版发行： | 四川大学出版社有限责任公司 |
| 地　　址： | 成都市一环路南一段24号（610065） |
| 电　　话： | （028）85408311（发行部）、85400276（总编室） |
| 电子邮箱： | scupress@vip.163.com |
| 网　　址： | https://press.scu.edu.cn |
| 印前制作： | 四川胜翔数码印务设计有限公司 |
| 印刷装订： | 四川省平轩印务有限公司 |

---

| | |
|---|---|
| 成品尺寸： | 170mm×240mm |
| 印　　张： | 18.25 |
| 字　　数： | 379千字 |

扫码获取数字资源

---

| | |
|---|---|
| 版　　次： | 2024年1月 第1版 |
| 印　　次： | 2024年1月 第1次印刷 |
| 定　　价： | 69.00元 |

四川大学出版社
微信公众号

---

本社图书如有印装质量问题，请联系发行部调换

**版权所有** ◆ **侵权必究**

# 前　言

国学大师季羡林认为，中华文化这条长河，有水满的时候，也有水少的时候，但从未枯竭，原因就是有新水注入。"新水"之得以注入，依靠的正是翻译，后者的重要性可见一斑。

当前语言科学与人工智能的深度融合，机器翻译等语言技术逐渐成为翻译行业的重要力量，造就了当前翻译著作的持续井喷。但在这繁荣的表象之下，国内的翻译领域仍然存在诸多问题，其中一大顽疾就是翻译的质量问题，不但影响读者的阅读体验，也给翻译事业的高质量发展造成了一定阻滞。这说明，利用好现代技术的同时，也要避免过度依赖现代技术，丢了基本功和判断力。

就汉英两种语言的翻译而言，译者要学习、把握汉英翻译领域的理论知识，并进一步探索新时代汉英翻译领域的前沿问题，提升自身的辨识水平和翻译技能。遗憾的是，近年来，国内学界对于人工智能技术在翻译领域的应用投入了极大的精力，但在语言文化等基本功方面，则出现了关注度相对下降、研究相对停滞的状况，某种程度上导致了相当多的翻译人才尚不能系统、准确地辨识汉英语言文化特征，难以采用有效的翻译策略，在翻译实践中向世界展现可信、可爱、可敬的中国形象。

《汉英语言对比与翻译策略》以强调规律性和可操作性的现代翻译理论为主要基础，努力总结、传承前人的诸多优秀研究成果，同时尝试着在一些领域做了开拓式的探索，力求梳理出一个系统、透彻、生动、实用的翻译图谱，以使学习者能够循序渐进地理解、欣赏、吸收可供操作的翻译理论与技巧，形成系统、有效的翻译思路，在翻译实践中心中有数。

在介绍翻译基本理论与策略、技巧的基础上，本书较为重视商务环境下对翻译员综合运用能力的需求，也因而把一些商务翻译题材适当地融入各章节中，包括选用一些原汁原味的翻译素材，附录在每一章节的"翻译欣赏"部分中，力求呈现翻译实践的真实面貌，使学习者能够管窥各类翻译任务的常用词汇、句式和行业信息，为翻译实践工作打下牢固的基本功，使其能够在不依赖于翻译工具的情况下，及时、准确、灵活地完成各种现场翻译任务。

  好的书籍具有较好的可操作性，能够使读者受益。本书在写作过程中，也一直循着这个方向努力，力争做到条理清晰，要言不烦，让读者在了然于胸的同时，又有一定的分析思考余地。

  本书可供本科阶段和研究生阶段英语专业的学生使用，也可供其他专业对翻译有兴趣的人士使用。

  由于水平有限，兼之时间仓促，不足之处在所难免，请读者不吝指正。

2023 年 12 月　重庆

# 目 录

**第一章　汉英语言类型对比与翻译**……………………………（1）
　第一节　语言对比的意义………………………………………（3）
　第二节　综合语与分析语………………………………………（10）

**第二章　汉英词汇对比与翻译**…………………………………（23）
　第一节　静态与动态……………………………………………（25）
　第二节　抽象与具体……………………………………………（40）
　第三节　替换与重复……………………………………………（56）

**第三章　汉英句法对比与翻译**…………………………………（73）
　第一节　主语显型与主题显型…………………………………（75）
　第二节　无灵主语与有灵主语…………………………………（90）
　第三节　形合与意合……………………………………………（109）
　第四节　主次与流水……………………………………………（128）
　第五节　首重与尾重……………………………………………（138）

**第四章　汉英修辞对比与翻译**…………………………………（147）
　第一节　汉英音韵修辞对比与翻译……………………………（149）
　第二节　汉英语义修辞对比与翻译……………………………（169）
　第三节　汉英结构修辞对比与翻译……………………………（188）

**第五章　汉英语用对比与翻译**…………………………………（205）
　第一节　语用功能与翻译………………………………………（207）
　第二节　委婉语的翻译…………………………………………（221）

第六章　汉英文化对比与翻译…………………………………………（231）
　　第一节　汉英价值取向对比与翻译……………………………（233）
　　第二节　汉英审美文化对比与翻译……………………………（247）

参考文献……………………………………………………………………（278）

## 第一章
# 汉英语言类型对比与翻译

汉、英分属不同语系，在文化系统上也差异极大，将汉、英两种语言文化进行系统的对比研究则是近二十年来的一种科学探索。研究证明，对比汉英语言与文化对翻译理论工作和实践有着极大的裨益。

# 第一节　语言对比的意义

## 一、译语优势

许渊冲先生在《翻译的艺术》指出，两种文字有时可以对等，那是均势；如果不对等，那时，一种文字就有优势或处于强势，另一种文字却处在劣势或弱势的地位。具体说来，两种文字都是各有优势，各有劣势的。如以中文而论，优势是精炼、含义丰富，成语典故较多，结构有四字词组等。而就英文来说，优势是精确，逻辑思维严密，语法结构清楚，有关系代词，有大词等。再以法文而论，优势是更精确，逻辑更严密，语法更清楚，关系代词更多等，但构词不如英文灵活。而英文和法文的强势就是中文的弱势。所以比较一下三种文字，大致可以说英文和法文相比有90％处在均势，中文和英文相比有45％处在均势，中文和法文相比只有40％处在均势。因此，在翻译的时候，应该尽可能发挥译语的优势，改变劣势，争取均势。《红与黑》是法国作家司汤达的一部有名的法语文学作品，许渊冲先生曾经以其第一章的一句翻译为例，来说明这个问题：

[例1]　ST：Ce travail, si rude enapparence, est un de ceux qui etonnent le plus le voyageur qui penetre pour la premiere fois dans les montagnes qui separent la France de l'Helvetie.

E：This work, apparently so arduous, is one of the things which most astonish the traveler making his first visit to the mountains that separate France from Switzerland.

C1：这种劳动看上去如此艰苦，却是头一次深入到把法国和瑞士分开的这一带山区里来的旅行者最感到惊奇的劳动之一。

C2：这种粗活看来非常艰苦，头一回从瑞士翻山越岭到法国来的游客，见了不免大惊小怪。

比较一下法文和英文，可以看出法文用了三个关系代词。英文只用两个，二者都发挥了优势，处在均势地位。汉译文C1用了三个"的"字来译三个关系从句，但定语、状语盘根错节的偏正结构是中文的弱势，用弱势来译强势，结果得不到均势，只能处在劣势地位。汉译文C2用了"翻山越岭"这个四字词组来译原文的关系从句,而四字词组是中文的强势,所以发挥了译语的优势,取得了结果的均势,甚至可以说是以少胜多,使译文处在优势的地位。

再来看看下面两个例子:

[例2] Vast flats of green grass, dull-hued spaces of mesquite and cactus, little groups of frame houses, woods of light and tender trees, all were sweeping into the east.

一片片茫茫的绿色草原,一簇簇色泽晦暗的牧豆树和仙人掌,一群群小巧的木屋,一丛丛轻枝嫩叶的树林——一切都向东奔驰。

叠词乃汉语独有的现象。通过上例中的英汉对比,汉语叠词的魅力即刻凸显。以上汉译文中叠词的迭现不仅让读者产生听觉美感,而且还有视觉美感。"一片片、一簇簇、一群群、一丛丛"本身已足够内涵丰富,美感满溢,再读到句末的"一切都向东奔驰",这些词都被自然赋予了动感——一片片……一簇簇……一群群……一丛丛……地从眼前掠过,生动、逼真。

[例3] The native grasses and weeds, the scattered patches of gorse, contended with one another for the possession of the scanty surface soil; they fought against the droughts of summer, the frosts of winter, and the furious gales which swept, with unbroken force, now from the Atlantic, and now from the North Sea, at all times of the year; they filled up, as they best might, the gaps made in their ranks by all sorts of underground and overground animal ravagers. One year with another, an average population, the floating balance of the unceasing struggle for existence among the indigenous plants, maintained itself. It is as little to be doubted, that an essentially similar state of nature prevailed, in this region, for many thousand years before the coming of Caesar; and there is no assignable reason for denying that it might continue to exist through an equally prolonged futurity, except for the intervention of man.

A:本地的牧草和杂草,分散着一小片儿一小片儿的金雀花,为了占据贫瘠的表面土壤而互相竞争,同一年四季时而从大西洋时而从北海不断吹来的狂风斗争;它们竭尽全力来填补各种地面上和地下的动物破坏者在他们行列中间所造成的空隙。年复一年,它们总维持着一种平均的类群数量,也就是本地植物在不断的生存斗争中维持着一种流动的平衡。无可怀疑，在恺撒到来之前的几千年中，这个地区就已存在着一种基本上类似自然的状态；除非人类进行干预，那么就没有任何明显的理由来否定它能够在同样长久的未来岁月中继续存在下去。

B：怒生之草，交加之藤，势如争长相雄。各据一抔壤土，夏与畏日争，冬与严霜争，四时之内，飘风怒吹，或西发西洋，或东起北海，旁午交扇，无时而息。上有鸟兽之践啄，下有蚁蝝之啮伤，憔悴孤虚，旋生旋灭，菀枯顷刻，莫可究详。是离离者亦各尽天能，以自存种族而已。数亩之内，战事炽然，强者后亡，弱者先绝。年年岁岁，偏有留遗。未知始自何年，更不知止于何代。苟人事不施于其间，则莽莽榛榛，长此互相吞并，混逐蔓延而已，而诘之者谁耶？

严复在《〈天演论〉译例言》里提出的"信、达、雅"论，长期被中国译界奉为圭臬，上例汉译 A 便是严复本人所译的《天演论》中的一段内容。从内容上说，译文 B 中有的句子不是按字面意思直译、顺译，而是将其内涵融会贯通后进行重新组织，如若细细推敲，并未脱离原文，其传递的信息仍然是忠实于原文的。但从语言风格上说，译文 B 完全摆脱了原文的窠臼，结合译文的受众（按勒菲弗尔三因素论的说法，就是赞助人）即中国士大夫阶层的语言审美习惯，充分发挥汉语的优势，音、形、意三美俱佳，取得了优于原文的语言效果。

比如，原文三个长句组成，译文 B 按汉语习惯将它们全部拆开，省掉连接词，略去主语，译成了汉语所擅长的短句，尤其是煞费苦心地大量采用汉语独有的四字格与叠词，使得译文铿锵有力、节奏分明。再如，"夏与畏日争，冬与严霜争……或西发西洋，或东起北海……上有鸟兽之践啄，下有蚁蝝之啮伤"等整齐划一的句子络绎不绝，让我们在沉浸于音乐美之余，也享受到了对偶句整饬的形式美。又比如，最后一句"苟……则……而已"等虚词的组合，"而诘之者谁耶？"的反问，原文都没有字面上对应的表达，属于创造性的翻译，大大增强了译文的意味。

由此可见，发挥译语优势可以改变劣势，争取均势，甚至可以转弱为强，超越原文。这在难度较高的文学翻译中尤为明显。

## 二、源语优势

先来看一个例子。

[例 4] Wherever I go, my little brother dogs my footsteps.

①：无论上哪儿，弟弟总是与我形影不离。
②：无论上哪儿，弟弟都像跟屁虫一样跟着我。
③：无论上哪儿，弟弟都像小狗一样粘着我。

抛却原文形象的意译往往面临美感丢失的危险，导致译文味同嚼蜡（汉译①），而替换成汉语熟知的形象也会面临受众的审美疲劳（aesthetic weariness）（汉译②），故宜尽量保持原文形象，能直译就直译，以求获得最大化的感染力（汉译③）。

翻译的上善之境，绝非单单是发挥译语的优势。译者既要懂得在哪些情况下必须采用归化法，将生涩的源语表达化为地道的译入语表达，更要善于利用自己的慧眼，能动地衡量哪些源语独有的表达是可以引入译语中，有意识地为译入语注入新鲜血液，从而丰富译入语的表达方式，提升其活力和生机。

## 三、语言对比的意义

我们了解了翻译一定要注意译文的可读性，要发挥译入语和源语的优势。那么，译入语和源语的优势在哪里呢？

答案是对比。

对比的这种裨益是双重的：（一）汉英对比研究可以使翻译获得双语转换的对应信息，使译者了解在哪些方面存在双语转换中的契合或平行模式；（二）这种研究也可以使翻译获得非对应信息，使译者明了汉英语言在思维方式、句式结构等方面的差异，并顺应这些差异，改变英汉翻译中的欧式思维定式和汉英翻译中的中式思维定式，最大限度发挥译入语优势，适当地对句子进行重组（recasting），甚至改写（rewriting）。概括来说，只有对其同异进行充分的对比研究，才能有的放矢，合理决定直译或意译，避免译入语的劣势，发挥其优势，产生通顺、地道、优美的上等佳译。

对汉英语言进行对比分析不仅有利于外语学习和翻译实践，也有助于语言交际。通过对比分析，人们可以进一步认识英语和汉语的特征，在进行交际时，能够有意识地注意英汉两种语言不同的表现方法，从而顺应这些差异，防止表达错误及语用失误，从而达到交际的目的。

就宏观的翻译交际策略而言，尽管输出中国文化因素越来越成为中国翻译人的共识，但翻译活动，尤其是商务翻译活动毕竟要以推广效能为根本出发点，不能一味强求大规模地保留汉语世界的语言文化元素，否则就是混淆了翻译人的沟通角色。因为过于着意自身的独特性而显得与世界格格不入，非但消化不良，更有可能招致反感，带来事与愿违的负面效果，使得华文世界的文化冤死在走向世界的战场上。换言之，高明的译者既不是源语的跟班，也不是译语的奴隶，他是"两脚踏中西之文化"的，是拥有一定的裁量权的！只不过，这种"引进"与"输出"一定要控制在可接受的范围之内。

总而言之，汉、英语言与文化千差万别，通过对比分析可以帮助我们梳理汉英间的区别和联系，从而对究竟何为"信、达、雅"的译文有一个科学、系统的思路，实实在在地提供一整套可操作的翻译方法。在本阶段，我们将主要从概况、词汇、句法、修辞、语用、文化等角度，微观与宏观并举，分析汉英两种语言基本特征的不同之处，探寻相应的翻译视角与策略。

## 【翻译欣赏】

**Our Guiding Principles**
**指导原则**

We act with integrity and fairness.
恪守原则，诚实正直
We are open and collaborative, yet decisive and unified.
开诚布公，精诚合作，求同存异，勠力同心
We trust, respect and care for the well being of each other.
相互信任，相互尊重，相互关心

We leverage our diversity to achieve competitive results.
文化多元，共达目的
We encourage and recognize risktaking.
激励进取，勇担风险
We work hard to accomplish our goals and have fun…always!
敬业乐群，实现目标

**Our values**
**英特尔价值观**

Risk Taking. Quality. Great Place to Work.
勇担风险、品质超群、敬业乐群
Discipline. Results Orientation. Customer Orientation.
纪律严明、注重成效、客户至上

**Innovate**
**创新**

When we innovate,
We advance.
开拓创新，锐意进取
We take informed risks to
realize new opportunities.
知难而进，大胆创新
We seek creative ways
to solve problems.
创造性地解决问题
We embrace change and
challenge the status quo.
崇尚变革，挑战现状

**Communicate**
**沟通**

When we communicate,
We clarify.
恰当沟通，明确目标
We are open and direct.
Always.
开诚布公，坦诚相待，持之以恒

We work towards
constructive outcomes.

直面问题，理智解决
We address what's
tempting to avoid.
处变不惊，迎难而上

## 第二节　综合语与分析语

连淑能先生在《英汉对比研究》中指出，综合语的特征是运用各种形态变化（即 inflected forms，也称屈折变化）手段来表达语法关系。现代英语具有较多的综合语特征，包括单复数、时态、语态、情态、比较级、人称、词性等。例如，letter 英语表示信件的单数，letters 则表示信件的复数。英语陈述句中现在时态单数第三人称（third-person singular）要加"-s"。又如，句子以限定动词为中心，各种语法范畴在现代英语中都有体现。现代英语具有较丰富的形态标志，有较鲜明的词类区分。同时，现代英语也具有分析语的特点：形态变化并不像典型的综合语那么复杂。词序相对稳定，虚词很多，且频繁使用，因此属于从综合型向分析型发展的语言，即综合－分析语（synthetic-analytic language）。

分析语的特征是：形式制约比较弱，句法关系缺乏形态标记，主要依靠词序及虚词来表示各种句法关系。汉语是典型的分析语，词没有形态标志，位置不能随便移动，词语之间的关系主要通过安排词序及使用虚词来表达。例如，在现代汉语中，如果孤零零来看，"学习""困难""危险"这些词，很难判断其是名词、动词，还是形容词。但在下列短语中，即①"业务学习""学习业务"，②"克服困难""困难问题"，③"脱离危险""非常危险"，我们就不难看出其词性。在①组中，"学习"分别为名词和动词；②组中的"困难"则分别为名词和形容词；③组中的"危险"分别为名词和形容词。可见，汉语词性往往要通过它在句中的词序或位置加以判别。可以说词序是汉语中最重要的语法手段。

下面我们就从形态变化、语序、虚词的使用三个方面来探讨英语和汉语之间的差别及对应的翻译技法或策略。

### 一、形态变化

英语有形态变化，汉语没有严格意义的形态变化。

#### （一）形态变化类型

所谓形态变化，即词的形式变化，主要包括以下两个方面：

1. 构词形态

构词形态，即起构词作用的词缀变化（affixation），包括大量的前缀和后缀。英语的词缀灵活多变，常常一缀多义，不仅规模大，数量多，而且种类齐全。汉语利用词缀构词仍处在发展中，不论规模、数量或种类，都不及英语。

一个英语单词，在用作句子的不同成分时，必须要适时地切换词缀，如：

[例1] 铁观音的加工非常复杂，需要专门的技术和丰富的经验。

铁观音需要专门的技术和丰富的经验来进行加工，非常复杂。

The processing of Tieguanyin is very complex and requires special techniques and rich experience.

The processing of Tieguanyin, which requires special techniques and rich experience, is very complex.

The processing of Tieguanyin, with a requirement for special techniques and rich experience, is very complex.

It is very complex to process Tieguanyin, requiring special techniques and rich experience.

It is very complex to process Tieguanyin, with a requirement for special techniques and rich experience.

To process Tieguanyin is very complex, requiring special techniques and rich experience.

Special techniques and rich experience are required for the complex processing of Tieguanyin.

The requirement for special techniques and rich experience makes it very complex to process Tieguanyin.

上例说明，英语通过词形变化，可以改变词性，用来灵活组句，表达一个基本相同的意思；汉语没有词形变化，就难以用这么多的句式来表达同样的意思。英汉互译时，很多时候都要改变词性、转换词类，才能通顺地表达原意。

2. 构形形态

构形形态，即表达语法意义的词形变化。如：

[例2] 我给了他一个鸡蛋。I gave him an egg.

他已给妹妹了两个鸡蛋。He has given his sister two eggs.

我妈妈常常给我鸡蛋当早餐吃。My mother often gives me eggs for breakfast.

汉语的"我""他"没有形式变化，同一个词可以表示主格、宾格或所有格;"鸡蛋"没有形式变化,可以表示单数或复数;动词"给"也没有形式变化,可以表示现在、过去或已完成的行为。但英语对应的词 I, me, he, him, his, egg, eggs, give, gave, has given 却有形式变化。

概括而言,现代英语的形态变化主要是动词的变化和名词、代词、形容词及副词的变化,以及上述的词缀变化。这些变化有:性(gender)、数(number)、格(case)、时(tense)、体(aspect)、语态(voice)、语气(mood)、比较级(degree of comparison)、人称(person)和词性(parts of speech)等。这类变化,往往是英语初学者首先遇到的难点之一。下面这一篇应试作文,大概是该考生把自己所看过的一则故事译成英文的结果,颇能体现汉英语言在形态变化上的差异:

[例3]　　　　Nothing Succeeds Without a Strong Will

Once, a player in the NBA. He *want* to be *a succeeds player* when he was young. One day he *meet a old* star in the NBA. The "old star" *see* the young man's *mean*, *ask he* "See me tomorrow". *Second day young man get bed 4 o'clock*. Old star *take* him to the sea. *Young man* didn't know what's *the mean* for the old star. *Older say*, "go to *the deep* in the sea." *Older ask* him, "How much do you *want succeed?* *younger*: "very". The older star put the young man's head in the sea, until he *can't breath*. *Older help* him and *say*, "When you *want succeed* like you want to *breath* you'll *be succeed*." Everything *like* this.

再来看一个翻译考试题译例:

[例4] 过去几年里,移动支付市场在中国蓬勃发展。随着移动互联网的出现,手机购物逐渐成为一种趋势。18岁到30岁的年轻人构成了移动支付市场的最大群体。由于现在用手机付款极为容易,许多消费者在购物时宁愿用手机付款,而不愿用现金或信用卡。为了鼓励人们多消费,许多商店给使用移动支付的顾客打折。专家预测,中国移动支付市场未来仍有很大的发展潜力。

In few years later, mobile pay market *is develop* highly in China. *Make* by mobile Internet, shopping on the cell phone *is become* a smart thing. Youngsters in 18 to 30 become the biggest people of the mobile *pay* market. Many people *shop use* cell phone to pay money, but they don't want to use money or bank ID card, because it is easy to pay by cell phone. For dangerous people shopping for more times, many stores have a sale for thing to person who will come. Person who have knowledge from pay *thinks*, mobile pay market in China, it *is have* big idea to develop itself in the future.

这种变化甚至也让 native speaker 头疼，如：

［例5］

香港文汇报报道，美国前总统布什拥有两所名牌大学的学位，先于耶鲁大学获学士学位，后在哈佛大学获得商业管理硕士。他学历虽高，但经常犯口误，惨成笑柄，其「名言」统称为「Bushism」。

美国《*Slate*》杂志编辑韦斯伯格出版《*Bushisms*》一书，辑录无数布什「名句」，极受欢迎，在全球各国也成畅销书，以下摘录数句：

【口误篇／文法篇】

Rarely is the question asked: is our children learning?

「很少人问：孩子在学习吗？」

－「children」是复数，不能用「is」，连基本的文法都错。

They misunderestimated me.

「他们『错误低估』了我。」

－不知布什是否太心急，将「misunderstood」（误解）和「underestimated」（低估）合成新词。

Our enemies are resourceful and innovative, and so are we. They never stop thinking about new ways to harm our country and our people, and neither do we.

「敌人机敏创新，我们亦然；他们不停找新方法来损害我们的国家和人民，我们也一样。」

——后半段吓坏人，说美国不停找新方法来损害自己的国家和人民，让人啼笑皆非。

汉语没有形态变化，虽然有时可借助一些半独立的词语来表示，但多数时候是隐含在句中或上下文里的。这就给汉翻英带来很大的麻烦，可以说是难上加难。

［例6］这样的风气的民众是灰尘，不是泥土，在他这里长不出好花和乔木来。（鲁迅《未有天才之前》）

A public like this is dust, not soil, and no lovely flowers or fine trees will grow from it. (杨宪益　戴乃迭　译)

[例7] 其既得之也，敲剥天下之骨髓，离散天下之子女，以奉我一人之淫乐，视为当然。（黄宗羲《原君》）

And when he has attained to kingship, he does not mind grinding out the bones and marrow of the people and breaking up families to labor and to serve that he alone may enjoy all the luxury and amusements of an easy living. (林语堂　译)

[例8] 而小儒规规焉以君臣之义无所逃于天地之间，至桀、纣之暴，犹谓汤、武不当诛之，而妄传伯夷、叔齐无稽之事，乃兆人万姓崩溃之血肉，曾不异夫腐鼠。（黄宗羲《原君》）

There are narrow-minded scholars who still say that the cardinal relationship between king and subject is eternal, to the extent they doubt the propriety of Tang and Wu in overthrowing their overlord tyrantsChieh and Chou, and try to sell the ridiculous story of those patriots like Poyi and Shuchi, who refused to serve a conqueror. It would seem to them that the lacerated flesh and bones of the millions of people were worth less than the mouse's head. （林语堂　译）

（二）形态变化的翻译转换

1. 英译汉

（1）英汉翻译时，原文中的时、体、语态、语气等语法上的形态变化手段可用汉语的时间指示词等词汇、句法手段来表达。

[例9] You are too concerned with what was and what will be. There's a saying: Yesterday is history, tomorrow is a mystery, but today is a gift. That is why it is called the present.

对于过去与未来，你想得太多了。俗话说得好，昨日种种昨日死，明日之事不可期，把握现在莫等待，所以我们要活在当下。

[例10] He is in the house, but he won't be.

他现在确实在我家里，但将来不会在我家里。

[例11] When I started deejaying at clubs, I wouldn't tell the managers I was deaf.

我刚开始在夜总会做打碟师的时候，总是瞒着经理们，不告诉他们我耳聋。

（2）但并非所有的形态变化都一定要在汉译时予以明示。比如，有时候，把数、时、体、语态、语气等形态变化手段译成汉语具体的数量、时间词汇等并无必要，不译反而更加简洁。

[例12] The sides fat people see are rounded blobs, usually gray, always nebulous and truly not worth worrying about. But the thin person insists. "If you consume more calories than you burn," says *one of* my thin friends, "You will gain weight, it's that simple." Fat people always grin when they hear statements like that. They know better. (Susan Britt Jordan  *That lean and Hungry Look*)

胖子所看到的各个方面是一团团难以名状的东西，通常是灰色的，黑白不甚分明，真不值得为之伤脑筋。但瘦子却很执着。"如果摄入的热量比消耗的多，"我的瘦子朋友说，"你的体重就会增加。道理就这么简单。"胖子听了这样的话，总是一笑了之。这个他们比谁都懂。（刘士聪　马会娟　译）

[例13] They will cry in your beer with you. They will put your name in the pot. They will let you off the hook. Fat people will gab, giggle, guffaw, gyrate, and gossip. They are generous, giving, and gallant. They are gluttonous and goodly and great. What you want when you're down is soft and jiggly, not muscled and stable. Fat people know this. Fat people have plenty of room. Fat people will take you in. (Susan Britt Jordan  *That lean and Hungry Look*)

他们同你一起借酒浇愁，他们凑钱买东西时会把你的名字也写上。他们会帮你摆脱困境。胖子喜欢闲聊、傻乐、狂笑、欢蹦乱跳、转来转去、爱传小道消息。他们慷慨、大方、豪爽。他们贪吃、漂亮、伟大。你心情不好时需要温柔和轻松，而不是强劲和持重。胖子懂得这个道理。他们度量大，容得下你。（刘士聪　马会娟　译）

[例14] Reuben, where were you? We were waiting for you to have dinner.

鲁本，你去哪里了？我们都在等你吃晚饭呢。

有时候，在汉语译文中加上时间指示词甚至会横生枝节，产生原文没有的歧义。

[例15] I am going to say this again: I did not have sexual relations with that woman, Miss Lewinsky.

我重申一遍,我和那个女人,莱温斯基小姐,没有发生性关系。

[例16] What he said to the American people was that he did not have sexual relations, and I understand you're not going to like this, Congressman, because you'll see it as a hairsplitting evasive answer. But in his own mind, his definition was not⋯

他告诉美国公民的是,他从未和她发生性关系。议员先生,我理解你不会喜欢这个说法,因为你会把这个看作是一种无聊的刻意回避,但他确实觉得这不叫性关系。

2. 汉译英

(1) 汉英翻译中,汉语原文中某些词汇(如时间指示词)和句法手段可免用英语的对应词汇,而改用数、时、体、语态、语气等形态变化来表达。

[例17] 二十岁那年,我就逃出了父亲的家庭。直到现在还是过着流浪的生活。(萧红《永远的憧憬和追求》)

When I was twenty years old, I escaped from my father's family, and since then I have led a vagrant life. (张培基 译)

(2) 汉英翻译中,须用心琢磨汉语原文中隐含的信息,并将未曾明示含义用英语中适当的数、时、体、情态、语态、语气等形态变化来表达。

[例18] 迷时师度,悟了自度。

WhenI was confused, you delivered me. Since my enlightenment, I am able to deliver myself.

[例19] 仿佛为探寻什么而来,然而,我永远不能寻见什么了,除非我也睡在花床的下面,土地连着土地,在那里面或许还有一种温暖的、爱的交流?(缪崇群《花床》)

I seem to have come here in search of something, but I'll never be able to find it, though except hoping that one day I will lie and sleep underneath a flowerbed where the land is one in which there is an interflow of warmth and love. (高巍 刘士聪 译)

[例20] 死生契阔,"Meet or part, live or die,"

与子成说:We made oath, you and I,

执子之手,"We shall stay hand in hand,

与子偕老。Till the end of the world."

吁嗟阔兮，Alas! So long we've parted,
不我活兮！CanI live broken-hearted?
吁嗟洵兮，Alas! The oath we swore,
不我信兮！Can be fulfilled no more!（《诗经·邶风·击鼓》刘士聪　马会娟　译）

[例 21] 昔者庄周梦为蝴蝶，栩栩然蝴蝶也，自喻适志与，不知周也。俄然觉，则蘧蘧然周也。不知周之梦为蝴蝶与，蝴蝶之梦为周与？周与蝴蝶则必有分矣。此之谓物化。（庄子《齐物论》）

Once upon a time, I, Chuang Chou, dreamt that I was a butterfly, fluttering hither and thither, to all intents and purposes a butterfly. I was conscious only of my happiness as a butterfly, unaware that I was Chou. Soon I awaked, and there I was, veritably myself again. Now I do not know whether I was a man dreaming that I was a butterfly, or whether I am a butterfly, dreaming that I am a man. Between a man and a butterfly, there is necessarily a distinction. The transition is called "the transformation of material things."（林语堂　译）

## 二、语序

英语语序比较灵活，汉语语序相对固定。英汉句子的主要成分如主语、谓语、宾语或表语的词序基本上相同。一般情况下，英汉的排列顺序都是：主－动－宾（表）。但与汉语相比，英语语序倒置的现象比较多，如：

[例 22] When I had once addressed your lordship in public, I had exhausted all the art of pleasing which a retired and uncourtly scholar can possess. I had done all that I could; and no man is well pleased to have his all neglected, be it ever so little.（让步倒装）（Samuel Johnson　*To Lord Chesterfield*）

仆本一介寒士，不求闻达于世，不善逢迎之术。前者于大庭广众之间得与阁下共语，曲尽所能，以期取悦于君，终不可得。人之竭尽绵薄，屡遭鄙夷而复能怡然自得者，鲜矣哉！（黄继忠　译）

[例 23] The notice which you have been pleased to take of my labours,

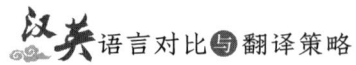

had it been early, had been kind; but it has been delayed till I am indifferent, and cannot enjoy it... (*假设倒装*) (Samuel Johnson *To Lord Chesterfield*)

阁下于拙著之锦注,若在昔年,诚不失为美意;惜于姗姗其来迟,今仆已兴味索然,难以欣赏……(黄继忠 译)

[例24] Not a finger did I lay on him. (*否定倒装*)

我从没有指责过他。

英语形态变化规则要求句中词语之间保持语法关系一致(grammatical concord),换言之,有了这种形态变化,词语之间的次序就容易灵活安排,而又保持其语法关系和表意的准确。汉语没有形态变化来确保语法关系的一致,只能按照相对固定的语序来表意,试看以下各句的翻译:

[例25] No man thinks more highly than I do of the patriotism, as well as abilities of the very worthy gentlemen who have just addressed the house.

刚才几位可尊敬的先生向全体代表发言了。对于这几位先生的爱国精神及才干,我个人比任何人都更钦佩。

[例26] I have been long wakened from that dream of hope, in which I once boasted myself with so much exultation. (Samuel Johnson *To Lord Chesterfield*)

盖仆昔时固尝陶醉于希望之美梦,今则梦醒久矣。(黄继忠 译)

## 三、虚词

英汉都有大量的虚词,但各有特点。

英语的虚词包括冠词、助动词、介词、并列连接词和从属连接词等。汉语的虚词包括介词、助词和连词等。英汉虚词都是与实词相对而言的,在句中主要起辅助和连接等作用。英汉虚词各有特色,不仅种类不同,用法也不同。对介词、并列连接词和从属连接词等,由于涉及衔接手段问题,我们将在"形合与意合"一章中另行讲述,此处只介绍英汉语中各自独有的几类虚词。

### (一)冠词

英语经常使用定冠词和不定冠词,这是英语的一大特点。用不用冠词,用什么冠词,常常有正误之分或意思之别。这是中国人学习英语的难点之一。因为汉语没有冠词,英译汉时可以省略。但有时一个冠词之差,意思大不相同,这时汉语就要用不同的词语来表达。如：

[例27] 只要流传的便是好文学，只要消灭的便是坏文学；抢得天下的便是王，抢不到天下的便是贼。莫非中国式的历史论，也将沟通了中国人的文学论欤？（鲁迅《文学和出汗》）

What has lasted is good literature, what has perished is bad literature. If you seize a country you are *king*, if you fail you are *a bandit*. Don't tell me the Chinese theory of history is going to be applied to the Chinese theory of literature!（杨宪益　戴乃迭　译）

[例28] I am never at a loss for *a word*; Pitt is never at a loss for *the word*.

我总能滔滔不绝，而皮特则是字字珠玑。

[例29] 写电视剧要比写广播剧容易一些。

It's easier to write plays for television than *for radio*.

[例30] 她打来电话时，我正在听收音机。

I was *listening to the radio* when she phoned.

[例31] 耻之一字，所以治君子；痛之一字，所以治小人。（张潮《幽梦影》）

Remind a gentleman of shame and threaten a sneak with pain. It always works.（林语堂　译）

（二）助词

汉语有丰富多彩的助词，这是汉语的一大特点。这些助词的作用，有一部分相当于英语的形态变化，有一部分却能左右结构、表达丰富的语气色彩：

[例32] Upset? I'm not upset. What makes you think I'm upset?

难过？我才没有嘞。你，你为什么这么说啊？

[例33] In other years, spring tiptoes in. It pauses, overcome by shyness, like my grandchild at the door, peeping in, ducking out of sight, giggling in the hall way. "I know you are out there," I cry. (James J. Kilpatrick *Spring, the Resurrection Time*)

四月有时又蹑手蹑脚，像我的小孙女一样，羞羞答答地倚在门外，向里探探头，一闪又不见了，只是在门口咯咯地笑。"我知道你在那儿藏着呢，"我喊道。（宋德利　译）

[例34] 是的，是的……乡下冷，你往人家门前的稻草堆上一钻就暖了哪……这街上，哼，鬼地方！……还有那些山里呵，比乡下更冷哩，咳，那才好哪！火烧一大堆，大大小小一家人，闹热呀！……（艾芜《冬夜》）

True, true… it's cold in the country, but when you get into somebody's straw stack, you get warmed up at once… But this street, humm, what a terrible place! In the mountains, it's even colder, but when they have a fire in the house with the whole family sitting around it, wow, it's heaven!（张培基 译）

[例35] 酒样酽的花香熏得人慵，
蜜蜂在花枝上尽着嘤嗡，
一阵阵的暖风向窗内送，
梦罢，
日光里的梦呀其乐融融！（朱湘《梦》）
Flowerscents befuddle like heady wine.
Honeybees hum loudly on the flowers.
A gentle breeze wafts warmly through the windows.
Dream!
A sunlit dream is full of joy. （庞秉钧 闵福德 高尔登 译）

## 【翻译欣赏】

4月6日那天早上，我看着窗外漫天飞舞的雪花，不禁想：今天的北京奥运火炬伦敦段的传递将会怎样？

In the morning of April 6th, looking at the snow flakes falling outside the window, I could not but wonder: what would the torch relay be like?

大约八个小时以后，当第80位火炬手，英国著名中长跑运动员霍尔姆斯手举祥云火炬，跑上千年穹舞台，点燃了圣火盆时，场内4000多名观众一片欢腾。

About 8 hours later, when the torch finally struggled through the route, Olympic gold medalist Dame Kelly Holmes ran up to light the Olympic cauldron at O2 Dome, 4,000 spectators cheered.

这一天将以北京和伦敦之间的一次碰撞留在人们的记忆中，这个碰撞火花四溅，充满躁动，中国是首次举办奥运会的发展中国家，而英国则是迎接火炬的第一个西方国家。

This day will be remembered as Beijing met London with splashes and sparkles. It was an encounter between China, the first developing country to host the Olympics, and Britain, the first western country to greet the torch.

在返回机场的大巴上，北京奥组委年轻的女士们，包括前奥运冠军乔，都坚定地认为是全英国的人在跟她们作对。一个女孩说，"这哪里是养育了莎士比亚和狄更斯的国家啊！"另一个说，"英国人的绅士风度到哪儿去了？"我花了很长时间试图说服他们，但从她们潮湿的眼睛中我明白，我没有做到。

On the bus to the airport, I was with some young girls from the Beijing team, including an Olympic Gold Medalist Miss Qiao. They were convinced that the people here were against them. One girl remarked she couldn't believe this land nourished Shakespeare and Dickens.

我完全理解她们的看法。她们一整天都在车辆间来回穿梭，照应火炬手，鼻子冻红了，双手冰凉，前一天晚上只睡了三个小时的觉，有些人刚刚吃上午餐留下来的三明治。更糟糕的是，她们一路上还要反复经受暴力冲抢火炬的行径。

I can't blame them. I fully understood how they felt. They were running between vehicles for the whole day, nose red and hands cold, trying to service the torch bearers. They had only about three hours of sleep the previous night and some were having lunch sandwiches just now. Worse still, they had to endure repeated violent attacks on the torch throughout the relay.

而我很幸运地坐在后面的车上，有机会看到数万伦敦人顶风冒雪前来欢迎火炬，有挥手致意的老人，也有在风雪中表演节目的演员们。

I was fortunate to sit at the rear bus and saw smiling faces of Londoners who came out in the tens of thousands, old people waving and young performers dancing, braving the cold weather.

夜幕降临，看着奥运包机慢慢滑动到跑道上，我不禁想，飞机是否变得更加沉重了？北京奥运火炬全球传递这个艰难的旅程将让13亿中国人民可以更好地认识这个世界，也让世界更好地了解中国。

In the darkness of London night, waving the chartered plane good-bye, I had a feeling the plane was heavier than when it landed. The torch will carry on and the journey will educate the over a billion Chinese people about the world and the world about China.

一个年轻朋友看了 BBC 对火炬伦敦传递的转播,他在给我的信中写到,此刻百感交集,有悲哀、愤怒,也有不解。像他一样,很多人可能从中领悟到,中国融入世界不是凭着一颗诚心就可以的,挡在中国与世界之间的这堵墙太厚重了。

A young friend in China wrote me after watching the event on BBC: "I felt so many things all at once —sadness, anger and confusion". It must have dawned on many like him that simply a sincere heart was not enough to ensure China's smooth integration with the world. The wall that stands in China's way to the world is thick and heavy.

(《如果西方能够倾听中国》傅莹)

第二章

# 汉英词汇对比与翻译

词是可以独立运用的最小语言单位,也是最小的语法单位。了解汉、英两种语言在动态与静态、具体与抽象、重复与替换等词汇层面上的不同倾向,对于发挥译语优势、产生地道的译文具有重要意义。

## 第一节　静态与动态

作为有丰富形态变化的综合型语言，英语句子中的谓语动词要受很多形态变化规则的约束，使用时有很多不便，所以一般每个句子只有一个谓语动词。英语中常用含有行为和动作含义的普通名词、形容词、副词和介词短语表示动作，使得英语具有明显的静态倾向。

相反，汉语动词缺乏形态变化，没有谓语动词与非谓语动词的形式之分，可以充当句子的各种成分，可以在句中多次连用，甚至重复、重叠，合成并用，使用起来十分自由、简便，读来叫人感到活泼、生动、流畅。因此，在汉语中，动词使用频繁，必然使得汉语的表达呈现动态倾向。

汉英两种语言的动态与静态差异，对写作和翻译训练都具有极大的影响。汉语概念中的动词，在英语中很多时候都可以用名词、形容词、副词、介词来表达，这就是说，摆脱了汉语味，读来更像是地道的英语。反过来说，英语中的名词、形容词、副词和介词，在汉语中很多时候都可以用动词来表示，更显通顺、地道。

### 一、英语静态倾向的表现类型

#### （一）名词化（抽象名词等）是英语常见的现象

名词化（nominalization）主要指用名词来表达原来属于动词（或形容词）所表达的概念，如用抽象名词来表达动作、行为、变化、状态、品质、情感等概念。英语有"名词优势于动词"的倾向，这种名词优势往往可以使表达比较简洁而清楚，造句比较灵活，行文比较自然，也便于表达比较复杂的内容。试比较：

[例1] C1：医生迅速到达，并非常仔细地检查了病人，因此病人很快就得救了。

　　　C2：医生的迅速到达和对病人非常仔细的检查导致了病人的快速得救。

　　　E1：The doctor arrived extremely quickly and examined the patient uncommonly carefully; the result was that he recovered very quickly.

E2: The doctor's extremely quick *arrival* and uncommonly careful *examination* of the patient brought about his very speedy *recovery*.

细细品味，可以发现，在汉语中，C1 的动态短句较之 C2 的静态长句更加轻快，但在英语中，E1 的动态短句却比 E2 的静态长句增加了理解和记忆上的负担。这大概是由于缺乏形态变化和介词等使得层次关系清楚的手段，所以汉语的静态长句结构就不如动态短句来得轻快、灵动。但同是静态长句，到了英语中，却由于有了形态变化和介词等凸显层次关系的衔接手段，而且可以使几个主谓结构简化为一个主谓结构，因而较之动态结构更加简洁、清楚，平添了一份沉着、理性的气度。

[例2] Don't get me wrong, I think my mother-in-law is a wonderful grandmother to my daughter, but my preference is for greater involvement from her daddy so that my daughter understands a strong parental unit.

别误会我。我真心觉得婆婆是我女儿的好奶奶，但我宁愿孩子他爹能多承担一些，这样女儿就会懂得父母是一个紧密相连的整体。

[例3] The cooking, the cleaning and the childcare were all amazing bonuses that I don't dare complain about, especially when I see friends back in Canada struggle with daycare or juggle working hours with only occasional help from family, but the hours she put in! The complete devotion to the task of helping us manage our household seemed extreme.

她做饭、打扫、带孩子，这一切都是期望之外的，我不敢有任何怨言，尤其当我看到在加拿大的朋友们将孩子日托，艰难维持，或是上班与家务兼顾，忙得不可开交，偶尔才有家人帮忙，再看看我婆婆付出了多少时间！她全身心投入帮助我们照料家务，远非常人所能做到的。

(二) 用名词表示施事者，以代替动词。

[例4] I have never used twitter. I notice that young people are very *busy* with these electronics. My thumbs are too clumsy to type in things on the phone. But I'm a big *believer* in technology. And I'm a big *believer* in *openness* when it comes to the flow of information. I think that the more freely information flows, the stronger the society becomes, because then citizens of countries around the world can hold their own governments *accountable*. They can begin to think for themselves. That generates new ideas. It encourages creativity. So I've always been a strong *supporter* of open internet use. I'm a big *supporter* of *non-censorship*.

我从未用过推特。我注意到年轻人非常热衷这些电子玩意儿。不过我的手指比较笨拙，难以在手机上操作输入。但是还是非常*相信*技术的作用，并完全*主张*信息流动要*开放*。我认为，信息流通越自由，社会就变得越强，因为这样一来，世界各地的公民就能让自己的政府*负责*。他们可以独立思考，激发新思想，提升创造力。所以，我一直坚定支持互联网的开放使用。

［例5］Sherlock is a real worrier.
夏洛克老是担心这担心那的。

［例6］You're all clock-watchers today!
你们今天老是看着钟表等待下课啊！

## （三）名词优势造成介词优势

名词与名词之间往往要用介词连接，名词与动词、形容词等其他词类之间也常用介词连接。换言之，由于英语多用名词，必然也要多用介词，因而产生了介词优势。介词优势与名词优势结合，使英语的静态倾向更为显著。

英语常常用介词短语取代动词短语，即以"静"代"动"，如：

［例7］I'm from Chicago, recently unemployed, and my fear is that the longer I'm unemployed the harder it is going to be for me to get employed. It seems that nowadays employers are hiring people who are currently employed because they're in touch with their skill set. What programs do you think should be in place for individuals such as myself to keep in touch with our skills, be in demand, marketable and eventually get hired?.

我来自芝加哥，最近刚刚失业。我所忧虑的是，失业时间越长，就越是难以找到工作。现在的雇主似乎都倾向于招那些有现职工作的人，因为他们技能没有生疏。您认为应该采取什么样的措施，可以让我这样的人保持技能,得到市场青睐,进而推销自己,最终获得工作?

[例8] We are in a rush. We are making haste. A compression of time characterizes many of our lives. As time-use researchers look around, they see a rushing and scurrying everywhere.

我们东奔西忙,我们仓促张皇。时间紧迫是我们许多人的生活特点。时间利用研究者环顾四周,只见人人生活忙乱,处处步履匆匆。

[例9] The family traveled by slow-boat up the river, then for 15 miles across the sweltering plain in chairs carried by local farmers to a rest house at the foot of the mountain.

一家人乘一叶扁舟沿江而上,然后坐上当地人的竹椅前行 15 英里,穿过一片湿热的平原,随后抵达庐山脚下的客栈。

介词与名词结合,组成介词短语。成串的介词短语又常常与弱化动词(如 be, seem, look, become 等)和沉闷的名词连用。这类短语往往削弱或淡化原来所要表达的动词、形容词和其他词语的意义,使叙述曲折迂回,因而增强了静态感。

(四)动词的弱化与虚化

英语里最常用的动词正是动作意味最弱的动词——to be,其各种形式(包括 must be, may be, should have been 等)都缺乏动态感。由"it"或"there"与"be"构成的句式,其静态意味更加明显。试比较:

[例10] A:It was the finding of the committee that there had been many bribes paid by company managers to foreign officials.

委员会发现公司经理向外国官员行贿。

B:The committee found that many company managers had bribed foreign officials.

委员会发现公司经理向外国官员行贿。

除了 be 之外,have, become, grow, feel, go, come, get, do 等也是英语常用的弱式动词。

英语还常常把动词转化或派生成名词,置于虚化动词(如 have, make, take, do 等)之后作其宾语,如 have a look, take a walk, make attempts, pay visits, do some damages, put up a proposal 等。这类动词往往显得虚弱而平淡

无味。试比较：

[例 11] 她喜欢远距离散步。

　　　　A：She takes delight in having long walks.

　　　　B：She delights in walking long distances.

[例 12] 我的两个儿子各自在很小的时候就有了惊人的发现。

　　　　A：Each of my sons made the discovery early.

　　　　B：Each of my sons discovered it early.

### （五）用形容词表达动词的意义

英语常用动词的同源形容词与弱化动词相结合的方式表达动词的意义，如：

[例 13] He was unaware of my presence.

　　　　他当时不知道我在场。

[例 14] 我怀疑他是否还活着。

　　　　I am doubtful whether he is still alive.

很多时候，native speakers 青睐这种形容词，乃是因其较之动词更有客观描述之感，可以传递出一种较为真诚的情态与存续的状态，如：

[例 15] We are thankful for the rescue teams. But our hearts ache alongside you.

　　　　我们深深感谢救援队员，但同时，我们心里深切感受着你们的悲恸。

[例 16] You should be supportive of my scheme.

　　　　你应该支持我的计划啊。

[例 17] John was very helpful.

　　　　约翰帮了很大的忙。

### （六）用副词表来达动词的意义，如：

[例 18] He'll be home in half an hour.

　　　　他将在半小时内到家。

[例 19] I'm afraid the president is out，but he'll be in soon.

　　　　总裁恐怕出去了，但是他很快会回来的。

总之，英语常常通过动词的派生、转化、弱化和虚化等手段，采用非动词的形式（如名词、介词、形容词、副词等）表达动词的含义，因而表达呈静态。

## 二、汉语动态倾向的主要表现类型

与英语的静态倾向相反,汉语则倾向于多用动词,除了大量的动宾结构外,还有两个以上动词连用的连动式、兼语式。此外,汉语动词可以充当句子的主语、宾语、定语和状语,从而形成了明显的动态优势。汉语的动态倾向有以下几种表现形式:

### (一)动词连用是汉语常见的现象

汉语连动式和兼语式句子都包含着两个或两个以上的动词。中国的英语初学者常写出"There was a person was injured in a car accident"的错误句子,就是受了汉语兼语式句子的影响。但在汉语中,连动式、兼语式、把字式和被字式这四个句式还常常互相包孕套用,构成各式各样的多动词谓语句:

[例20] 让我儿子来接电话吧。
  Put my boy on the phone.
[例21] 我去叫他们派一个专业人员到这儿来帮你做勘测吧。
  Let me go and ask them to send a professional here to help you with your survey.

### (二)动词词组可以充当汉语句子的各种成分

汉语动词及动词词组,包括连动式词组、兼语式词组,无须改变形式就可以充当句子的各种成分。如此一来,就显得汉语句子处处都有动词了:

[例27] 空谈误国,实干兴邦。(动词词组作主语、谓语)
  Empty talk endangers the nation and practical work brings prosperity.
[例28] 革命不是请客吃饭。(兼语式词组作表语)
  Revolution is not a dinner party.

### (三)汉语动词可以充当助动词

[例29] 她带了一盒精美的生日蛋糕来。
  She's brought a delicate birthday cake.
[例30] 他筹款去了。
  He's out to raise money.

## （四）汉语动词还可以充当介词

严格说来，汉语的介词大多是由动词演变来的，因而仍然保留着动词的某些特征，如：

[例 31] 他一心向着祖国和人民。（动词）

He is devoted to his country and people.

[例 32] 不眠的夜，梦幻和烛火

一同摇落，一同

向夜角缭绕又低翔。（介词）（陈敬容《铸炼》）

On sleepless nights, dreams and candlelight

Vanish together, waft together,

Curling and covering, toward the corner of night. （庞秉钧　闵福德　高尔登　译）

汉语没有形态变化，动词与介词常常难于区分，因而也常常互相替用。汉语动词可以用来代替介词，这就大大加强了汉语的动态倾向。

## 三、英汉互译策略

鉴于英汉语言静态和动态特性的差异，英汉翻译过程中必然会经历静态和动态之间的转换。这种转换主要发生在整个句子或句内某个成分层面上的转换。

### （一）英译汉中静态到动态的转换

1. 名词（抽象名词、施事者名词、实指名词）译成动词

[例 33] We can nowhere find a better type of a perfectly free creature than in the common house fly. Not free only, but brave. There is no courtesy in him; he does not care whether it is king or clown whom he tastes; and in every step of his swift, mechanical march, and in every pause of his resolute observation, there is one and the same expression of perfect egotism, perfect independence and self-confidence, and conviction of the world's having been made for flies.

无论走遍天涯海角，也找不到像普通家蝇那样更为自由自在的生物了。苍蝇不仅无拘无束，而且胆大妄为。它可不讲什么谦恭礼

让，也不管你是一国之君，还是一介草民，想叮就叮。每当它敏捷而机械地迈出一步，或者果断地驻足观察时，总是流露出一副自命不凡、不求他人、自信满满的神情，全然认为世界就是为苍蝇而创造的。

英语原文选自 John Ruskin 的文章 The Freedom of the Fly。对比上例的原文和译文，不难发现下划线部分的英语原文中除了一个弱化动词"is"之外，没有第二个动词，然而却把苍蝇的动作描写得栩栩如生。汉语译文中，动词丰富，不但没有杂沓堆砌之感，而且叫人感到活泼、生动、流畅，这主要是动词使用所形成的效果。再看几个例子：

［例 34］He is a great farmer.

他种地是把好手。

［例 35］I want to extend a warm welcome to President Hu as he attends this APEC Summit. We are glad to be host to him and other world leaders altogether.

我想向胡主席表示热烈的欢迎，欢迎参加亚佩克峰会。很高兴接待胡主席和其他的世界领导人。

［例 36］The chimp figured out that if he did tasks like cleaning his room, he'd earn coins to spend on treats and rides in Miles's car.

这只大猩猩悟出，如果它干些诸如清理房间的事，它就能挣些硬币，好用来买好吃的，还可以坐迈尔斯的车外出兜风。

不难看出，在以上各例中，译者均将英语名词转译成汉语动词。该方法的应用，不仅使译文与汉语语言动态特性相符，而且为顺译法这一最常用（尤其是在口译中）翻译技巧的运用创造了客观现实条件。

2. 介词短语译成动词

通过把介词转译为动词，往往能取得很好的效果，如：

［例 37］*Between* teaching, writing and lecturing, he has little time for reading.

因*忙于*教学、写文章，以及*作*讲座，他*读*书时间甚少。

［例 38］*Beside* the previous year's outputs of steel in China, the figures for 2015 have fallen slightly.

和前一年的钢产量*相比*，中国 2015 年的产量有所下降。

［例 39］Millions of people in the mountainous areas are finally *off* absolute poverty.

千百万山区人民终于*摆脱*了绝对贫穷。

[例40] Horticulture furnishes the setting for many recreational events, *from* picnics in the outdoor living area of a home *to* the tough turf of a football field and the "carpet like" putting green of a golf course.

园艺还为许多娱乐活动提供环境，*包括*家庭户外生活区的野炊地，足球场上的耐寒草皮，以及高尔夫球场"绿色地毯式"的球穴区。

3. 形容词转译成动词

英语形容词（不包括动态形容词）作定语、表语或主语补语时，如果译成动词，则将会使整个句子由静态转变成动态。

[例41] Residents of western states tend to marry younger, and younger people are generally more *divorce-prone*.

西部各州的居民结婚的年龄一般很小，而越年轻的人通常也就容易*离婚*。

[例42] The small gift was *indicative* of his best wish for your family.

这件小礼物*表达*了他对您家人的良好祝愿。

[例43] His words were *suggestive* of his *determination* to finish the tough job on schedule.

他的一番话*表明*他*决心*按时完成这件棘手的工作。

4. 副词转译成动词

有些英语副词，先由动词构成分词或形容词，再由分词、形容词加上后缀 -ly 构成副词。这类副词本身具有某种动态性，所以在汉译时可以转换成动词。有些副词虽不是由动词或形容词转换而来，但译成汉语时往往不得不转译成动词。

[例44] He is *wonderfully* patient.

他的忍耐功夫着实*令人惊叹*。

[例45] He will talk *quickly* and *eagerly* about *nothing* at all.

他*口若悬河*，*讲得眉飞色舞*，其实*什么内容都没有*。

[例46] All of them left when the meeting was *over*.

会议*结束*后大家都离开了。

## (二) 汉译英中动态到静态的转换

由于汉语具有这种动态特点,汉译英过程常常就是在译文中强化英语静态色彩的过程,也就是说,由汉语动词充当的主语、宾语、定语和状语,或表示动态意义的句子成分翻译成英语时,可以译成英语非限定动词形式、名词、形容词或介词短语。

1. 汉语动词译作英语名词(实指名词、抽象名词、施事者名词)

[例47] 忽而庄严说教,忽而插科打诨,忽而高歌一曲,忽而舞步翩翩。帝王将相,牛鬼蛇神,无不具备,应有尽有,场面各有不同。(金克木《老来乐》)

Come upon the screen, now serious preaches, now comic gestures and remarks, now resounding songs, now twists and dances. The cast may be emperors, generals, monsters or demons, of all kinds and of all sorts, but in different situations. (萧立明等译)

[例48] 我们有幸邀请到欧美社区服务学者以及来自东南亚地区的朋友们参加这次研讨会。

We are very fortunate to have the *attendance* of many European and American scholars in community service and friends from Southeast Asia.

[例49] 人际关系就是一种善于听取别人的意见,体察别人的需要,虚心接受批评的能力。

Interpersonal skills are nothing but the ability to be an empathizer, and *a listener* with an open heart to different opinions, even criticisms.

[例50] 以后见着狗,我总是逃,它也总是追,而且屡屡望着我的影子猖猖狂吠。

From then on, I always played the *fugitive* while the dog the *pursuer*. He would bark furiously at the sight of me.

2. 汉语动词译作英语形容词

[例51] 这船能*抗*得住大浪的击打吗?

Is this boat *good enough* for big waves?

[例52] 根据一项调查,在美国,年纪越轻,便越容易离婚。

A survey revealed that the younger people are more *divorce-prone* in the U. S.

［例53］在叙利亚、伊朗和阿富汗问题上，美国热衷于武力。

Americans are trigger-*happy* when it comes to the issue of Syria, Iran and Afghanistan.

3. 汉语动词译作英语介词或介词词组

［例54］你在想什么呢？

What's *on your mind*?

［例55］一个新的富裕阶层正在形成。

A new class of nouveau riches is *in the making*.

［例56］你这样看着我，叫我没法做事。

I can't do it with you *in my face*.

（三）动静转换的相对性

我们说英语倾向于静态，并不意味着英语就排斥动态表达。相反，在完整的英语语篇中，静态表达固然有多过动词结构的时候，如：

［例57］I would not be standing here *without the unyielding support of my best friend for the last 16 years*, *the rock of my family*, *the love of my life*, *the nation's next first lady. Michelle Obama.* Sasha and Malia, I love you both more than you can imagine, and you have earned the puppy that's coming with us into the White House. Although she's no longer *with* us, I know my grandmother is watching us along with the family that made me who I am. I miss them tonight. I know *my debt* to them is *beyond measure. To my sister Maya*, *my sister Alma*, *all my other brothers and sisters*, thank you so much *for all the support* that you've given me. I'm *grateful* to them. *And to my campaign manager*, *David Plouffe*, *the unsung hero of this campaign*, who build the best political campaign, I think, *in the history of the United States of America*, *to my chief strategist David Axelrod*, *who's been a partner with me every step of this way*, *to the best campaign team ever assembled in the history of politics*, you made this happen and I'm *forever grateful for* what you sacrificed to get it done.

如果没有一个人的坚决支持，我今晚就不会站在这里，她就是我这 16 年里最好的朋友，是我家庭的支柱，我一生的挚爱，也是我们国家的下一位第一夫人：米歇尔·奥巴马。还有我的女儿，萨沙和玛丽亚，我好爱你们，我们会带着你们刚赢得的小狗一起搬进白宫。而我的外祖母，虽然此刻已经离开我们，但我知道她和塑造了今日之我的家人们一道，正在看着呢。今夜，我想念他们。我知道我欠他们太多的爱，无法估量，难以偿还。我的妹妹玛雅，我的妹妹阿尔玛，我的所有其他的兄弟姐妹们，感谢你们给了我这么多的一切支持，我感谢他们。感谢我的竞选主管大卫·普劳夫，他打造了在我看来是美利坚合众国历史上最好的*政治竞选*，感谢我的首席战略师大卫·阿克塞罗德，在这条路上的每一步都有他与我风雨同行，感谢美国政治史上最棒的竞选团队，是你们造就了今天，我永远感谢你们的付出和牺牲。

但多数语境中，静态表达并不占有绝对的数量优势。只是由于汉语中静态表达出现的概率实在太小，类型也远不如英语丰富，我们仍然说英语相对于汉语而言具有明显的静态倾向。在完整的英语语篇中，静态表达哪怕只是隔三岔五地出现，但相对于汉语一面倒的动态倾向，差异也会非常之大的，构成了翻译的突出障碍。

[例58] Let's imagine a different case. This time you are a doctor in an emergency room, and six patients come to you. They've been *in a terrible trolley car wreck*. Five of them sustain moderate injuries. One is severely injured. You could spend all day caring for the one severely injured victim, but in that time the five would die. Or you could look after the five, restore them to health. But then at that time, the severely injured person would die. Now as a doctor, how many would save the five? … (*Many students raised hands.*) How many would save the one? … (*Few students raised hands.*) Very few people, a handful of people. Same reason, I assume: *one life vs five*?

我们来想象一个不同的情况。这次你是一名急诊室的医生，有一天送来了六个病人。他们刚刚经历了一场惨重的电车事故。其中五人伤势不算严重，另外一人受重伤。你可以花上一整天的时间来救治这名重伤员，但另外那五人就会病死。你也可以选择医治这五人，但那位重伤员就会死。有多少人会选择救那五人？……（很多学生举手）有多少人会选择救那一人？……（很少学生举手）很少。我猜想，理由还是一样：牺牲1个保全5个。

同理，汉语的动态倾向也具有相对性，并不排斥静态表达。

这种相对性还有另一面。我们发现，汉英翻译中动态转换为静态的现象，以及英汉翻译中，静态转换为动态的现象固然突出，但也不排除在某些极端情况下，甚至可能出现汉语名词转译成英语动词，英语动词或副词转译成汉语名词的情况：

[例59] 学生在上外语课时应该学习如何理解陌生的文化习俗，学会与外族人交际时应有的*言谈举止*。
While attending foreign language classes, students should learn how to interpret unfamiliar cultural conventions and how to *behave* appropriately when communicating with people of a foreign culture.

该例中，汉语名词"言谈举止"转译成英语动词"behave"。

另外，我们还应辩证地看到，静态结构是英语的优势所在，但如果静态表达法过多，则又会势必给动词增加太多的负担，因而阻碍思路畅通，显得缺乏活力。甚至容易造成意思含混不清。很多时候，当静态结构开始恣意汪洋，读者就要望洋兴叹，翻译员更是要丢盔弃甲，伤心太平洋了：

[例60] Thus a very large mass of writers, among whom are poets, novelists, philosophers, political theorists, economists, and imperial administrators, have accepted the basic distinction between East and West as the starting point for elaborate theories, epics, novels, social descriptions, and political accounts concerning the Orient, its people, customs, "mind," destiny, and so on.

A：这样一个非常大的作家，其中是诗人、小说家、哲学家、政治理论家，经济学家和帝国管理员接受了东西方之间的基本区别作为复杂的理论起点，史诗，小说，社会的描述，和政治账户关于东方，它的人民，风俗，"看来，命运，等等。

B：这样非常多的著述者，他们当中有诗人、小说家、哲学家、政治理论家、经济学家和帝国管理者，都接受了东西方之间的基本区别作为起点,展开关于东方的复杂理论、史诗、小说、社会描述和政治记述,内容涵盖了东方的人民、风俗、"思维"、命运,等等。

上例的译文 A 是国内居于行业领先地位的人工智能翻译的结果,这里引用它,意在展示在近年来人工智能翻译水平已经取得长足进步的背景下,这段译文能比较客观地反映出静态结构过多所带来的理解和翻译上的突出障碍(至少不是英汉语水平不好的人所翻译),导致错译、漏译、胡乱译。这也说明,对于英语的静态结构优势,在用英语写作或进行汉-英翻译时,宜把握好一个度,谨慎使用;在英-汉翻译时,也应仔细斟酌,不可迷信人工智能翻译。

总之,通过本节的分析,给我们打开了一扇观察汉英翻译转换的窗口,大家可以据此多关注常见的动静转换形式,灵活掌握汉英动静态特点,根据具体情况进行动静态转换,使译文符合目的语的语言特征。

## 【翻译欣赏】

Good morning everyone and welcome to the opening of Communicate, an exhibition which celebrates the creativity of Independent British Graphic design since 1960s.

各位早上好!欢迎参加"沟通"展览,尽情欣赏英国六十年代以来独立平面设计的创意大餐。

As Director of the British Council in Guangzhou, I am very proud to open this exhibition which was developed by the Barbican Art Gallery in London and which starts its world tour with Guangzhou. I would like to give my thanks and appreciation to Rick Poynor, who is responsible for putting Communicate together as curator.

我是英国驻广州总领事馆文化教育处主任。非常荣幸主持今天的开幕式。本次展览由伦敦巴比肯艺术馆策划组织,广州是其全球巡展的第一站。在此,我想对里克·派纳先生表示感谢。派纳先生是"沟通"展览的策展人。

We are very fortunate to have someone of Rick's status in the UK and international design world with us today. Just to give you an idea of his background: Rick was the founding editor of "Eye", the highly acclaimed international review of graphic communication and is a respected author of a large number of books and article in the UK's design and business media. Rick has been a visiting professor at the School of Communication at the Royal College of Art in London and now delivers lectures on Graphic design around the world.

我们能够邀请到派纳先生这样一位在英国如雷贯耳、在国际设计界也是响当当的专家光临出席，真是非常幸运。我简要地介绍一下派纳先生的背景吧：他一手创办了世界上誉名卓著的平面设计杂志《视觉》；他也是令人称道的撰稿人，在英国的设计和商业媒体上发表过大量著作和文章。除此之外，他还身兼伦敦的英国皇家艺术学院传播学院客座教授，并在世界各地举办平面设计讲座。

The Communicate exhibition brings together work of over 100 independent UK graphic designers and provides the best examples of how UK designers have worked with the music industry, the web, with social issues and politics, with business on developing corporate identity and on independent projects.

"沟通"平面设计展汇集了超过100位英国独立平面设计师的作品，展示了英国设计师与音乐界、网络、社会问题、政治、企业等互动合作，设计企业标识，以及独立项目等多个领域里的最佳范例。

We hope that the exhibition will provoke dialogue and spark off relationships between UK and South China design professionals. In our Communicate seminar yesterday, we explored the relationship between graphic design, branding and corporate identity. This provoked some stimulating discussions which we hope will continue.

我们希望本次展览能够促成大家积极开展对话、在英国和华南地区设计专业人士之间架起一座联系的桥梁。在昨天我们举办的"沟通"研讨会上，大家探讨了平面设计、品牌和企业标识的关系。这次研讨会已经激发了许多讨论，这样的探讨大有裨益，我们希望能够继续下去。

（节选自 Christine Skinner 在 "Communication—UK Graphic Design since 1960's" 上的致辞，仲伟合　赵军峰　莫爱屏　译）

## 第二节 抽象与具体

在翻译实践中,很多技巧,比如"增词法""减词法""转译法""分切法"等,都要落实到对语言美感差异的对比上来,系统地了解汉英语民族规律性的语言审美习惯,否则就会沦为玄之又玄、无从捉摸的"感觉"或"经验之谈"。

因此,即便本节介绍的翻译策略中有一部分从其译文结果和形式上看来与上一节有着些许相似之处,但鉴于它代表了另一种语言审美角度和思路,我们还是将其也纳入一个章节,以便为读者打开另一扇窗口,开启另一条思路,从而更加自信、熟练地应对一些翻译难题。

更重要的是,在翻译实践中,开启了本节所论述的抽象语言 vs 具体语言的审美视角后,译文的效果很可能会有较大的提高。譬如小说《蜗居》的译文,同样是意译法,但是"Dwelling Narrowness"就是要比"The Narrow Dwelling"要厚重得多,原因就在于前者的抽象表达 narrowness 作为中心词,读来"曲"而"隐",要好一阵才能回过味来:我住的不是 Dwelling,而是 Narrowness 啊。这股子冷幽默,含义隽永,回味悠长,可算是对汉语的具体形象之美做出了适当的补偿,较之原文效果不遑多让,不过是各有千秋罢了。

### 一、英语里抽象表达法得以流行的原因

由于英语倾向于使用名词化结构,往往导致过度地依赖名词,而削弱了动词的作用,相应地,作家的思想也跟具体时间地点的现实情况分离,跟事情发生的过程和发生时的心情分离,不知不觉地产生一种习惯性的泛化、抽象和模糊。换言之,英语的名词化往往导致表达的抽象化。

抽象表达法在英语里使用得相当普遍,尤其常用于社会科学论著、官方文章、报刊评论、法律文书、商业信件等文体。

这种表达法得以流行,还有以下几个主要原因。

首先,抽象表达法便于表达复杂的理性概念和微妙的情绪,被认为是一种高级思维。随着科学技术的发展和文明社会的进步,原有的感性表达方式已不足以表达复杂的理性概念,因而需要借助于抽象、概括的表达法。英语的抽象表达法含义概括,指称笼统,覆盖面广,往往有一种"虚""泛""暗""曲""隐"的"魅力",因而便于用来表达复杂的理性概念和微妙的情绪。如:

[例1] It is the web culture itself rather than mobile devices and social channels that are driving some of the negative aspects of language standards. (＝The web culture itself rather than mobile devices and social channels are driving the language ungrammatical.) ("the negative aspects of language standards"比"ungrammatical"虚泛、弱化、委婉)

造成语言不规范的是网络文化本身,而不是移动设备和社交渠道。

[例2] No year passes now without evidence of the truth of the statement that there exist prevailing prejudices and discriminatory practices in the legal system. (＝Every year shows how true it is that...) ("statement"似在暗示这是别人说过的,显得"暗""曲",委婉。)

法律系统中存在的具有强大势力的偏见和歧视行为,每年都证明确实如此。

[例3] Given that many people already feel strongly about state-of-the-art social robot "abuse", it may soon become more widely perceived as out of line with our social values to treat robotic companions in a way that we would not treat our pets. (＝Given that many people already feel strongly about state-of-the-art social robot "abuse", it may soon become more widely perceived as betraying our social values to treat robotic companions better than we treat our pets.) ("out of line"较之"betraying"或"challenging",显得笼统、委婉,留有余地,"in a way that we would not"比"better than"来得"泛""曲""隐"。)

鉴于许多人已经对最先进的社交机器人"欺骗"有强烈的感受,用比对待宠物更好的方式对待机器人同伴,可能很快就会被更广泛地认为偏离了我们的社会价值观。

其次,由于抽象表达法被认为是一种高级思维(superior mind),是文明人的一种象征(mark of civilized man),许多作者为了显耀其思想深奥而故弄玄虚、追随时尚,也嗜好抽象表达法。如:

[例4] There is an exaggeration of the sense of insecurity with a probable consequence of increasing demand for protection and greater pressure for the authorization of the use of force by law enforcement. (＝It is exaggerated that people feel more and more insecure, and therefore more and more people may call for the police to use force to protect them.)

危险和不安全感越来越被夸大了,越来越多的人或许会因此而要求获得更多的保护,要求赋予警察更多的动武权。

［例 5］ The respondent correspondent gave expression to the unqualified opinion that the subject missive was anterior to his facile comprehension. (＝He replied that he didn't understand our letter.)

他回复说,我们的信他没看明白。

［例 6］ We are assigning major priority to the early completion of the preliminary stages of the program. (＝A successful beginning will merit our attention.)

开头开得好,会更加吸引我们。

由此可见,抱残守缺地坚守"质朴"的直观具体固然不好,故弄玄虚般执着于"高级"的深邃抽象亦未必佳,不过半吊子文明而已。语言表达的"善境",仍在于灵活机变,拿捏好一个度,以免"宽严皆误"。

另外,抽象词语便于掩饰作者含混(cloudy)或真实的思想,以迎合某种表达的需要。这种不良文风常常表现在过分使用含义抽象、内容虚泛、语气庄严的大字眼(pompous words),有时简直到了装腔作势、令人难以捉摸的地步,在政府、商业、学术或技术等部门里甚为盛行,譬如 liquidity(流动性)、quantitative easing(量化宽松)等。

## 二、英语的抽象表达手段

英语有丰富的抽象表达手段,从而大大方便了抽象表达法的使用。这些手段主要包括:虚化词缀构词、用介词表达比较虚泛的意义、用 wh－词表达比较虚泛的含义。

### (一) 虚化词缀构词

通过-ness、-ment、-ity、-ship 等词缀,可以将原来含义比较明确的动词、形容词等转化成为比较虚泛、抽象的名词,如:

［例 7］ I thanked her for the years of eating her good cooking, the equal of which I had not found since.

我感谢她多年来让我吃到她烧的美味菜肴，离开她后我再也没吃过那么可口的菜肴。

[例8] To help myself live without fault, I made a list of what I considered the 13 virtues. These virtues are *1 Temperance*, *2 Self-control*, *3 Silence*, *4 Order*, *5 Firmness of mind*, *6 Savings*, *7 Industry*, *8 Honesty*, *9 Justice*, *10 Cleanliness*, *11 Calmness*, *12 Morality*, *13 Humbleness*.

为了使自己生活中不犯错误，特列出我认为应该身体力行的13条守则。这些守则是：*1. 节制饮食*；*2. 自我克制*；*3. 沉默是金*；*4. 有条不紊*；*5. 坚定信念*；*6. 勤俭节约*；*7. 工作勤奋*；*8. 忠诚老实*；*9. 办事公正*；*10. 衣履整洁*；*11. 平心静气*；*12. 品行高尚*；*13. 谦虚恭谨*。

（二）用介词表达比较虚泛的意义

介词（某些介词可能会活用成副词或形容词）本来就是虚词，在英语里十分活跃。两个甚至更多的介词还可以构成各式各样的短语或成语，其意义有时虚泛得难以捉摸，读者既要分拆了解各单个介词的基本含义，再将各个基本含义加以引申、综合，结合上下文反复琢磨，才能揣测其意思，如：

[例9] Kids don't say "Wait". They say "Wait up. Hey, wait up." Because when you are little, your life is up, your future is up, everything you want is up. "Wait up! Hold up! Shut up!" "Mama, clean up! Let me stay up." parents of course are just the opposite. Everything is down. "Just calm down! Slow down!" "Come down here. Sit down. Put that down!"

孩子不会说"等一会儿"，他们会说"等上一会儿"，因为当你还小的时候，你的生活在上面，你的未来在上面，你所要的一切都在上面。"等上一会儿！举起来！闭上嘴！""妈妈打扫一下。让我再玩上一会儿吧。"父母则相反，一切都在下面。"冷静下来！慢一点！""下来！坐下。给我放下！"

[例10] He's just not that into you.

他只是不那么爱你。

[例11] China: her history no unitary, but made up of many histories; as she is made up of many different peoples, altogether 56 nations.

Yet she is a oneness, coherent, whole. THE GREAT WITHIN. (Han Suyin  *Han Suyin's China*)

中国的历史并不是一部单一的历史,而是由许多部历史组成,因为中国是由许多不同的民族组成的——总共有为五十六个民族。然而她却是一个紧密完整的统一体。

真是一个伟大的、自成一统的国家。(邹海波  译)

[例12] I understand he is in for a position in the new administration.
我知道他在申请政府中的一个职位。

[例13] Bob has it in for George because George told the teacher that Bob cheated in the exam.
因为乔治向老师告发鲍伯考试作弊,鲍伯就对乔治怀恨在心。

(三) 用 wh-词表达比较虚泛的含义

[例14] Fortunately at Harvard we had helped them, as we do now, to understand how we got where we were, and what the future might hold.
幸运的是,我们哈佛大学曾经像今天一样,帮助他们廓清迷雾,了解危机的前因何在,未来又会怎样。

[例15] I love you not because of who you are, but because of who I am with you.
我爱你,不是因为你的样子,而是因为跟你在一起时的,我的样子。

[例16] It's almost got to the point where there's stress envy. Everyone wants to have a little bit of this stress to show they're an important person.
这几乎是到了羡慕压力的程度。人人都想表现几分时间紧迫感,以显示自己的重要。

### 三、汉语的具体化倾向及具体表达手段

与英语相比,汉语的用词倾向于具体。因为汉语缺乏像英语那样的词缀虚化手段,汉语常常以实的形式表达虚的概念,以具体的形象表达抽象的内容。这种倾向的好处是,措辞具体、含义明确,叙述直接,常常借助于比喻和形象,因而比较平易、朴实。

具体说来，汉语的具体化倾向往往表现为：抽象名词少、动词多、范畴词多、形象化的俗语多。

［例 17］ 我只想到项羽，力举千鼎，气盖山河。（贾平凹《我读何海霞》）

At this point I think of Xiang Yu, the ancient heroic general, who had unusual physical strength and overwhelming will power.

（刘士聪　译）

［例 18］ 友听毕，掩口笑道：君言差矣，常言道：以为最安全的却是最危险，岂不闻情人眼里出西施吗？

On hearing this, his friend couldn't help a smile and the following comment: "Forgive me, sir, for pointing out that you are wrong there. As the saying goes, the greatest danger resides in the false sense of security. Haven't you heard of love being blind?"

［例 19］ 真搞不懂，你为什么老对我横挑鼻子竖挑眼呢？

I don't understand why you're always so judgmental toward me.

## 四、抽象化倾向与具体化倾向的翻译转换

### （一）英译汉中抽象到具体的转换

无论汉语抑或是英语，都是既有抽象化表达手段，也有具体化表达手段。鉴于翻译应当尽可能地兼顾表层形式的对应与深层含义的对等，尊重上下文的具体语境的考量下，英语虚泛模糊的抽象化表达自然也可以译成汉语的抽象、模糊表达。请看下面这一则某学术会议场合的实例：

［例 20］ You helped us better understand optimal auctions, bargaining and regulation. You have also established the great generality and usefulness of the revelation principle.

您使得我们能够更好地理解最优拍卖、议价和监管。您还证实了显示原理的通用性和实用性。

［例 21］ I love you not because of who you are, but because of who I am with you.

我爱你，不是因为你是谁，而是因为跟你在一起的时候我是谁。

但是，相对而言，英语的抽象化倾向更加突出一些，汉语则是具体化倾向更为明显。这样，在英译汉中抽象转换为具体的情况就往往更多一些，也更加陌生一些，因此，我们这里主要谈一谈这种不同倾向之间的转换。

1. 用具体的动词解释抽象的词义

英语抽象词的含义比较笼统、概括、虚泛，在汉语里往往找不到对应的词来表达，这时常常要借助具体的动词、名词、形容词等词语来解释其抽象的词义，正如 Peter Newmark 所说的："As a last resort, explanation is the translation." 例如：

[例 22] It is incredible coming to America to find you are somewhere else — in Seoul, in Taipei, in Mexico City. You can travel inside this Korean culture right on the streets of Los Angeles.

行走在美国，却恍若置身他乡—首尔、台北、墨西哥城，这种奇妙的感觉真是不可思议。你在洛杉矶街头行走，就可以感受到韩国的文化氛围。

[例 23] Instantaneity rules.

急功近利大行其道。

[例 24] My question is: Would you please raise my taxes? I would like very much to have the country to continue to invest in things like Pell Grants and infrastructure and job training programs that made it possible for me to get to where I am.

我的问题是，您能否提高我的税负？我希望国家能够继续投资于佩尔奖学金、基础设施、职业培训等，因为我现在所拥有的一切都是拜它们所赐。

需要指出，上面这类翻译如果仅仅是理解为静态与动态之间的转换，是不能反映它的全貌的，操作起来也是吃力的。必须辅以抽象与具体的观察角度，才能豁然醒觉。

2. 用具体的名词解释抽象的词义

[例 25] The stars twinkled in transparent clarity.

星星在清澈的晴空中闪烁。

[例 26] Greatness of names in the father ofttimes overwhelm the son; they stand too near one another. The shadow kills the growth.

伟人之名常常压垮他们的儿孙。他们彼此站得太近；大树荫摧残了小树苗的生长。

[例 27] The English language would not have been what it is if the English had not been for centuries great respecters of the liberties of each individual and if everybody had not been free to strike out new paths for himself.

如果不是多少世纪以来英国人一向崇尚个人自由，如果不是每个人都能自由地为自己开拓新的道路，英语就不会成为今天这个样子。

3. 用具体的形容词解释抽象的词义

［例 28］No country should claim infallibility.

任何国家都不应自称一贯正确。

［例 29］The countryside was, in fact, famous for the abundance and variety of its bird life, and when the flood of migrants was pouring through in spring and fall people traveled from great distances to observe them.

事实上，这里的乡村鸟类品种繁多、数量庞大，久已闻名遐迩。每当春秋时节，候鸟纷纷飞来栖息，四方游人不辞路遥前来观赏。

4. 用范畴词使抽象概念具体化

范畴词（category words）用来表示行为、现象、属性等概念所属的范畴，是汉语常用的特指手段。如：

［例 30］That happy tolerance, that willingness to accept words from anywhere, explains the richness of English and why it has become, to a very real extent, the first truly global language.

这种乐意包容的胸襟，这种不管源自何方都愿意接纳的心态，解释了英语为什么会这样丰富多彩，解释了英语缘何在很大程度上成了第一种真正的国际语言。

［例 31］The power of gratitude takes just a few minutes a day. But it requires consistency and an open mind—and dedication.

每天只需花几分钟，感恩就会产生力量，但是它需要始终不渝，心胸开阔以及奉献精神。

［例 32］Any reduction in the risk of real-world acts would be worth it.

任何降低现实世界行为风险的举措都是值得的。

5. 用形象性习语使抽象意义形象化

汉语虽缺乏抽象词语，但形象性习语却相当丰富。汉语常借助这类生动具体的词语来表达英语抽象笼统的意义，如：

［例 33］Stress is an ignorant state. It believes that everything is an emergency.

紧张是一种无知。它以为什么事都是十万火急的。

［例34］Youth means a temperamental predominance of courage over timidity, of the appetite for adventure over the love of ease. (Samuel Ullman  *Youth*)

青春气贯长虹，勇锐盖过怯弱，进取压倒苟安。（王佐良  译）

［例35］There is more to their life than political and social and economic problems, more than transient everydayness.

他们的生活远不止那些政治、社会、经济问题，远不止柴米油盐问题。

（二）汉译英中具体到抽象的转换

如果说，英译汉时，"化虚为实"的方法往往可以通行文、添文采，增加译文的可读性，那么，汉译英时，则往往要"化实为虚"，以期化症结、消梗滞，提高转换的可译性。

1. 用抽象名词代替汉语动词

［例36］有一整套的技术专门用来促进一心多用。

An entire class of technologies is dedicated to the furtherance of multitasking.

［例37］无忧无虑，无人打扰，不必出门而自有天地。（金克木《老来乐》）

There being no worry and disturbance, I need not travel far in my own world so vast. （萧立明等  译）

2. 用抽象名词代替具体的汉语名词

［例38］为什么谎话也有市场

因为轻信的人太多（艾青《无题》）

Lies thrive

On credulity. （庞秉钧  闵福德  高尔登  译）

［例39］给黑夜开一个窗子，

让那儿流进来星辉，月光，

在绝静的深山，一片风

就能激起松涛的巨响。（陈敬容《铸炼》）

Open a window to darkest night,

Let in the starlight and moonbeams;

In the deepest mountain stillness, a breath of wind

May rouse deafening echoes from the sea of pines. (庞秉钧　闵福德　高尔登　译)

3. 用抽象名词代替形象的汉语形容词

[例40] 脑海中充斥的种种并行不悖的任务，给我们带来了一种*幸福的满足感*。每次我们都宁可大干一番而不愿厌倦懈怠。

A sense of *well-being* comes with this *saturation* of parallel pathways in the brain. We choose mania over boredom every time.

[例41] 这几天，岛内的选情*波谲云诡*，急转直下，用尽了权谋手段。

For the past few days, the campaign in Taiwan has been conducted with every possible *treachery and craftiness*, and there has been a significant and dramatic change with regard to the campaign. And every trick possible has been employed and used.

4. 汉语的范畴词略去不译

[例42] 许多场所和物件都表明人们有急躁情绪。

There are places and objects that signify impatience.

[例43] 总之，就全国范围来说。我们一定能够逐步顺利解决沿海同内地贫富差距的问题。

In short, taking the country as a whole, I'm confident that we can gradually bridge the gap between the coast and inland areas.

上例中，"解决沿海同内地贫富差距的问题"翻译时如果把范畴词照实译出，"solve the problem regarding the wealth gap between the coastal and hinterland areas"，就没了简洁流畅的感觉，不是地道英语的味儿了。

5. 用抽象名词代替形象的汉语习语

[例44] S君听毕，顿悟，叹道：听君一席话，胜读十年书，差一点大意失荆州！

Suddenly and thoroughly enlightened by his friend's kind warning, Mr. S sighed with feeling, "How true it is that one can learn more from the talk of a wise person than from ten years' reading! Otherwise I may lose her through oversight."

[例45] 在我看来，他这是"司马昭之心，路人皆知"。

His ill intention of doing so, in my view, is all too clear for anyone to see.

6. 用介词、wh-词代替具体的汉语词语

［例46］我们今天的成绩着实来之不易。

We have been through a lot to get to where we are.

［例47］要是给你妈妈看到你的裤子撕破了，你准得吃苦头。

When your mother sees your torn trousers, you'll *be in for it*.

虚化的抽象表达和静态表达结合在一起，是英语魅力的重要体现。有些抽象、静态的英语句型，与相应的汉语表达相比，其遣词显得累赘，不乏冗词余语，在初学者看来，大可"删繁就简"，以更明快更简洁的表达取而代之。但事实上，"简化"，只能剪去表达的风采和魅力。相反，正是这种"冗余"，才是其"地道"之所在，才能展示出英语表达的优雅、委婉和从容，散发出更沁人心脾的英语馨香，试比较下例译文 A 与译文 B：

［例48］你可以想象得出，成千上万的影迷的那些表示敬慕和恳求的信件一定把她弄得应接不暇。

    A：You can imagine, she is besieged with adoring and pleading notes from thousands of fans.

    B：It doesn't take too much stretch of the imagination to realize that she is now besieged with adoring and pleading notes from thousands of fans.

许多形象性词语有很强的民族色彩或特定的文化含义。这类词语往往难以对应翻译，因而不得不借助于虚化手段或其他方法，英汉互译都有这种情况。不过，这种虚化方法有时会冲淡甚至洗尽原文的形象色彩，使翻译成了一门"令人遗憾的艺术"。有经验的译者，往往能会想方设法在别处增添一些形象化的、可读性强的译笔以作补偿，下例中的"slip through our fingers"就是很好的例子。

［例49］我以为世间最可宝贵的就是"今"。最易丧失的也是"今"。因为它最容易丧失，所以更觉得它可以宝贵。

Of all things in the world, I think, the present is the most precious, and also the most apt to slip through our fingers. We, therefore, treasure it all the more because of its *transience*.

【翻译欣赏】

1

Your Majesties, Your Royal Highnesses, Honored Laureates, Ladies and Gentlemen,

This year's Economics Prize is about design. Let me explain.

尊敬的陛下、尊敬的殿下、尊敬的获奖人，女士们，先生们：

今年的经济学奖是有关于设计的。下面让我来解释一下。

Mechanism design theory provides general methods for the analysis and development of mechanisms for resource allocation. This analysis is carried out in three steps. First, one makes a prediction of the behavior that is expected under given rules. Here, game theory comes into use. Thereafter, one evaluates, according to the given goal, the resource allocations—such as consumption, production and environmental stress—that result. Finally one looks for the mechanism, with due regard to its behavioral implications, that best meets the goal. The last step is the hardest.

机制设计理论为资源配置机制的分析和发展提供了一般性的方法。此分析包括三个步骤。首先要预测在给定规则情况下最可能产生的行为。在这里要用到博弈论。其次，根据给定的目标来评估这些行为所导致的资源配置方式，比如消费、生产和环境压力。最后，充分考虑行为的影响，去寻找最能达到目标的机制。最后一步是最困难的。

The theory of mechanism design currently plays a major role in many areas of economics and in parts of political science, and has led to many fruitful applications. Its domain of application has expanded in recent years, due to globalization and growing Internet trade, phenomena that improve new demands on old institutions.

机制设计理论在很多经济学领域和部分政治科学领域里发挥着重要作用，并已在实践中得到有效的运用。近些年来，由于全球化和不断增长的网络贸易，对旧机制提出新要求，使得该理论的应用范围得以扩展。

Dear Drs. Hurwicz, Maskin and Myerson: You have laid the foundation of the theory of mechanism design, thereby providing a systematic and rigorous approach to central questions in economics. This has enabled economists not only to study the performance of existing economic institutions but also to suggest how these can be improved, and to identify the theoretical limits to what can be achieved when we take into accounts the constraints that emanate from individuals' incentives and private information.

尊敬的赫维茨、马斯金、迈尔森博士：你们以奠定了机制设计理论的基础，由此为研究经济学中的核心问题提供了一套系统而缜密的方法。这使得经济学家们不仅能够研究现行经济体制的执行效果，而且能够就如何改进执行效果提出建议，同时，在考虑到个人动机和私人信息所导致的制约因素以后，经济学家们还能够识别出这些机制的理论局限。

Dr Hurwicz: you pioneered this whole field and introduced some of the key perspectives and concepts. In particular, you suggested that economic institutions be conceived of as information systems within which agents send messages, and where these messages together determine an allocation of the available resources. In this context you also introduced the key notions of incentive compatibility.

赫维茨博士：您发起了这个领域的研究并引入了一些重要的观念和概念。特别需要提出的是，您建议把经济制度设想成信息系统，在这些系统里，行为者发送各种信息，将这些信息整合起来就可以决定可用资源如何配置。在此背景下，您还引入了动机相容这一关键概念。

Dr Maskin: you did pioneering work on implementation theory, that part of the theory of mechanism design which deals with the problem of the potential co-existence of inferior equilibrium along with the desired ones. You have also made numerous other important contributions, both to the pure theory of mechanism design and to its application to areas such as auctions, monopoly and social choice.

马斯金博士：您在实施理论方面做出了开创的贡献。这一理论是机制设计理论中的重要部分，解决的是次均衡解与理想解有可能同时存在的问题。此外，您还做出了许多其他方面的重要贡献，如机制设计的纯理论方面，还有它在拍卖、垄断、社会选择等领域中的应用方面。

Dr Myerson: you have been the leader in applying mechanism theory to games of incomplete information, that is situations in which different agents do not know each other's goals, costs or actions. This helped us better understand optimal auctions, bargaining and regulation. You have also established the great generality and usefulness of the revelation principle.

迈尔森博士：您始终引领着把机制设计理论应用到非充分信息条件下的博弈中去的研究方向。在信息不充分的状态下，不同行为者不了解彼此的目标、成本和行为。这有助于我们更好地理解最优竞卖、议价和监管。您还证实了显示原理的通用性和实用性。

It is an honor and privilege to convey to you, on behalf of the Royal Swedish Academy of Sciences, our warmest congratulations. I now ask you to receive your Prizes from His Majesty the King.

我非常荣幸能够代表瑞典皇家科学院向你们表示我们最热烈的祝贺。现在请你们来接受国王陛下为你们颁奖。

2

今天，我很高兴有机会和各位一起，共同探讨世界可持续发展领域的问题。各位刚才的发言充满智慧，深受启发。如何使这次会议的行动计划和大家的承诺真正落实，不仅直接关系到本次会议的成效，更关系到人类社会的未来发展。

Today I am delighted to be with you here to discuss issues relating to global sustainable development. The speeches of previous speakers were full of wisdom and most enlightening. The question of how to implement the plan of action of this summit and to honor our commitments in real earnest bears not only directly on the success of the summit, but even more on the future of human society.

中国作为世界上人口最多、国土面积最大的发展中国家，高度重视可持续发展问题。我们在处理经济发展与人口、资源、环境的关系方面，有以下几点体会：

As the world's largest developing country in terms of population and land area, China attaches great importance to sustainable development. In handling the relations between economic development and population, resources and environment, we have learned the following from experience:

——坚持经济发展与资源、环境保护相协调。作为发展中国家，首要的任务是发展经济，消除贫困。经济不发展，人民生活改善和环境治理就没有物质基础。但发展经济绝不能以破坏环境、浪费资源为代价。不注重资源、环境保护，经济不可能实现持续发展。

—Emphasis on harmony between economic development and resource and environmental protection. The primary task of developing countries is to develop the economy and eradicate poverty. Without economic growth, there would be no material basis for a better life or better environment for the people. But economic growth must not be achieved at the cost of environment or resources. In the absence of proper resource and environmental protection, there could be no sustainable economic development.

——坚持以人为本的发展道路。发展经济、保护环境，都要着眼于提高人民生活水平和质量，着眼于人的全面发展和长远发展。要努力开创生产发展、生活富裕、生态良好的文明发展道路。

—Adherence to the road to human-oriented development. Economic development and environmental protection are both aimed at improving the level and quality of people's life and ensuring an all-round and long-term development of human beings. We should strive to find a civilized road to development featuring higher productivity, a well-to-do life and sound ecosystem.

——坚持依靠科技进步和加强管理。科学技术特别是高新技术，是可持续发展的强有力支撑。要围绕增强可持续发展能力，不断增加科技投入，加强环境基础设施建设，采用清洁生产工艺，发展环保产业，完善资源和环境管理体系。通过改革体制，完善机制，健全法制，推动可持续发展战略的有效实施。

—Continued reliance on scientific and technological advancement and stronger management. Science and technology, hi-tech in particular, gives strong backing to sustainable development. We should focus on enhancing our capacity for sustainable development, further increase our input in science and technology, intensify our efforts in the development of environmental infrastructure, apply clean manufacturing technology, develop the industry of environmental protection and improve the resource and environmental management system. We should improve the mechanisms and the legal system through institutional reforms so as to facilitate the effective implementation of sustainable development strategies.

——坚持积极参与环境与发展国际合作。当今世界，一个国家的经济发展和环境保护，离不开国际交流与合作。通过开展双边、多边的国际环境合作，一方面承担责任，履行承诺；另一方面，可以引进资金、先进技术和管理经验，增强本国可持续发展能力。

—Continued active participation in international environmental and development cooperation. In today's world, a country could not fully ensure its economic development and environmental protection without international exchanges and cooperation. Through bilateral and multilateral cooperation, it could introduce the capital, advanced technology and managerial experience to enhance its capacity for sustainable development, while assuming responsibilities and honoring commitments.

## 第三节 替换与重复

无论英语还是汉语，抑或是任何其他的语言，都是既有替换，也有重复。但就总体特征来说，英语倾向于替换，汉语则倾向于重复。

### 一、英语的"替换"倾向

特定情况下，比如出于修辞或强调的需要，或在润色较少的口语中，或者在涉及法律术语时，英语同其他语言一样，会浓墨重彩地求诸重复：

[例1] I believe in America, I believe in our democracy. I believe that if you just stay ahead long enough, eventually, after they have exhausted all the options, folks do the right thing. But we've got to give them a little help to do the right thing. So I'm asking all of you to lift up your voice, not just here in Richmond. — anybody watching, listening, following online — I want you to call, I want you to email, I want you to tweet — I want you to fax, I want you to visit, I want you to Facebook, send a carrier pigeon. I want you to tell your congressperson, the time for gridlock and games is over. The time for action is now. The time to create jobs is now. Pass this bill. If you want construction workers on the worksite, pass this bill! If you want teachers in the classroom, pass this bill! You want small business owners to hire new people? Pass this bill! You want veterans to get a fair share of opportunities that they help create? Pass this bill! You want a tax break? Pass this bill! Prove you will fight as hard for tax cuts for workers and middle-class people as you do for oil companies and rich folks. Pass this bill! Let's get something done.

但是，总的来说，英语有一个很大的倾向：尽量避免重复。讲英语的人对于随意重复相同的音节、词语或句式往往感到厌烦。英语文体学家批评这类重复是粗心的、笨拙的，因而也是令人厌烦的。在能明确表达意思的前提下，英语宜尽量采用替代、省略或变换等方法来避免无意图的重复。这样不仅能使行文简洁、有力，而且比较符合英语民族的语言心理习惯。

下面我们就把英语的"替换"倾向从表现形式上进行分类梳理并介绍相应的汉译手段。

## 二、英语的"替换"类型及汉译

### （一）替代（Substitution）

用替代的形式（pro-forms）来代替句中或上文已出现过的词语或内容，这是用英语说话或写作的一项重要原则。这些替代的形式主要有：

1. 名词性替代（nominal substitution）

用代词或某些名词来取代名词（词组），这类词如：第三人称代词、指示代词（this, that, these, those）、关系代词（who, whom, whose, which）、连接代词（who, whom, whose, what, which）、不定代词（all, each, every, both, either, neither, one/ones, none, little, few, several, many, much, other, another, some, any, no），以及名词（enough, half, the same, the kind, the sort, the former, the latter）等。

总的说来，英语多用代称，以避免重复；汉语少用代称，多用实称，因而较常重复。汉语代词的使用远远不如英语广泛。人称代词的性别之分，大约只是新文化运动以后的事，显然是受了英语的影响。"他""它"和"她"除了因发音相同而不便在口语里使用之外，即使是书面语，在同一句子或语段里经常出现这类代词不仅会使指称混乱，还会令人感到不是中国话的味儿。

［例2］我随时可以在家里接待客人了。

I'm now ready to meet my guests at my home.

［例3］他耸耸肩，摇摇头，两眼望天，一语不发。

He shrugged his shoulders, shook his head, cast up his eyes, but said nothing.

相对而言，英语常用代词，汉语少用代词，因而较常重复，这在汉译英时也可以看出来：

［例4］秦淮河里的船，比北京万生园、颐和园的船好，比西湖的船好，比扬州瘦西湖的船也好。这几处的船不是觉着笨，就是觉着简陋、局促；都不能引起乘客们的情韵，如秦淮河里的船一样。秦淮河里的船约略可分为两种……（朱自清《桨声灯影里的秦淮河》）

The ships on the Qinhuai are better than those in Beijing's Myriad Creature Garden and Summer Palace and Hangzhou's West Lake, better than those on Yangzhou's Shouxi Lake. The vessels in those places are either clumsy or crude and cramped, less inviting than those on the Qinhuai, which fall roughly into two categories...

[例5] 一定的文化（当作观念形态的文化）是一定社会的政治和经济的反映，又给予一定社会的政治和经济以巨大的作用和影响。

Any given culture (as an ideological form) is a reflection of a given society's politics and economics, and the former in turn has huge effect and influence on the latter.

英语的代词在汉译时常常采用还原（restoration）、复说（repetition）或省略（omission）的办法加以处理。

[例6] He sat in front of me, taking his time to talk, while a scene rose from behind him: A blue sky projected white clouds, which rode the breeze, which swung a tree full of golden-colored, withered leaves by the window.

他就坐在我的对面，不紧不慢地说着，就有一种风景从他的背后冉冉升起，蓝天衬着白云，白云托着微风，微风轻抚着窗前一树金黄的枯叶。

[例7] One is not born a woman, one becomes one.

女人并非生就的，而是长成的。

2. 动词性替代（verbal substitution）

用替代词来取代谓语动词（词组），这类替代词主要有：代动词 do，复合代动词 do so, do it, do that, do this, do the same，以及替代句型 so+do+主语，so+主语+do, so+be+主语, so+主语+be, so+will+主语, so+主语+will 等。汉语也有替代的方式，但也常常重复其所代替的动词（词组），如：

[例8] The fight takes hours, because the system keeps crashing. I say a line, then he does, then crash! And yet we keep on, doggedly.

由于系统常出故障，两人一吵就是几个小时。我写一句，他回一句，接着网络故障！可我们俩还是锲而不舍地吵个没完没了。

[例9] You've been pretty wired lately. You know you have.

你最近一直很兴奋，这你是知道的。

3. 分句性替代（clausal substitution）

用替代词 so 或 not 来取代充当宾语的 that 从句，用 if so 或 if not 来取代条件从句，用 so、as 来取代分句的一部分，等等。汉语也有替代的方式，但为了使表达正确、清楚，也常常重复其所代替的词语，如：

[例10] 我站住，狗也就站住。它望着我狂吠，它张大嘴，它做出要扑过来的样子。但是它并不朝着我前进一步。它用怒目看我，我便也用怒目看它。它始终保持着我和它中间的距离。（巴金《狗》）
I stood firm and so did he. He barked angrily with his mouth wide open as if he were about to run at me. But nevertheless, he never moved a single step towards me. He glowered at me, and so did I at him. But he always kept the same distance between us. （张培基 译）

[例11] 黑与白交，黑能污白，白不能掩黑；香与臭混，臭能胜香，香不能敌臭，此君子与小人相攻之大势也。（张潮《幽梦影》）
Black can besmirch white and a bad odor wipe out a fragrance easily, but not vice versa. This is what happens when a gentleman is confronted by a cad or a sneak. （林语堂 译）

（二）省略（Omission）

省略和替代一样，也是避免重复的一种常用手段。两者常常互相替换使用，有的语言学家甚至把省略称为"零位替代"（zero-substitution）。

（1）英语省略的类型很多，有动词性省略、名词性省略、分句性省略；有句法方面的省略，也有情景方面的省略。在并列结构中，英语常常省略前面已经出现过的词语，而汉语则往往重复这些词语，如：

[例12] By the time I missed home so much that soup dumplings and sautéed eels popped up in my head as I read, Nietzsche had replaced Plato on the chronological reading list and Flaubert Homer.
等到我的思乡情绪越来越浓，读书时脑海里会蹦出小笼包和清炒鳝丝的时候，我那个按年代顺序排列的必读书单上，尼采已经取代了柏拉图，福楼拜已经取代了荷马。

[例13] Some people go to priests; others to poetry; I to my friends.
有人求诸牧师，有人求诸诗歌，我则向朋友寻求慰藉。

［例14］ Since ancient times, winners have been crowned and losers vilified.
　　　　 成者为王败者寇，自古皆然。

［例15］ It's not me who broke the rule. It's you.
　　　　 不是我破坏了规则，而是你破坏了规则。

（2）英语常常承前省略相同的谓语动词或谓语动词的一部分；汉语则较常承前省略相同的主语而重复相同的动词。试比较：

［例21］ The devil you know is better than the devil you don't.
　　　　 跟认识的魔鬼打交道，总比跟不认识的打交道好。

［例22］ 人生就是台阶，我们得一级接一级地去拾。
　　　　 拾得天荒地老，拾得辗转难眠，拾得泪流满面，拾得心静如洗。（郭翠华《煮熟的蚕茧》）
　　　　 Life is a flight of steps. We have to climb it step by step. And this climbing may be time-consuming, exhausting, and filled with emotion, but it is all for the purpose of pacifying your heart. （刘英才 译）

［例23］ 古者以天下为主，君为客，凡君之所毕世为经营者，为天下也。今也以君为主，天下为客，凡天下之无地而（人民）得安宁者，为君也。（黄宗羲《原君》）

　　　　 In ancient times, the people were the masters, and the kings the guests, and the object of the kings' labors was the people. Now it is the kings who are the masters and the people the guests, and there is not one corner of the earth where people can live peacefully their own lives, all because of the rulers. （林语堂 译）

（三）变换（Variation）

广义的变换也包括上述的替代和省略。此外，英语还常用同义词替代，近义词复现和句式变化等方法来避免重复。汉语也讲究用词造句形式的多样化，以避免单调、枯燥，但英汉表现方法不尽相同。

1. 英语同义词替代

英语同义词替代的现象常见于用不同的名称来表示同一人或事物，即所谓"同名异称法"。例如，小说里提及某一人物时，有时用其名，有时用其姓，有时用其昵称，有时则用其职务等同一意思的变换说法。对于这类同名异称，读者或听众往往是根据上下文或特定的背景知识才明白其所指。中国人较不习惯于这种名称替换法,因而较常重复同一名称。

[例24] 这些价值观和孔子宣扬的一些思想有很多相似之处。孔子的思想强调的是中庸适度。但是我尊重孔子的思想,并不是要把他的思想搬到现代社会。

These values have much in common with some of the *virtues* of Confucianism, the Chinese *philosophy* that stresses moderation. However, although I respect the *spirit* of Confucianism, I have not tried to adapt this ancient Chinese *philosophy* to modern society.

2. 近义词复现

近义词复现常常是概括词(generic word)和下义词(specific word)之间的互相替换,如用 the furniture 来替换 the table,用 the animal 来替换 horse。汉语一般较少采用英语的这种变称,而较多重复同一名称,又如:

[例25] 人们常把闯红灯看成是小错,不当一回事,然而闯红灯一旦形成习惯,则远非是违反交通规则的问题了。

Red-light running has always been regarded as a minor wrong, and so it has never been taken seriously. When the violation become habitual, however, a great deal more than a traffic problem is involved.

## 三、汉语的重复类型及英译

汉语的重复无论在使用范围、出现频率和表达方式的多样性等方面都远远超过英语。英语的重复一般是修辞、强调性质的,而汉语的重复除了修辞、强调的需要之外,还往往出自语法的要求。

### (一) 强调型重复

很多时候,汉英语言中都会通过重复来表示突出强调,其翻译也比较简单:保留重复。例如:

[例26] 沉默啊!沉默啊!不在沉默中爆发,就在沉默中灭亡。

Silence! Silence! Unless we burst out, we shall perish in this silence.

## (二) 结构型重复

有时是为了促成结构整齐匀称，节奏缓急协调的修辞效果，也会重复某些词语或句子成分。不过这里说的是"修辞"，并非比喻排比之类的修辞格，而是就其广义而言，系指语言的润色，比如四字结构等等，其翻译可以根据英语的表达习惯，将汉语中重复出现的结构删去或替换，从而避免重复，使译文简明扼要，如：

[例27] 风幡非动，*动自心耳*。

It's neither the wind nor the banner that's moving. *It's your mind*.

[例28] 好哇，大风，你就*使劲地刮吧*。你现在刮得越大，秋后的雨水就越足。*刮吧*，*使劲地刮吧*，刮来个丰收的好年景，刮来个富强的好日子。

All right, wind! Roar *as hard as* you like. The *stronger you blow* now, the more rain we will get in autumn. Come on! You'll give us a good harvest and bring us a good life.

[例29] 西陵峡以险峻闻名，巫峡以秀丽著称，瞿塘峡以雄伟见长。

The Xiling Gorge is famed for its breath-taking steepness, the Wu Gorge, elegant serenity, and the Qutang Gorge, enchanting magnificence.

汉语中有一个特别有趣的重复类型：重叠。英语也有音节重叠的现象，但一般属于谐音或拟声现象，有许多来自儿语，通常用于口语、俚语或非正式文体，如 yo-yo, tut-tut, zig-zag, criss-cross, dangle-dangle, walkie-talkie 等，其构词能力和使用范围都受到很大的限制，远远不如汉语普遍。这主要是因为英语词的音节参差不齐。

汉语单音节文字的特点便于字和词的重叠。汉语的叠字叠词不仅是音节的重叠，而且有词法和句法的因素。重叠构词不仅使得词语音节匀称，形式整齐，而且赋予词语以新的意义和感情色彩。

在英汉转换中，适当地运用汉语的重叠形式可以加强译文的表现力，使之更加符合汉语的习惯：

[例30] Is not a Patron, my lord, one who looks with unconcern on a man struggling for life in the water, and, when he has reached ground, encumbers him with help? The notice which you have been pleased to take of my labours, had it been early, had been kind; but it has been delayed till I am indifferent, and cannot enjoy it... (Samuel Johnson  *To Lord Chesterfield*)

伯爵阁下：见人挣扎于水中则默默然袖手旁观，见人安然登岸则遽遽乎殷勤相助，此非恩主之为人乎？阁下于拙著之锦注，若在昔年，诚不失为美意；惜于姗姗其来迟，今仆已兴味索然，难以欣赏……（黄继忠　译）

[例 31] Thin people make me tired. They've got speedy little metabolisms that cause them to bustle briskly. They're forever rubbing their bony hands together and eyeing new problems to "tackle". I like to surround myself with sluggish, inert, easygoing fat people, the kind who believe that if you clean it up today, it'll just get dirty again tomorrow. (Susan Britt Jordan  *That lean and Hungry Look*)

瘦人让我感到累。他们新陈代谢快，手脚总是忙个不停。他们总是搓着两只皮包骨头的小手，东瞧西望，看看有什么新问题需要"着手解决"。我喜欢和那些慢腾腾、懒洋洋、随随便便的胖人在一起，那种认为你今天打扫干净了明天还会变脏的人。（刘士聪　马会娟　译）

而在汉英转换中，汉语的叠词叠字极难原汁原味地重现。大多只有采用英语的头韵、尾韵、半韵等音韵修辞手段予以一定的音效补偿，却极难像汉语那样意义对应而又词语重叠。

[例 32] 小路两边，是两行小柳树。树枝细细的，柳叶沙沙响。嫩叶上刷着一层白色的绒毛。
Two rows of small willows lined the paths. The twigs were slender, with rustling leaves covered by a layer of white villus.

[例 33] 大知闲闲，小知间间；大言炎炎，小言詹詹。（《庄子·齐物论》）
Great wisdom is generous; petty wisdom is contentious. Great speech is impassioned, small speech cantankerous. （林语堂　译）

[例 34] 黄鹤一去不复返，
白云千载空悠悠。
晴川历历汉阳树，
芳草萋萋鹦鹉洲。（崔颢《黄鹤楼》）

The yellow crane has never returned once again,
The 1000-year lonely clouds leisurely remain.
The river is so clear to mirror the tree shadow,
The grass on the Parrot Islet luxuriantly grow. （朱曼华 译）

李清照的"寻寻觅觅，冷冷清清，凄凄惨惨戚戚"连用七对叠字，有两个重要特点：（1）单从字义上看，意蕴层层推进，不断深化，但无法排遣之中放而又收，因而周而复始地循环；（2）音律齐整，且在长度不断增加的字数中强化了节奏，并与词义的深化彼此渲染，相生相成，涌起一浪紧似一浪悲苦愁绪；但叠字同样也有舒缓的一面，具备了在激昂时放中有收，无休无止地循环下去的效果。

这也难怪，目前为止，众多的译家殚精竭虑，惜乎理解尚难到位，遑论翻译。

诸多译本中，林语堂的版本可算是音美、形美、意美兼具的典范，从音律、词义都体现了不断强化的气势，再加上富有想象力的排版，似非其他译本所能及。然而它仍然难免顾此失彼，语义上的循环不息固然付之阙如，原文叠字所营造出的旋律、意境上收放自如的循环感，在译文中亦已"一水茫茫"，渺然无踪了。

[例35] 寻寻觅觅，冷冷清清，凄凄惨惨戚戚。（李清照《声声慢》）
So dim, so dark,
　　So dense, so dull,
　　　　So damp, so dank,
　　　　　　So dead! （林语堂 译）

（三）语法型重复

汉语的重复现象远比英语普遍。英语的重复一般是修辞性的（rhetorical），而汉语的重复除了修辞的需要之外，还往往出自语法的要求。限于篇幅，本部分着重分析语法上的重复倾向及翻译技巧。

连淑能先生在《英汉对比研究》中，对汉语的语法型重复进行了梳理，归纳为大致八种情形：

（1）主语与表语重复，即主语与判断语重复，表示对于别的判断的排斥，英译时可能照搬重复，也可能用替代或省略。如：

[例36] 但为什么人类成了人，猴子终于是猴子呢？（鲁迅《革命时代的文学》）

How is it then that *men have become men*, while *monkeys remain monkeys*?（杨宪益　戴乃迭　译）

[例37] 这人现在也已经"寿终正寝"了，但在那里继续跋扈出没着的也还是这一流人，所以秋瑾的*故乡也还是那样的故乡*，年复一年，丝毫没有长进。（鲁迅《论"费厄泼赖"应该缓行》）

Since then this informer has died peacefully in bed. But because there are still many of his sort lording it in that district, Chiu Chin's *native place has remained unchanged* from year to year, and made no progress at all.（杨宪益　戴乃迭　译）

（2）主语与宾语重复，即宾语就是主语加"的"字，表示互不相干，类似英语的"do your own part"，如：

[例38] 你们吵你们的，我就不参与了。

You just go on with your fight. I won't take part.

（3）主语与谓语重复。这种格式用两个以上相同的结构，有列举的性质，英译时可能照搬原文结构，但更多是用替代和省略来回避重复。如：

[例39] 去的尽管去了，来的尽管来着；去来的中间，又怎样地匆匆呢？（朱自清《匆匆》）

*What is gone is gone*, *what is coming keeps coming*. How swift is the transition in between!

[例40] *崩溃者自崩溃，纠缠者自纠缠，设立者又自设立*；毫无戒心，也想不到改革，所以如故。（鲁迅《我们现在怎样做父亲》）

*While what must crumble crumbles, the trouble-makers still make trouble, and the rule-makers still make rules.* They are not on their guard in the least and have no desire to change, hence all goes on as before.（杨宪益　戴乃迭　译）

[例41] 我们几姊弟和几个小丫头都很喜欢——买种的买种，动土的动土，灌园的灌园；过不了几个月，居然收获了。（许地山《落花生》）

At that my brother, sister and I were all delighted and so were the young housemaids. And then *some went to buy seeds, some began to dig up the ground and others watered it and*, in a couple of months, we had a harvest!（刘士聪　译）

[例42] 有时候许先生一面和我们谈论着，一面检查着房中所有的花草。

看一看叶子是不是黄了？*该剪掉的剪掉，该洒水的洒水，因为不停地动作是她的习惯。*（萧红《鲁迅先生记》）

Mrs. Lu would chat with us while moving from one plant to another, checking if any of them had turned yellow or needed clipping or watering. She would keep herself busy in her room. （刘士聪 译）

（4）主语与宾语的修饰语重复，一般表示评估。英语一般用替代来避免重复。例如：

[例43] 大家庭有大家庭的热闹，小家庭有小家庭的温馨。

Big families may enjoy their lively togetherness, while small ones may have their own cozy moments.

[例44] 每个小家庭都是各住各的房，各吃各的饭，各自有各自的亲戚和朋友，比方说，我们就各自有自己的"外婆家"。（冰心《祖父和灯火管制》）

The smaller families lived and ate separately. They each had their own relatives and friends, for example, their own in-laws. （张培基 译）

（5）重复谓语。这种格式可分为三小类：表示转折，译成"but"；表示让步，译成"even"；表示假设，译成"if""as"等。

[例45] 所以倘有谁要预知令夫人后日的丰姿，也只要看丈母。*不同是当然要有些不同的，但总归相去不远。*（鲁迅《这个与那个》）

If you want to know what your honorable wife will look like in later life, you have only to watch your mother-in-law. Of course, there will be some difference, but not a great one. （杨宪益 戴乃迭 译）

[例46] 你是个大忙人，平素请都请不到。

You are a busy man, and won't come at ordinary times even if you are invited.

[例47] 他们都是自私自利的沙，*可以肥己时就肥己*，而且每一粒都是皇帝，可以称尊处就称尊。（鲁迅《沙》）

They are all self-centered, self-seeking grains of sand, out to better themselves while they can; and each particle is an emperor, who lords it over others whenever they can. （杨宪益

戴乃迭 译）

(6) 重复带宾语的及物动词。英译时可移植重复，或者采用省略的办法。例如：

[例 48] 现在一听到了这一个提议，自然是心里急跳了起来，两只脚便也很轻松地跟他出发了，并且还只怕翠花要出来阻挠，*跑路跑得*比平时只有得快些。（郁达夫《我的梦，我的青春！》）

Now that Ah Qian offered to take me along, I readily set out with him, my heart throbbing with excitement and my feet floating with light steps. As I was afraid that Cuihua might rush out to pull me back, I began to run, and run faster than usual. （刘士聪 译）

[例 49] 我找他找了十几年了！

It's over a decade for me trying to make contact with him.

(7) 重复"也好""也罢"之类，置于并列的谓语形式之后，表示假设或选择，其翻译相对简单，用"whether"或者其变体即可。例如：

[例 50] 只要有人向孩子演示该如何做某件事——把钥匙塞进钥匙的槽口也好，画只鸡也好，或者是弥补过错也好——那他就不太可能自行想方设法去完成这件事。

So long as the child is shown exactly how to do something — whether it be placing a key in a key slot, drawing a hen or making up for a misdeed — he is less likely to figure out himself how to accomplish such a task.

[例 51] 其实，生命这种东西轰轰烈烈也好，默默无闻也罢，归根结蒂，都不过是一种悲壮的过程而已。正因为有了这种悲壮的过程，所以"太阳每天都是新的！"（赵红波《怀念那片青草地》）

In fact, in final analysis, life, being dynamic or unknown, is nothing but a solemn and stirring process. Yet just because of this solemn and stirring process, "the sun is new everyday!"（张晔 译）

(8) 重复"各"或"自己"，英语则往往使用代词以回避重复。

[例 52] 所以，要是说得苛刻一点，也就是*自家掘坑自家埋*，怨天尤人，全是错误的。（鲁迅《论"费厄泼赖"应该缓行》）

So, strictly speaking, they are digging their own graves, and have no right to blame fate or other people. （杨宪益 戴乃迭 译）

## (四) 汉语的"意复"现象

除了词语的重复之外，汉语还常常运用相似、相对或不同的词语来重复同一意义，在译成英语时大可以采取省略、替换等方法处理。

［例53］这真是所谓"你不说我还明白，你越说我越糊涂"了。

This is truly a case of: *"The more you explain the more confused I grow."*

［例54］有的人能够正视困难，而有的人却在困难面前垂头丧气，怨天怨地，大叹生不逢时，缺少机遇。（张大锁《生命的启示》）

While some face up to them, others lose heart and become dejected, complaining all the time about their bad luck, about not being favored by chance, etc.... （陈文伯 译）

汉语的意复现象尤其常见于四字成语和谚语。英语也有类似的同义重复，只是数量相对少一些。

(1) 四字成语的意复，很多时候不需要重复翻译，例如：

［例55］譬如好花从泥土里出来，看的人固然欣然的赏鉴，泥土也可以欣然的赏鉴，正不必花卉自身，这才心旷神怡的——假如当作泥土也有灵魂的说。（鲁迅《未有天才之前》）

For when a beautiful blossom grows from the soil, all who sees it naturally take pleasure in the sight, including the soil itself. You need not be a blossom yourself to *feel a lifting of your spirit*—provided, always, that soil has a spirit too. （杨宪益 戴乃迭 译）

［例56］海峡两岸的人民都是血肉同胞、手足兄弟。

The Chinese on both sides of the Taiwan Straits are of the same flesh and blood.

［例57］她可真有沉鱼落雁之容，闭月羞花之貌。

Her beauty would put the moon and the flowers to shame.

有时则可借用英语中类似的成语，例如：

［例58］我们光明正大地赢了他们，这是一场精彩的比赛。

We beat them fair and square. It was a wonderful game.

(2) 谚语的意复。这类重复往往可以归入惯用法、语法或修辞等范畴之内。

[例59] 人不可貌相,海水不可斗量。

  Judge not a book by its cover.

[例60] 月亮圆缺缺复圆,花儿开谢谢又开。

  The moon waxes and wanes; the flowers bloom and fade.

  总体而言,英语是尽量避免重复;汉语则较常重复。但另一方面,汉语很多时候也讲究变化,而且随着对外交往的增多,还有进一步加强变化的意识。换言之,英译汉时,由于中文读者既习惯了重复,又能接受一定的变化,译者的操作空间相对较大;而汉译英时,由于英文读者更加挑剔,这就决定了译者在汉翻英时面临着更大的挑战,需要花费更多的心思对原文的重复进行变化处理。

  然而,变换要适度,替代也要明确,不应引起语义的含混。如果为了追求"优雅的变换"而给人以炫耀言辞之感,甚至影响了表达的清晰和准确,那就过犹不及,违背语言交际的初衷了。

## 【翻译欣赏】

  甘肃历史悠久,文化源远流长,是中华民族的发祥地之一。自古以来,甘肃就是中外经济、文化交流的重要通道之一,是中华文化与西方文化交流、融汇的热土。著名的古丝绸之路全长7000多公里,在甘肃大地就绵延1600多公里。广袤的陇原大地已经形成了具有甘肃地域特色的敦煌文化、丝绸之路文化、黄河文化和伏羲文化、民族和民间民俗文化、戏剧舞台艺术等文化品牌。

  Gansu has a long history and ever-lasting culture. It is a birthplace of the Chinese nation. Since the ancient times, Gansu has been an important path for economic and cultural exchange between China and foreign countries, as well as a place where Chinese and Western cultures exchanged and blended with each other. The famous 7,000-kilometer long Silk Road passes through 1,600 kilometers of Gansu province. The province is also home to a number of distinctive cultures, such as the Dunhuang Grottoes, the Silk Road, the Yellow River, the Fuxi Worship, as well as the colorful cultures of different minorities, their folk customs, and arts.

  彩陶文化、长城文化、石窟文化等在陇原大地交相辉映,不仅成为甘肃多彩的文化,也成为中国文化和世界文化的宝贵财富。以《丝路花雨》《大梦敦煌》《敦煌乐舞》等为代表的优秀剧目和舞台艺术,竞相彰显着甘肃特色文化独特的内涵和大西北的风情,向世人展现了悠悠中华数千年的文明传承。

  Many resplendent cultures, featuring painted pottery, the Great Wall, grotto art, etc., cluster here. They not only add to Gansu's colorfulness, but also make precious treasures of China and the world. Represented by "Romance on the Silk Road", "Dunhuang, My Dreamland" and "Dance and Music of Dunhuang", the province's dramatic arts and stagecraft, unique and excellent, showcase the charming flavors of northwest China. They also display to the world China's age-old civilization.

为更好地保护历史文化遗产，科学合理地开发利用特色文化资源，2002年省委、省政府决定将甘肃特色文化建设纳入经济社会发展总体规划，把发展社会主义先进文化作为带动经济发展，推动社会和谐进步的重要战略，特色文化建设得到了前所未有的发展，全省初步构建起特色文化战略格局。

For the purpose of further protecting the historical cultural heritages and scientifically and reasonably utilizing the resources of the distinctive local culture, Gansu Provincial Party Committee and Gansu Provincial People's Government decided in 2002 to incorporate the development of the distinctive culture with the general plan of provincial economic and social development, taking the development of socialist advanced culture as an important strategy to stimulate provincial economy and push forward a harmonious and progressive society. Gansu has made unprecedented progress in its distinctive cultural development. A strategic pattern of the distinctive culture has been basically formed.

建成了文溯阁《四库全书》藏书馆、省博物馆新展览大楼等一批重点文化基础设施；推出了《大梦敦煌》《敦煌韵》等一批舞台艺术精品工程和精品剧目；形成了兰州黄河风情文化周、天水伏羲文化旅游节、平凉崆峒文化旅游节、庆阳香包民俗文化节、武威天马国际文化旅游节、甘南香巴拉旅游节等一批特色文化品牌。

An array of key cultural infrastructure projects have been completed, e.g., the Wensu Pavilion of *Si Ku Quan Shu*, a complete series of Chinese classics, the new Exhibition Center of Gansu Provincial Museum, etc. A batch of great plays, such as "Dunhuang My Dreamland" and "Dunhuang Rhythm", have been staged. A series of distinctive cultural brands have sprung up, for example, Lanzhou Yellow River Cultural Week, Tianshui Fuxi Cultural Tourism Festival, Pingliang Kongtong Cultural Tourism Festival, Qingyang Sachet Folk Custom Festival, Wuwei Tianma Tourism Festival, and Hi

Shambhala Festival.

同世界五大洲的许多国家和地区开展了文化交流和合作；23项非物质文化遗产列入国务院公布的首批非物质文化遗产保护名录；礼县大堡子山遗址考古发掘、张家川马家塬战国墓地考古发掘入选2006年度全国十大考古新发现；享誉海内外的《读者》杂志，成为中国期刊的著名品牌。概括地讲，地域性、多样性和特色性三个方面构筑了甘肃特色文化建设的骨干体系。目前，甘肃特色文化已成为经济社会发展新的增长点。

We have carried out cultural exchanges and cooperation with countries and regions all over the world. As many as 23 items of Gansu are high on the intangible cultural heritage list certified by the State Council. Archaeological studies of Dapuzishan Historical Site in Lixian County and Majiayuan Warring States Tomb in Zhangjiachuan are included among the Top 10 Archaeological Discoveries of 2006. *Reader*, a magazine renowned at home and abroad, enjoys even greater prestige as a Chinese brand. Generally speaking, locality, diversity and uniqueness constitute the cornerstone of Gansu's cultural distinctiveness, which has now become a new growth pole of economic and social progress.

各位朋友，在推进我省特色文化建设进程中，一年一度的伏羲公祭大典即将来临。2007年6月22日，也是中华民族的传统节气——夏至，甘肃省人民政府将在中华人文始祖伏羲、女娲故里——天水市隆重举行2007（丁亥）年公祭中华人文始祖伏羲大典。这是全世界华夏儿女共同朝觐祖先，共襄民族发展，增进文化认同感和民族凝聚力的一件盛事。

Friends, in the process of pushing forward Gansu's cultural development, the annual Memorial Ceremony to Chinese Ancestor Fuxi is around the corner. On June 22, 2007, the day of the Summer Solstice, Gansu Provincial People's Government will hold the Memorial Ceremony in Tianshui City, the hometown to Fuxi and Nüwa, two important ancestors of the Han Chinese. This is a grand occasion for Chinese people from every corner of the world to worship our ancestors with an eye on promoting the nation's economic development, cultural identification and national cohesion. （原文节选自时任甘肃省长在伏羲大典新闻发布会上的讲话）

第三章 ▶▶
# 汉英句法对比与翻译

语句是表达思想和观点的基本单位，语句的选用是英汉翻译的核心内容。对比英汉句法结构的差异，译者可以根据英汉语言的句法特点，选用自然、地道的句式传递原文所表达的意义

## 第一节　主语显型与主题显型

### 一、主语与主题

英语和汉语的不同思维模式决定了两种语言在建构句子表达思想时具有各自的特性。西方哲学深深植根于相对宽松自由的土壤之中，其发展更多地立足于逻辑和客观的基石。所谓"人是万物的主体"，在多元化的西方，并非主体哲学观。相反，崇尚自由、平等的西方人，在写作、交谈中，所使用的句式的主语很少束缚，很少一律化。人称可以作主语，非人称的一切事与物，无论具体的、抽象的、意念的、心理的，都可以"拉"来充当主语。既然主语可以五花八门，那么，就不难理解为什么英语的主语就不能像汉语那样可以随便缺席。因为既然主语不具备汉语主语的那种"一律"，一旦省略，受众必然如坠云雾。因此，英语句型结构较严谨完整，一个句子通常要有主语，主谓（subject-predicate）结构在英语所有句型中占绝大比例。英语本质上是主语显型（subject-prominent）语言。

道家、儒家思想是中国人的主体哲学观，他们提出的"万物与我为一""万物皆属于我""事在人为"的观点，使得汉民族思考问题、认知事物，都是以人的角度为出发点的。在语言组织上，这种思维习惯会使中国人以人为主语展开表述，从而导致人称主语句成了遣词造句的一种定式而深入人心了。但是，既然汉语句型之主语几乎千篇一律以人称作主语，就需要经常省略主语，以免单调乏味；同时，由于人称主语句已经深入人心，国人对这种句式的使用和接受已经发展到了"心有灵犀一点通"的地步，它的省略不但不会影响到交流，反而可以令行文或言辞更趋简洁，并且把注意力集中在真正重要的问题——主题上。因此，在汉语中，严格意义上的"主谓"句或"主动宾"句并非都是汉语句子的常态，没有主语的句型很普遍，属于主题显型语言。

具体说来，这两种语言分别表现出以下两种倾向。

### （一）主题句和无主句在汉语中很突出

有两种情况在汉语中比较突出：（1）主题显型（topic-prominent）句。中国人重主题，经常把句首成分看作主题加以评论，句子无论有无主语，突出的都是主题，而不是主语。（2）没有主题的无主句。很多情况下，汉语句子里既没有主语，也没有主题。

[例1] ①男人令人首先感到的印象是脏！当然，男人当中亦不乏刷洗干净洁身自好的，甚至还有油头粉面衣冠楚楚的，但大体讲来，男人消耗肥皂和水的数量要比较少些。②某一男校，对于学生洗澡是强迫的，入浴签名，每周计核，对于不曾入浴的初步惩罚是宣布姓名，最后的断然处置是定期强迫入浴，并派员监视，然而日久玩生，签名簿中尚不无浮冒情事。③有些男人，西装裤尽管挺直，④他的耳后脖根，土壤肥沃，常常宜于种麦！⑤袜子手绢不知随时洗涤，常常日积月累，到处塞藏，等到无可使用时，再从那一堆污垢存货当中拣选比较干净的去应急。⑥有些男人的手绢，拿出来硬像是土灰面制的百果糕，黑糊糊粘成一团，而且内容丰富；⑦男人的一双脚，多半好像是天然的具有泡菜霉干菜再加糖蒜的味道，所谓"濯足万里流"是有道理的，小小的一盆水确是无济于事，然而多少男人却连这一盆水都吝而不用，怕伤元气。两脚既然如此之脏，偏偏有些"逐臭之夫"喜于脚上藏垢纳污之处往复挖掘，然后嗅其手指，引以为乐！⑧多少男人洗脸都是专洗本部，边疆一概不理，洗脸毕，手背可以不湿，有的男人是在结婚后才开始刷牙。⑨"扪虱而谈"的是男人。……男人的脏大概是由于懒。（梁实秋《男人》）

①What strikes us first of all *in men* is their uncleanliness. There are of course no lack of men who always make a point of keeping themselves spick-and-span. And some of them even make up heavily and dress respectably. But, generally speaking, men consume a smaller quantity of soap and water than women. ②*A certain boys' school* makes it compulsory for its students to take a bath regularly. Every student had to sign his name before taking a bath so that the school authorities could conduct a weekly checkup. Those who violated the regulation for the first time would have their names published. The drastic measure for those who repeat the offense was to force them to take a bath regularly under surveillance. Nevertheless abuses crept in with time. Forgery was often discovered among the signatures. ③*Some men*, although they wear smooth-ironed Western style pants, ④ leave much dirt behind their ears and around their necks—so much that it is good enough for growing wheat! ⑤Their unwashed socks and handkerchiefs accumulate and are left here and there in unseen corners. When no more clean ones are available, some of the less dirty ones are picked out from the filthy stock to meet an urgent need. ⑥Men's handkerchiefs, curled up into blackened balls, look like fruit cakes made of wholemeal flour and have a very rich content of their own. ⑦Men's feet, for the most part, seem to have a distinctive smell of their own, like that of pickles, dried vegetables and sweetened garlic all mixed together. There is some truth in the saying: "The running water of a long river is good for washing one's feet." Therefore, it goes without saying that a small basin of water will hardly suffice for the same purpose. But lots of men begrudge using even a mere basin of water to wash their feet—perhaps for fear of sapping their vitality and spirit! Dirty as their feet are, some men are so eccentric as to indulge in passing their fingers repeatedly among their stinking toes and then smelling their fingers with gusto. ⑧Some men, when they wash up, they concentrate only on the face proper, without touching the rest of the head and without wetting the back of the hand. Some do not brush their teeth until after they get married. ⑨The addiction to "chatting while cracking body lice with fingernails" is unique to men only. ……Probably, men's uncleanliness is due to their laziness.

（张培基 译）

例1原文当中，画线部分的单词都不是主语，而是评论的对象，是显型主题。各个句子无论有无主语，突出的都是主题。在英译里，各个句子都有主语，是主语显型，原文句子里的主题，大多转换成了主语或者状语，只有第五句例外，采用了英语里极少出现的类主题+主语结构。

再来看看下例：

[例2]　说出来，有谁相信呢？我已经四天没吃饭了。

起初是一天吃四个烧饼，或者两个小面包；后来由四个减成两个，再由两个减成一个，最后简直穷得连买开水的一个铜板也没有了。口渴时就张开嘴来，站在自来水管的龙头下，一扭开来，就让水灌进嘴里，喝得肚子胀得饱饱的，又冷又痛，那滋味真有

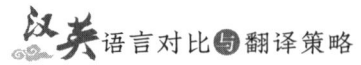

说不出的难受。

……

如果有人问我:"饥饿的滋味怎样?"我立刻干脆地回答他:"朋友,请你四天不吃一点东西,饿一下试试吧。"老实说,饥饿的确比死还要难受,比受了任何巨大深刻的痛苦还要苦。当你听到肠子饿得咕咕地叫时,好像有一条巨蛇要从你的腹内咬破了皮肉钻出来一般;有时你饿得头昏眼花,坐起来又倒下去了,想要走路,一双腿是酸软的,拖也拖不动;有时一口口的酸水从肚子里翻上来,使你呕吐,但又吐不出半点东西;更有时饿得实在不能忍受了,就想在自己的胳膊上咬下一块肉来吞下去,这时我才相信古时"易子而食"和现在有些地方把死人的肉煮来当饭吃的惨事是真的。(谢冰莹《饥饿》)

Believe it or not, I've been starving for four days on end.

At first, I ate nothing but four baked cakes or two small buns per day, then I cut them down by half and then by another half, until I didn't even own a copper for buying boiled water. When I was thirsty, I would stand under a tap and let its running water pour down my throat through my wide-open mouth. I felt bloated. *There* was a pain and chill in my stomach. I cannot tell you enough how miserable I was.

…

If *I*'m asked what it is like to go hungry, my answer is prompt and clear-cut, "Keep starving yourself for four days, my dear friend, and *you*, ll know." Honestly, hunger is even more painful than death. It is the greatest of all human sufferings. When you hear your own stomach rumbling with hunger, *you*'ll feel as if a large snake were trying to gnaw its way out of your belly. Sometimes, you feel so giddy that you cannot rise from your bed no matter how hard *you* try to, and your legs feel like jelly so that *you* cannot walk. Sometimes, *you* feel nauseous, but *you* throw up nothing but the gastric juice. *You* may even feel like gulping down a piece of flesh bitten off your own arm so as to appease your unbearable hunger. That made me believe as true the tragic story of ancients driven by hunger "to eat the flesh of each other's son" and victims of some calamity-stricken areas cooking corpses as food.（张培基　译）

例 2 中，汉语原文多数句子都没有主语，也没有显型主题，译成英语时都加上了主语。

## （二）英语是主语显型语言

英语则与汉语很不一样。除非是口语，英语极少使用主题句与无主语句，而是以主语作为必不可少的核心，成了组织句子结构的灵魂。这就意味着，在翻译过程中，译者不能照搬原文结构，而必须要考虑到汉语重主题，多主题句和无主句，而英语则重主语这一差异，根据译文的表达习惯，处理好英汉句子主语和主题的转换。切忌思维定式于汉语，误把汉语的主题当作英语的主语，或把汉语中能作主语而英语中不能作主语的句子成分直接译作主语。

试看以下几例：

[例 3] 许仙想和我说的话，我要听。

What Xu Xian has to say, I want to hear.

尽管该例的译文从语法角度来讲也正确，属于英语中的主题结构。不过，英语主题结构的使用大多表示强调，并非常例。因此，该译文译成"I want to hear what Xu Xian has to say."更为妥当。

正因为英语和汉语中都有主题结构，译员（特别是口译员）有时会按汉语的句子顺序把汉语主题直接翻译成英语的主语。例如：

[例 4] IT 产业，我认为在中国深圳最好。

The IT industry I think Shanghai is the best in China.

该例中译者误把汉语的主题"IT 产业"当作英语的主语。实际上，英语译文中的"The IT industry"并非英语的主语，因为它不是句子中的倒装成分，无法还原到正常的句序中。因此，原文应译作："In my opinion, the IT industry in Shenzhen is the best in China."

此外，受汉语影响，译者往往会把汉语的主题直接译作英语的主语，忽略了英语自身固有的语法要求，出现翻译错误。

[例 5] 我们宾馆能住六百多人。

Our hotel can stay more than six hundred guests.

如果仔细一点，就会发现"hotel"与"stay"不能搭配，就不会犯上述错误。然而，有时，翻译（口译）的即时性容不得他们有过多时间去认真考虑，仔细端详，往往会出现一些低级翻译错误，确属无奈。

当然，如前所述，英语口语中也会有一些类主题句：

[例6] The final exam: you should do well if you read, if you come to lecture, and if you attend section.

期末考试：如果你做了阅读，来听了讲座，参加了小组讨论，就应该不会有什么问题。

[例7] But those that we make more intelligent, that we give emotions to, and that we empathize with, will be a problem.

但是那些我们使之变得更聪明的，那些我们给予情感的，那些我们感同身受的机器人，它们将会是一个问题。

## 二、英—汉翻译转换

### （一）省略主语

在翻译中，由于学生思维受源语影响，忽略源语与目标语之间的差异，因而在英汉翻译中会出现欧化的汉语，而在汉英翻译中则会造出生硬的中国式英语。具体而言，在英汉翻译过程中，受英语思维定式的影响，汉语译文中本可以省略的主语却啰唆地一一照实译出，听起来就像一个外国人刚学汉语，洋相百出。

[例8] I'm glad to have the pleasure of meeting you in my hometown.

我很高兴能在我的家乡接待您。

[例9] I hope you will enjoy your stay here.

我希望您在这里过得愉快。

在上面两个例子中，"我"在汉语口语中通常是省略的，因为在特定语境中听话人知道说话人是谁。译文中使用"我"反倒别扭，虽非大的语法错误，却不是十分通顺。

### （二）增加主题结构

英语中极少出现主题结构，而汉语中则非常乐见主题结构，这种差异意味着很多英语句子在汉译时，如果能够深挖内涵，"无中生有"地添上主题结构，往往会显得更加清楚明了。

[例10] Sometimes the heart sees what is invisible to the eye.

有时候，眼睛看不见的，心灵却能看见。

[例11] Tender tailoring. Feminine but far from frilly... gentle on your budget, too.

做工,精巧细致;式样,娇美自然;价格,低廉宜人。

[例12] TE says: "Shop with confidence."

TE百货,值得信赖的商店,充满自信的选择。

[例13] Who ever loved that loved not at first sight?

对真正的所爱,有谁不是一见钟情?

(三) 保留主题结构

英语原文中的主题结构和无主句不仅数量远远不如汉语中那么突出,而且往往被归入不规范的语言现象,一般只出现在广告、口语(或模拟口语)中。在译成汉语时,正好可以按照汉语的习惯,保留主题结构。

[例14] Featherwater: light as a feather.

法泽瓦特眼镜:轻如鸿毛。

[例15] So, your obligation to your aged parent, that's greater than to aged parents around the world, (*and it*) is only because and insofar as you're repaying a benefit that your parent gave you when you were growing up?

所以,你对自己年迈的父母所尽的义务,要远远大于对世界上其他人的年迈父母所尽的义务,仅仅是因为你要报答他们在抚养你的过程中所带给你的好处?

[例16] To try and reach some much desired goal—the favours of a beautiful lady, high public office, running like mad after some such objective, when it is quite certain that it is ultimately only leading to death—sooner or later, the vanity and pointlessness of it all, the absurd overestimation of the importance of such short-term goals, make the situation of the persons who are after them essentially comic. (Martin Esslin *Who's Afraid of Samuel Beckett?*)

执着于某个孜孜以求的目标——窈窕佳人,高级公职,在必然引向死亡的路上仍然亡命地追逐此类目标——追逐者迟早都会因为目标的毫无价值和索然无味,会因为荒唐地高估了此类短期目标的重要性而沦为滑稽的笑料。(张云 译)

## 三、汉—英翻译转换

### （一）汉语无主句的英译

在翻译汉语无主句时，经常使用以下三种方法解决主语隐含的问题，以符合英语语法习惯。

1. 添加人称代词作为主语

［例17］岂曰无衣？Are you not battle-drest?

与子同袍。Let's share the plate for breast!

王于兴师，We shall go up the line.

修我戈矛，Let's make our lances shine!

与子同仇。Your foe is mine! （《诗经·秦风·无衣》许渊冲译）

［例18］曲则全，Stooping, you will be preserved.

枉则直，Wronged, you will be righted.

洼则盈，Hollow, you will be filled.

敝则新，Worn out, you will be renewed.

少则得，Having little, you may gain.

多则惑。Having much, you may be at a loss. （《道德经》许渊冲译）

［例19］闻人善则疑之，闻人恶则信之，此满腔杀机也。

Beware of a man who is always doubtful when he hears something good about you, but is quick to believe something bad.

［例20］打铁还需自身硬。

To forge iron, one must be strong.

2. 用"it"，或"there be"当主语

［例21］又是一个似曾相识的周末，又是一个欲说还休的阴雨天。我突然感到一种对于友情的深切的渴望，我的星散于海角天涯的友人们啊，你们现在都在哪里？（段和平《朋友》）

It is such a weekend as reminiscent of another similar one, a cloudy day threatening to rain which suggests something one would rather hold back on the point of expressing, that stirs in me a strong longing for my friends. Where are you now, scattered far away from me?

[例22] 一向没有整理照片的习惯，却有喜欢盲目拍照的毛病。

I've never got into the habit of sorting out photos. However, it's almost a habit of mine, a bad habit at that, to have photos taken thoughtlessly.

[例23] 在社会各级都有许多监督委员会。

There are numerous watch-dog committees at all levels of society.

[例24] 菩提本无树，　　Wisdom has never been a tree,
明镜亦非台；　　And the bright mirror has no stand.
本来无一物，　　There has never been anything,
何处惹尘埃？　　So whereupon can the dust land?

3. 转为被动语态

[例25] 搞好治理整顿也离不开深化改革。

The success of improvement and rectification cannot be separated from deepened reform.

[例26] 未经审批机关批准，合同中不得规定禁止受方在合同期满后继续使用技术的条款。

Unless approval has been obtained from the review organ, a contract should not include provisions prohibiting the recipient from continuing to use the technology after the expiry of the contract term.

（二）汉语主题句的英译

在翻译实践中，汉语主题句的英译到底有哪些具体的操作路径呢？下面是几个较为典型的做法：

1. 译成主语

[例27] 祸兮福之所倚，
福兮祸之所伏。

Weal comes after woe;
Woe lies under weal.

[例28] 美人之胜于花者，解语也；花之胜于美人者，生香也，二者不可得兼，舍生香而取解语者也。（张潮《幽梦影》）

Women are flowers that can talk, and flowers are women who give off fragrance. Rather enjoy talk than fragrance. (林语堂 译)

［例29］夫天地者，万物之逆旅；光阴者，百代之过客。而浮生若梦，为欢几何？古人秉烛夜游，良有以也。（李白《春夜宴从弟桃花园序》）

The universe is a lodging house for myriad things, and time itself is a traveling guest of the centuries. This floating life is like a dream. How can one enjoy oneself? It is for this reason that the ancient people held candles to celebrate the night. (林语堂 译)

［例30］临皋亭下不数十步，便是大江，其半是峨眉雪水，吾饮食沐浴皆取焉，何必归乡哉！江山风月，本无常主，闲者便是主人。问范子丰新第园池，与此孰胜？所不如者，上无两税及助役钱耳。（苏轼《临皋闲题》）

The Great River lies only a few steps below me and half of its water comes from the Omei Mountain, so that it isalmost as good as seeing our hometown. The hills and the river, the wind and the moon, have no owner; they belong to anyone who has the leisure to enjoy them. How would your new garden compare with mine? I suppose you have the advantage of paying the summer and autumn taxes on it, and the draft exemption tax besides, while I don't. (林语堂 译)

2. 译成主题+解说性短语结构（这一结构多用于诗歌、人物简介、文章标题等特定的语域）

［例31］忌妒——

是心灵上的肿瘤（艾青《无题》）

Jealousy—

A cancer in the soul. （庞秉钧　闵福德　高尔登　译）

［例32］气球　飘浮在高空的斑斓的巨物，但是，哪怕是针尖大小的批评也受不了。

Balloon A gigantic colourful object floating high in the sky, but in capable of withstanding the slightest pin-prick of criticism.

3. 译成状语

[例33] 泉水上，天雨次，井水下。其山水，捡乳泉、石池漫流者上。其江水，取去人远者。井，取汲多者。（陆羽《茶经》）

Spring water is best for making tea, next rain water, and next well water. Among spring waters, those that come in swift, clear currents over rocks can be used. River water must be taken from places far from close human habitation. In well water, wells that are constantly drawn are preferred. （林语堂 译）

[例34] 花不可见其落，月不可见其沉，美人不可见其夭。
种花须见其开，待月须见其满，著书须见其成，美人须见其畅适，方有实际，否则皆为虚设。（张潮《幽梦影》）

Avoid seeing the wilting of flowers, the decline of the moon, and the death of young women. One should wait to see the flowers in bloom after planting them, see the full moon after waiting days for it, and complete writing a book after starting it, and should see to it that a beautiful woman is happy and gay. Otherwise, all the labors are in vain. （林语堂 译）

[例35] 楼上看山，城头看雪，灯前看月，舟中看霞，月下看美人，另是一番情境。（张潮《幽梦影》）

Things may strike you as charmingly breathtaking when looked at from a particular place, such as hills seen from a tower, snow seen from the top of a city wall, the moon seen from the lamplight, river haze seen from a boat, and pretty women seen in the moonlight. （林语堂 译）

[例36] 面对失控的网络暴力，我感到无力、痛心、愤怒！我还是那句，一星期前说的那句："非要耍流氓的来这里好了！"多行不义必自毁，请自重。

These internet violence has gotten out of hand. I feel helpless, hurt and enraged in the face of thesecyberbullies! But I stick to what I said a week ago: if you want to act like a hooligan, you have come to the right place. For those who delight in unrighteousness, you will reap what you sow.

[例37] 今之武将讲武事，亦属纸上谈兵；今之文人论文章，大都道听途说。（张潮《幽梦影》）

Nowadays, when a military man discusses wars and battles, it is also mostly an armchair strategy, and when a literary man discusses literature, it is mostly based on rumors picked up from hearsay. (林语堂 译)

4. 译成宾语

[例38] 傲骨不可无，傲心不可有；无傲骨则近于鄙夫，有傲心不得为君子。(张潮《幽梦影》)

A man must have pride in his bones, i. e., in his character, but not in his heart. Not to have pride in character is to be with the common herd, and to have pride in one's heart is inappropriate for a gentlemen. (林语堂 译)

[例39] 不要相信牧师的话——
上帝在他嘴上，
魔鬼在他心里。(艾青《无题》)

Don't believe the preacher:
He has God on his lips
And Satan in his heart. (庞秉钧 闵福德 高尔登 译)

[例40] 基本路线要管一百年，动摇不得。

We should adhere to the basic line for a hundred years with no wavering.

5. 译成主题式状语+主语结构

这一种情况主要是源于原文的主题本身就是以状语的形式呈现的。

[例41] 爱逐臭争利，锱铢必较的，请到长街闹市去；爱轻嘴薄舌，争是论非的，请到茶馆酒楼去；爱锣鼓铿锵，管弦嗷嘈的，请到歌台剧院去；爱宁静淡泊，沉思默想的，深深的小巷在欢迎你！(柯灵《巷》)

To those who strive after fame and gain, and haggle over every penny, please go to the downtown area! To those who are sharp-tongued and quarrelsome, please go the teahouse or restaurant! To those who love deafening gongs and drums as well as noisy wind and string instruments, please go to the opera house or theatre! To those who are given to profound meditation and a quiet life without worldly desires, welcome to the lane! (张培基

译）

[例42] 至于何时可以推广到更高的层次、到什么层次，我希望越快越好。至于我的任期，确实已经过半了。在我今后不到三年里面，我将恪尽职守，奋力拼搏，以不辜负人民对我的信任。

As to when such a system can be extended to a higher level and as to what level they may possibly be upgraded to, my hope is, the sooner the better. As to my term of office, it is true that I'm half way through. So in the less than three years remaining in my current term, I shall do everything to discharge my duty and devote all I can to my job, so that I can live up to the trust of the people.

6. 译成类主题结构

[例43] 那双清明无邪的眼睛，在这个万山环绕不上二百五十户人家的小村落中，看过了些什么事情？那张含娇带俏的小嘴，到想唱歌时，应当唱些什么歌？还有那颗心，平时为屋后大山豺狼的长嗥声，盘在水缸边碗口大黄喉蛇的歇凉呼气声，训练得稳定结实，会不会还为什么新事情而剧烈跳跃？我难道还不愿意放弃作一个画家的痴梦？（沈从文《湘西散记·雪晴》）

Those limpid, innocent eyes, what had they seen in this little village of no more than two hundred and fifty households surrounded by countless hills? What songs should float from that pouting rosebud mouth if she was moved to sing? And her heart, trained to steady staunchness by the drawn-out howls of wolves on the mountain behind the house and the hisses of the yellow snake, as thick as the mouth of a rice bowl, which coiled by the water vat, would it beat faster because of some new event?（杨宪益 戴乃迭 译）

当主题句在语篇中大量连续出现时，可以变化着交替使用以上手段，可以丰富英语译文的结构，显得地道、自然，如上例。

【翻译欣赏】

**1**

提高自主创新能力，建设创新型国家，这是国家发展战略的核心，是提高综合国力的关键。

We need to enhance China's capacity for independent innovation and make China an innovative country. This is the core of our national development strategy and a crucial link in enhancing the overall national strength.

要坚持走中国特色自主创新道路，把增强自主创新能力贯彻到现代化建设各个方面。

We need to keep to the path of independent innovation with Chinese characteristics and improve our capacity for independent innovation in all areas of modernization.

认真落实国家中长期科学和技术发展规划纲要，加大对自主创新投入，着力突破制约经济社会发展的关键技术。

We need to conscientiously implement the Outline of the National Program for Long-and Medium-Term Scientific and Technological Development (2006-20), increase spending on independent innovation, and make breakthroughs in key technologies vital to our economic and social development.

加快建设国家创新体系，支持基础研究、前沿技术研究、社会公益性技术研究。

We will speed up forming a national innovation system and support basic research, research in frontier technology and technological research for public welfare.

加快建立以企业为主体、市场为导向、产学研相结合的技术创新体系，引导和支持创新技术向企业聚集，促进科技成果向现实生产力转化。

We will step up our efforts to establish a market-oriented system for technological innovation, in which enterprises play the leading role and which combines the efforts of enterprises, universities and research institutes, and guide and support the concentration of factors of innovation in enterprises, thereby promoting the translation of scientific and technological advances into practical productive forces.

深化科技管理体制改革，优化科技资源配置，完善鼓励技术创新和科技成果产业化的法制保障、政策体系、激励机制、市场环境。

We will deepen reform of the system for managing science and technology, optimize the allocation of relevant resources, and improve the legal guarantee, policy system, incentive mechanism and market conditions to encourage technological innovation and the application of scientific and technological achievements in production.

实施知识产权战略。充分利用国际资源。

We will implement the strategy for intellectual property rights. We will make the best use of international resources of science and technology.

进一步营造鼓励创新的环境,培养造就世界一流科学家和科技领军人才,使创新智慧竞相迸发、创新人才大量涌现。

We will continue to create conditions conducive to innovation, work to train world-class scientists and leaders in scientific and technological research, attach great importance to training innovative personnel in the frontline of production, inspire the creative wisdom of the whole society and bring forth large numbers of innovative personnel in all areas.

## 2

我觉得外国舆论对中国国有企业的困难看得太大。我们讲中国国有企业的亏损面现在有百分之四十几,是按企业的个数来统计的。中国目前的工业企业有七万九千个。你按这一种——有时是很小的,只有几十个人或者几个人——按这个数目来统计,当然亏损面很大。但是,请大家注意,其中500个特大型的国有企业,它们向国家缴纳的税收和它自己的利润,就占了全中国利润和税收的85%。而这500个特大型企业,亏损面只有10%,也就是说50个。所以我们认为从总体上讲,国有亏损企业摆脱困境,三年够了。

I think the foreign media have overestimated or played up the difficulties of China's state-owned enterprises. When we say that the loss-making percentage of the state-owned enterprises is 40%, we are referring to the number of loss-making SOEs. You know, in China there are 79,000 industrial enterprises which are state-owned, and some are very small, employing only several or dozens of people. So, in terms of the number of these SOEs, it seems that the loss-making percentage is high. But here I'd like to call your attention to this fact that in China we have 500 extremely large or mega SOEs, whose profits and taxes turned in to the state account for 85% of the nation. And among the 500 mega SOEs, the loss-making percentage is only 10%, that is, only 50 of them are at a loss. So, that's why I say that three years are enough for us to bring most of the loss-making enterprises out of their difficult situation.

## 第二节 无灵主语与有灵主语

### 一、英语的无灵主语 & 主谓"混搭"倾向

无灵主语（inanimate subject）句指非人称主语（Impersonal Subject）后续一般为人称主语所使用的表示感觉、意识、情感或动作之类的动词作谓语，从而构成的句式。通常折射一定生命内涵的动词被挪用于不具生命的主语，因此，这样的句式就自然而然地抹上了拟人（personification）的色彩。除了表达顿趋活泼之外，此句型新意拂面，结构严谨，言简意丰，语体活泼。试比较以下各例中的 A、B 两种译文。

［例1］发怒之后，我不难过，也不后悔。

A：AfterI got angry, I felt neither sorrow nor regret.

B：Neither sorrow nor regret followed my passionate outburst.

［例2］进入青年期，他工作了，恋爱了。

A：After he became a youth, he got a job and then fell in love with a girl.

B：Youth sees him on a job and in love.

［例3］2019 年 10 月我在欧洲学习。

A：I studied in Europe in October 2019.

B：October 2019 found me studying in Europe.

［例4］二十岁的时候，和某个人晚上一起去看了场电影，不经意中拉了一次手，结果幸福了整整一个夏天。三十岁之后，坐在香格里拉酒店的旋转餐厅陪客户吃自助餐，在缓缓的转动之中，莫名其妙地一阵空虚，突然间对一切感到索然无味……

A：At the age of twenty, I went to see a film on a night with someone who casually took my hand in his palm, and this sweet happiness lingered for the whole summer. After I have turned thirty, I feel an aching void in the slow movement of the rotating restaurant, where I dine with my clients upon a buffet meal, in Shangri-la hotel and all of a sudden I lost

　　　　interest in everything.
　　B: At the age of twenty, one evening, I went to see a film. In the darkness, an incidental touch of hands filled me with joy all that summer. Now thirty, I am seated with my clients at a buffet in the revolving restaurant of Shangri-la hotel. In the slow rotating, an indescribable emptiness, all of a sudden, seizes me, and I find everything dull and dreary.

在以上例句中，可以看到，译文 B 由于使用了非人称主语，较之译文 A 更有英语味，而汉语原文则更习惯于使用人称主语。

有趣的是，英语的非人称主语还经常"混搭"具备人称意味的、充满灵动的谓语动词，相较于汉语的"常规搭配"，显得别有风味。

英语和汉语的这一习惯差异可以通过非人称主语句的数量对比来说明——英语的非人称主语句已成习惯，而且偏好"混搭"，美不胜收，一如春日满山遍野的绚丽山花；而汉语的非人称主语句，尤其是"混搭"的那种，尚在花蕾阶段，往往就已经被标准化的教育机器当作"花妖"给掐了，仿佛仅有天才才可以搞些疏落有致的"灵光一现"，一如点缀于天幕的寂寥晨星。

具体而言，英语无灵主语及其混搭倾向大体可以分为以下几大类，其相应的汉译句子大都改成了有灵主语的正配。

## （一）无灵主语"混搭"有灵动词

英语用无灵主语搭配有灵动词的句式使用的场合频率比汉语广。

英语这类句子采用无灵主语，即用抽象名词或无生命的事物名称作主语，表示抽象概念、具体事物、自然现象、心理、感觉、体貌、见闻或时间地点等，但谓语却常使用有灵动词（animate verb），即本来表示人的动作或行为的动词，如 see, find, bring, give, escape, surround, kill, deprive, seize, send, know, tell, permit, invite, take, drive, prevent... from 等。这种句式往往语气活泼，令人回味，带有拟人化（personification）的修辞色彩，其广泛使用反映了英美民族无所不在的幽默感。

1. 时间名词

[例 5] In reality, however, the Putin years saw Russia turn into a petro-state.

实际上，在普京时代，俄罗斯却变成了一个石油国家。

2. 见闻名词

[例6] 进入耶鲁大学的校园,看到莘莘学子青春洋溢的脸庞,呼吸着书香浓郁的空气,我不由回想起 40 年前我在北京清华大学时的美好时光。

The moment I step into your Yale, with its distinctive academic flavor, the sight of your young and eager faces brings back in a flash memories of my wonderful days at Qinghua University in Beijing 40 years ago.

[例7] "也许,多年后的一个黄昏,像现在,你一人独坐的时候,你会想起眼前的这一刻的。"沉默了很长时间的丈夫,突然说出这样的话来,而且在声音中还带着一丝藏不住的伤感。(王亚丽《珍惜感情》)

"Perhaps, this scene will come back to you years later when you sit alone at sunset like this." A tinge of melancholy was tangible in my husband's voice, which broke the long silence. (陈文伯译)

3. 体貌名词

[例8] The little chap's good-natured honest face won his way for him.
这小伙子长相老实,看上去脾气也好,到处有人缘。

[例9] 她们或许是我们的奶奶,满头银丝,满脸皱纹,世人多用"慈祥"去形容她们,但很少有人能品位皱纹背后那岁月与历史拂过的幽香。她们无须再用铅华刻意雕饰,我却分明看见她和她老伴共同演出那首动人的歌——《牵手》。

She is very charming when singing "Hand in Hand" in a duet with her lifelong companion. White-haired and wrinkled, she may be one of our grannies, a perfect image of kindness as she is often described. The furrows ploughed by time deny replenishment with cosmetics, for they are fertile soil radiating the fragrance of history.

4. 心理名词

[例10] 哦,时光流逝太快,还没有很好地一览风光,怎么就已入秋境了呢?便觉得有三分怅惘,三分无奈。然而,思之又觉释然。(风舒青《风采翩然》)

A touch of frustration and helplessness comes over me as I realize how time flies. Before I have sufficiently admired the scenery and enjoyed the beauties of life, it's already autumn. However, a second thought brings me relieved calm. (陈文伯 译)

[例 11] 有的人如游客，不急不慌，走走停停，看花开花落，看云卷云舒。有时也在风中走，雨里行，心却像张开的网，放过了焦躁苦恼。

Others travel leisurely like tourists. They would take time off now and then for a look at blooming flowers or fallen petals. They would stop to admire clouds gathering and dispersing. Even when they go against the wind or are caught in the rain, they never get annoyed. For worries slip their minds as from an open net.

[例 12] 当一个女人突然之间意识到自己是一个女人并且为自己的性别感到自豪时，是女人最美的时候。

A woman is never more beautiful than when the full sense of being a female dawns on her and makes her very proud of the sex.

[例 13] The happiness—the superior advantages of the young women round about her, gave Rebecca inexpressible pangs of envy.

丽贝卡看见她周围的小姐那么福气，享受种种优越的权利，却有说不出的眼红。

5. 自然现象名词或其它具体的"物"的名词

[例 14] Along the roads, laurel, viburnum and alder, great ferns and wildflowers delighted the traveler's eye through much of the year.

在道路两旁，月桂、荚蒾、桤木、蕨菜，还有那各色的野花，一年四季竞相开放，实让路人赏心悦目，乐此不疲。

[例 15] 就这样，面对着满院子灿烂的花，不说一句话，心里的怨恨已全消失了。(王亚丽《珍惜感情》)

The blooming flowers in the yard presenting a riot of colors before my eyes quietly dispelled all my grudges.

[例 16] 又过了几个月，我看见他们手上戴了结婚戒指，可是他们不像以前那样健谈了，她又在看书，他在看报。

Months later, rings appeared glistening on their fingers but chatting was gradually replaced by reading, one with a book the other with a newspaper.

［例17］于是，暮色中匆匆的人群里，总有我赶路的身影，雨里，雾里，雪里，只盼着早些回家，洗去一身的疲劳，泡上一杯清茶，点上一炷檀香，打开半卷的书卷，一任轻柔的旋律把我带进一个美丽的境界……

Thus the gathering dark often finds me hastening home in a hurrying crowd. Whether it is windy or foggy, amid all the rains and snows, it is the longing to be home that quickens my steps. To be home means to end a day's fatigue and enjoy myself in a world of my own. With a nice cup of tea and a burning sandalwood incense by my side, I can resume my suspended reading with a soft melody, which gets me carried away to a wonderful fairyland …

（二）用非人称代词"it"作主语

代词"it"除了用来代替除人以外的生物或事物之外，还广泛用作填补词（expletive），包括：

1. 用作先行词（preparatory "it"）

［例18］For some reason we are satisfied to think we are well-protected; it does not occur to ask ourselves: Why are we having to barricade ourselves against our neighbors and fellow citizens?

出于某种原因，当我们觉得防范周密时我们才觉得安心；我们从来没有想到问问自己：为什么非得在自己和邻居之间、和同住一城的市民之间垒起一道墙来呢？

［例19］To the man, whatever his place on the paper, nothing should satisfy short of the best. It is here that ability counts and that character counts, and it is on these that a newspaper, if it is to be worthy of its power and duty, must rely. (C. P. Scott  *On Journalism*)

至于报人，不管他在报社内处于何种地位，都不满足于次佳。正是在这一点上能力很有关系，性格也很有关系。一张报纸要不辱没其享有的力量和应负的责任，就必须依靠这些。（陈文伯　译）

2. 用作虚义词（unspecified "it"）

代替的主语是难以言明的现象或情形，如用以表示自然现象、时间、空间以及用于惯用语之中。

[例 20] It doesn't take too much stretch of the imagination to realize how difficult it would be to live in a wild place like that.
你可以想象得出，生活在那样一个荒野之地是何等艰难！

[例 21] How is it going with the patient?
那个病人怎么样了？

3. 用作强调词（emphatic "it"）

引导所要强调的成分，也是一种形式主语：

[例 22] It is a silly goose that comes to the sermon of the fox.
再蠢的鹅也不会来听狐狸布道。

[例 23] It is not so much the hours that tells as the way we use them.
起作用的与其说是时间多少，不如说我们善于利用时间。

英语的非人称代词"it"往往使句子显出物称倾向，汉语没有这类用法的非人称代词，因而常使用人称，或省略人称，采用无主句。

（三）"There be +"句式

英语的"There be +"句式也具有非人称倾向，汉语则采用比较具体的人称或事物作主语，或者是不用主语（但是逻辑主语为人）。

[例 24] There is a growing acceptance by the husband of the wife's employment.
越来越多的丈夫接受了妻子参加工作的事实。

[例 25] There are places and objects that signify impatience.
许多场所和物件都表明人们有急躁情绪。

## 二、汉语的有灵主语 & 主谓"正配"倾向

汉语虽然也有用拟人法来描述抽象的概念或无生命的事物，如"高山低头，河水让路"，"什么风把你给吹来的？"但这种表达法较常见于形象的比喻或轻松的文体，无论从使用的语境范围还是出现的频率来看，都远远不及英语。

汉语的有灵动词（animate subject）一般只能与人称主语搭配（有时候以省略了人称主语的无主句形式呈现），因为根据中国人的思维习惯，人或社会

团体才有这类有意识、有意志的行为，非人类的、无生命的事物只能有一些无意识、无意志的状态、运动或变化。从另一方面来看，这也反映了汉语民族不苟言笑，说话、思维相对严肃、沉重的特点。如：

[例26] 来这儿观光的人无不赞叹美国这块土地幅员广阔、多姿多彩。

The American scene awes the viewers with both its variety and size.

[例27] 上海的一位女网友留言说："手底下的人实在是太无能了，他也不容易。"

"His job is not easy, with everyone below him being completely incompetent," read one post, from a woman in Shanghai.

[例28] 又是一个似曾相识的周末，又是一个欲说还休的阴雨天。我突然感到一种对于友情的深切的渴望，我的星散于海角天涯的友人们啊，你们现在都在哪里？（段和平《朋友》）

It is such a weekend as reminiscent of another similar one, a cloudy day threatening to rain which suggests something one would rather hold back on the point of expressing, that stirs in me a strong longing for my friends. Where are you now, scattered far away from me?。（陈文伯 译）

[例29] 近来忙于公司事务，未能及早登门探视，深感抱歉。

I am very sorry that the pressure of corporate business has prevented me from paying an earlier visit to you.

[例30] 从小到大，聚沙成塔，所以家里放着不少照片。（水月《老照片》）

Thus like the saying "Many a little makes a mickle", photos have been piling up in my home throughout the years from my childhood to womanhood.（陈文伯 译）

## 三、英语无灵主语 & "混搭"倾向的汉译

相对来说，英语有灵主语句多属常规搭配，直译就可以了，在此略过。而其无灵主语句不但出现频率远高于汉语，而且经常采用汉语中少见的"混搭"，翻译起来就要多花一些心思。

通过比较我们发现，汉英语言中主语表现出来的差异，是由于持两种语言的人认知思维方式差异和两种语言本身的特点所致。可以说，汉语言表达突出

了以人为出发点的认知特点，而英语语言表达则体现了以事物即客观实在为出发点的思维认知模式。因而，在英译汉时，要遵循英语语言的认知思维特点，根据英语的"有灵"主语及其"混搭"倾向，在英语译成中文时选用有灵主语的"正配"，从而使译文更加地道、准确。

具体而言，译员可以灵活地将英语无灵主语转化为汉语的谓语、宾语和状语等。

1. 无灵主语转译成谓语，主谓"混搭"转换为"正配"

汉语表达有一种动态倾向，即本来属于名词表达的概念，用动词来表达。因而英译汉时，经常要将英语中的主语译成汉语的谓语。

[例31] When loneliness comes over you as a result of too much thinking, a favorite book will ease your mind and broaden your horizons.

如果静思太久，觉得孤单了，不妨翻开你喜爱的书，书会使你轻松让你充实。

[例32] The thought of spending another week at home makes me sick.

一想到还要在家里再呆一个星期我就难受。

2. 无灵主语转译成宾语，主谓"混搭"转换为"正配"

[例33] In the home, washing machines promised to free women from having to toil over the laundry. In reality, they encouraged us to change our clothes daily instead of weekly, creating seven times as much washing and ironing.

在家里使用洗衣机的初衷，本是要让妇女摆脱繁重的洗衣劳作。但事实上，它们促使我们每天，而不是每星期换一次衣服，这就使得熨洗衣物的工作量变成了原来的7倍。

[例34] A letter or telephone comes from someone you have not met, and you find yourself imagining what the person looks like, putting a face to the hidden voice.

一个素未谋面的人给你寄来一封信或打来一通电话，你不知不觉地想象这个人是个什么样儿，猜测这个隐秘声音的主人究竟长着一张什么样的面孔。

3. 无灵主语转译成状语，主谓"混搭"转换为"正配"

[例35] I was one of the Murzim's several cooks and, quite the same as for folk ashore, this Thanksgiving morning had seen us busily preparing a traditional dinner featuring roast turkey.

我是"军市一号"上的一名厨师，跟岸上的人们一样，那个感恩节上午，我们在忙着烹制一顿以烤火鸡为主的传统菜肴。

[例36] Your nomination just bobbled its way up to the top.

你在提名人选中排名已经上升到第一位啦。

4. "it""there be"句转译成无主句或有灵主语句，主谓"混搭"转换为"正配"

[例37] After a while, like a dawn's brightening, a further answer did come—that there were people to thank, people who had done so much for me that I could never possibly repay them.

过了片刻，如同晨曦初现，一个更清晰的念头终于涌现脑际——要感谢他人，那些赐我以诸多恩惠，我根本无以回报的人们。

[例38] Chinese teachers are fearful that if skills are not acquired early, they may never be acquired; there is, on the other hand, no comparable hurry to promote creativity.

中国老师担心，如果年轻人不及早掌握技艺，就有可能一辈子都掌握不了技艺；另一方面，他们并不同样地急于促进创造力的开发。

## 四、汉语"正配"倾向的英译

汉语的"混搭"往往被视作修辞手段，多数可以直译，不难操作，即使少数需要特殊处理的，本课程也将在后面的"修辞对比与翻译"中另做分析。这里主要讲的，是其"正配"倾向的英译，包括两种情况：

### （一）汉语有灵主语 & 主谓"正配"倾向的英译

如前所述，汉语语言表达突出了以人为出发点的认知特点，而英语语言表达则体现了以事物即客观存在为出发点的思维认知模式。因而，在汉译英时，宜遵循英语语言的认知思维特点，根据英语的"无灵"主语倾向，在汉语译成英文时选用无灵主语，从而使译文更加地道、准确。

具体而言，译员可以灵活地将汉语谓语、宾语和状语转化为英语主语。此外，译员还可选用形式主语"it"和"there be"结构。

1. 谓语转译成无灵主语，主谓"正配"转换为"混搭"

英语表达有一种静态倾向，即本来属于动词（或形容词）表达的概念，用抽象名词来表达动作、行为、变化、状态、体貌、心理、见闻、情感等，这也符合了现代英语的"名词化"趋势。因而汉译英时,经常要将汉语中的谓语译成英语的主语。

[例 39] 能和你相遇,我不知道交上什么好运。只因为你的一个吻,我相信万世的轮回,只为那一瞬间,一瞬间尝尽甜蜜与幸福。以后的每一分,每一刻,我都会守护在你身边,让你幸福一辈子。

I don't know what strike of good fortune allows me to make you mine. All it took was one kiss. The wheels of fortune turned and brought me to a perfect moment... of tenderness and happiness. From now on every moment, every second I have, I will spend beside you.

[例 40] 难道把头仰起来
就以为比别人高了吗(艾青《无题》)
Will raising the head skywards
Add a cubit to one's stature? (庞秉钧　闵福德　高尔登　译)

[例 41] 奢望它第二次出现是不实际的,结果是找不回第一次的感觉,反而破坏了原有的美好回忆。(何松《第一次》)

A second occurrence, if possible, would be a bare resemblance in which one seeks in vain such feelings one had before. Or even worse, it might spoil one's original impression that has been fascinating so far. (陈文伯　译)

2. 宾语转译成无灵主语,主谓"正配"转换为"混搭"

因为英语强调突出客观世界的存在实体,以自然为认知对象。因而根据英语的表达习惯,常常把汉语的宾语译成英语的主语,从而把客观事物对人产生的效果生动、形象地表达出来。

[例 42] 有时,父亲的手伤得很重,伤口大得吓人,要是换了我或者别人,肯定跑到急诊去缝针了,可父亲从来没往心里去过。

Sometimes, the cuts in his seriously wounded hands were scaring, which would send others like me immediately to the emergency room for stitches. But instead, such things never created a ripple in father's mind.

[例 43] 春日的傍晚,在北海边一家室外的冷饮店闲坐,看着波光粼粼的水面,嗅着枝叶的清香,觉得空气中充满了生命气息。(伊萍《分心》)

It was late in a spring afternoon. I was sitting idle at a cold drink stall near Beihai Lake enjoying the sight of shining ripples. The faint fragrance of foliage in the air awoke me to a full sense of life. (陈文伯 译)

[例44] 步入沟中，便可见林中碧海澹荡生辉，瀑布舒洒碧玉。一到金秋，满山枫叶绛红。盛夏，湖山幽翠。仲春，树绿花艳……，四时都呈现出它的天然原始，宁静幽深。

Mystic lakes and sparkling waterfalls captivate your eyes as you enter the ravine. The trees are in their greenest in spring when intensified by colourful flowers. In summer, warm tints spread over the hills and lakelands. As summer passes into autumn, the ample trees turn fiery red, splashing color through the thick forest hills... Tranquility pervades primitive Jiuzhaigou throughout the year.

3. 状语转译成无灵主语，主谓"正配"转换为"混搭"

按照英语的表达习惯，把原来汉语的状语结构，如原因、方式状语以及表示自然现象的时间、地点变成英语的主语。

[例45] 中年以后，多爱中国茶。中国茶那股若有若无的幽香，是深藏不露的。

Middle age turns him to Chinese tea, which gives a pleasant scent only discernible off and on.

[例46] 多情自古伤离别。

Parting especially saddens the sentimental.

[例47] 二十岁的时候，挤在人头攒动的公共大巴上，吃着甜筒，挺开心。三十岁之后，看见破旧肮脏的的士都心烦，拜托！油价一跌，就去买车吧，一路开往小康。

At the age of twenty, I felt so contented sandwiched in a jammed bus, eating ice cream. After thirty, even the sight of a shabby and sordid taxi may sicken me. Ok! When the oil price goes down, I'll buy a car and drive along the road of well-to-do.

4. 用 it 作无灵主语

[例48] 前几日，一位阔别多年的文友经过辗转曲折的多方"寻觅"，终于通过另一位朋友向我转达了他急于同我重建联系的渴望。这位友人多年前跻身商海，今日已很有成就，他对中间传话的友人

说:"我找他找了十几年了!"(段和平《朋友》)

A friend of mine in literary circles, of whom I lost track, has now become a successful businessman. It is said that he has had a hard time sending a message to me and eventually succeeded through a mutual acquaintance. He said, "It's over a decade for me trying to make contact with him."

[例49] 我渐渐地长大起来。有一天不知道因为什么,我忽然觉得怕狗是很可耻的事情。看见狗我便站住,不再逃避。(巴金《狗》)

As I was growing up, one day it suddenly dawned on me somehow that it was shameful to be afraid of a dog. Hence instead of shying away in fear, I stood confronting him. (张培基译)

[例50] 小玲?天啊,我忘记邀请她了。我偏偏就忘掉小玲了!她会生气的。

Xiaolin? Oh my gosh, I forgot to invite Xiaolin. It just slipped my mind. She'll be mad at me.

[例51] 我不是做发财的梦。为了发财我的几个好朋友都下海了,当了个体商贩。

It wasn't a dream after gold, which enticed some of my close friends to engage in business as self-employed traders.

5. There be 作无灵主语

[例52] 事已如此,后悔也没用。

There is no use crying over spilt milk.

[例53] 越来越多的家长接受了孩子们去参加各种各样的社会活动。

There is a growing acceptance among the parents of their children's participation in various social activities.

## (二) 汉语无灵主语+无灵动词的英译

无灵主语句虽然在汉语的整体结构上所占比重较小,但在特定的情况下——比如法律文体、科技文体、学术交流论坛——却占据了很大的篇幅。相较而言,汉语的此类句子采用无灵主语+无灵动词的"常规搭配"较为普遍,译成英语时,可考虑发挥英语优势,适当增加无灵主语+有灵动词的"混搭"。试比较下例的译文 A 与译文 B:

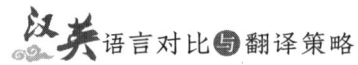

[例54] 父亲的手伤痕累累，旧疤没掉，又添新伤，指甲常常是青的青，紫的紫。

A：His hands were covered with scars, healing cuts, freshly blackened nails.

B：Scars crawled on his hands, where new ones came before old ones healed. The nails were often in black and blue.

再看几个例子：

[例55] 尽管公租房建设已经取得了众所周知的成绩并且好评如潮，成了全国保障性住房建设的模范与样板，但公租房建设作为保障性住房建设中的全新课题，各地可供借鉴的成熟经验并不多……

With its much-publicized accomplishments, the PRH program has grown into a popular role model in China's indemnificatory housing. However, PRH is an entirely new subject with few mature practices to learn from.

[例56] 尽管存在一些不足之处，但人们殷切期盼、政府积极行动、制度开始完善、建设已经展开、成果正在显现，第一批申请入住的市民已经陆续开始入住。

Despite some blemishes, the program, bearing rosy and eager hopes of the public, is presenting itself with convincing achievements: active government involvement, substantive construction, increasingly systematic and effective regulation, the move-in of its first batch of tenants....

## 五、变异句式（deviational subject）

在个别情况下，英语可能使用有灵主语而汉语则习惯于无灵主语

[例57] What? You have a selective memory. You tried to pay last time, but your credit card failed, so I ended up paying. It's definitely your turn.

什么？你这是选择性失忆。上次你刷卡失败，结果是我买了单，今天毫无疑问轮到你买单啦。

[例58] 宗教不得干预政治和干预教育。

No one is allowed to intervene into political and educational affairs in the name of religion.

[例 59] 我们的事业从胜利走向胜利。

We will make great strides in our socialist modernization drive.

[例 60] 已有成绩也并不能掩盖所有的问题与挑战,唯有正视现实、未雨绸缪、防患未然,才能更好地推动公租房的建设和发展。

Therefore, despite all the achievements, one can hardly ignore the existing challenges. Instead, only through facing up to the reality and providing necessary precautions for it can one better help promote the smooth development of the program.

[例 61] 一个音符无法表达出优美的旋律,一种颜色难以描绘出多彩的画卷。

A composer cannot write enchanting melody with only one note, nor can a painter portray a gorgeous landscape with just one color.

【翻译欣赏】

## 1

史书记载中国的建筑发端于"有巢氏筑巢而居",这"巢"也就是人类最早的住宅之一了吧?因此,作为人类生活衣、食、住、行的基本要素之一,住房的重要性不言而喻。符合人性的良好的居住环境是保障人的安全、健康、幸福以及尊严的基础,也是社会平安的基础。建立和完善城市低收入居民的住房保障制度、提供公共住房既是政府同时也是社会全体成员义不容辞的责任和义务,这不仅是为了保护社会低收入阶层的利益,同时也是为了全体人民福利最大化,每个社会成员都应该认识到任何一个社会成员对社会总体利益的扩大都有贡献。世界各国的历史经验已经表明,只有通过政府的主导作用,制定和实施良好的住房保障政策,才能实现全体社会成员住有所居、社会和谐的目标。

According to historical records, Chinese buildings originate from the days when "Youchaoshi (*literally* The Nester tribe) built nests to dwell in". Simple as they were, those nests—probably among the earliest houses for man—pointed exactly to the vital importance of owning a dwelling place. As a basic element of human life along with clothing, food and transportation, a sound, humanistic living environment not only is the prerequisite for human safety, health, happiness and dignity, but also constitutes the cornerstone of social stability. Therefore, to establish and improve a housing security system for low-income urban residents through public housing schemes is the unshakable obligation of the government as well as the society. This serves not only to protect the interests of the low-income class, but also to maximize the well-being of all people. Judging from the experiences of countries all over the world, only through a sound government-led housing security system can we achieve the goal of building a harmonious society with a decent home for all people.

近几年,我国各地的保障性住房建设在中央政府的高度重视下迅速发展,颇有井喷之势。这其中,我市由于市政府在公共租赁房(以下简称公租房)建设上的果断决策、大胆投入、迅速行动而在全国引发了热议。中央和各地相关部门纷纷前来考察、不少媒体呼吁以我市公租房建设模式为范本,用大量建设公租房来增加市场的房屋供应量,实现更多人的安居梦想。在这样的热潮背后,我市的公租房建设到底有哪些特点?存在着怎样的困惑?又有怎样的解决之道?这些正是本文试图探讨的问题。

In recent years, China has witnessed a booming development of indemnificatory housing construction. The PRH program, with the Municipal Government's courageous decision-making, bold investment and prompt action over public rental housing (hereinafter called PRH) construction, has attracted nation-wide attention. Amid the incoming visits by many departments from the central government as well as peer provincial governments, there is a growing public demand in the media to help people fulfill their dream of comfortable housing by increasing home supply in the market through great PRH programs with our city as a role model.

However, behind all this hustle and bustle, one can't help wondering: What, indeed, are the basic features of the PRH program? Are there any puzzles, or challenges? If there are, what are the solutions? These are the central questions this article tries to address.

## 2

尊敬的各位来宾,女士们、先生们:
　　是梧桐树的落叶铺就林荫大道的10月,是形形色色的文化活动纷纷登场的秋天,中国文化年就在这金色的收获季节来到法国。
Distinguished guests, ladies and gentlemen,
　　The broad avenues carpeted with fallen leaves of plane trees ushers in the

Year of Chinese Culture in October, the golden fall in France.

昨天,中国文化年在法国首都巴黎隆重开幕,我们见到的法国各界朋友,都为灿烂的中华文化以如此气派的场面、如此缤纷的色彩和多样的形式在法兰西登场而感到欣慰。国务委员陈至立在开幕新闻发布会上回答记者提问时说:"闭上眼睛想一想,中国首次在国外举办文化年,不选择法国选择谁?"

The Year of Chinese Culture was inaugurated on Oct. 7 in Paris. Our French friends we met here all felt pleased and hailed the splendid Chinese culture from afar. In response to a question at the press conference Chen Zhili, member of the State Council, put it like this, "Close your eyes and muse upon it. Is there any other choice better than France for the Year of Chinese Culture to make its maiden show out of China?"

是啊,舍法国其谁?法国是世界性文化大国,它向世人展示的形象,既是世界第四经济强国,又是独具魅力、散发着文化气息的国度。特别要指出的是,当今法国领导人对坚持文化多样性特别执着,他们在联合国的讲坛上,在外交、文化等众多国际活动领域,强调对其它文化和文明应持欣赏和学习的态度。众所周知,法国总统希拉克热爱东方文化,他对青铜器的鉴赏能力达到专家水平。前年巴黎集美博物馆(即法国国立亚洲艺术博物馆)修复竣工重新开放,希拉克在参观瓷器馆时,对着展品毕恭毕敬地鞠躬。当法国报纸刊出这幅照片时,我们的心灵受到震动。有这样的文化理解基础,中法这两个东西方文化大国携手合作互办文化年,显然是合乎逻辑的。

It is true that France, the fourth economic power in the world, is a country featuring a unique charm and flavor of culture. And what we must especially stress is that the present French leaders are always persistent in advocating the diversity of different cultures. At the UN pulpit and various international occasions diplomatic and cultural we've often heard their strong voices for the appreciation of and learning from cultures and civilizations other than that of their own. Chirac, French president himself dotes on oriental culture and is even a connoisseur in ancient Chinese bronzeware. The year before when paying a visit to the porcelain exhibition at the French National Museum of Asian Arts reopened after the restoration he bowed respectfully to the exhibits there. And when the photo was published in French papers, the hearts of the people were greatly moved. With such a basis of mutual understanding, the two cultural giants, China Oriental and France Occidental, to hold the cultural year in cooperation.

法国外长德维尔潘爱好文学，擅长诗文。许多人还记得今年2月安理会辩论辩论对伊动武问题时，他那充满激情和义愤的话语"你们面对的老欧洲，像山一样高峻，象海一样深沉。"在昨天的开幕仪式上，他对几百年来法中文化交流的描述行云流水般舒展，他诚挚而优美的致辞令人感动。他说"我们可以通过中国文化年的活动，从各个角度去领会中国，尤其是她的文化多样性、她的活力和她沸腾的创造力。"

Dominique de Villepin, French minister of foreign affairs, writes beautiful essays and poems as he took a liking in literature. Many remember his passionate and outraged words during the Security Council debate on the use of force against Iraq in February："The old Europe you face is as high as the mountains and as deep as the sea." At the opening ceremony, he made a sincere and moving speech in which he says："The Year of Chinese Culture offers us an opportunity to understand China from different angles, especially from her diversified forms of culture, her vigorous and enthusiastic creativeness."

中国文化年将向法国公众展示一种全然不同于西方文化的中华文化和文明。数百年来，中国文化令他们感到神秘，又使他们心往神驰。今天，在"古老的中国、多彩的中国、现代的中国"这一主题的统领下，中国传统文化、民族和地方文化、现代文化将使法国人民得到一次更全面、更深刻的精神享受，它向法国公众展示的是中国文化异彩纷呈、百花齐放的繁荣景象。

The Year of Chinese culture is a showcase of Chinese culture and Oriental civilization, which is utterly different from that of the West. For hundreds of years, people in the West marvel at the mystery of Chinese culture. Now, the event under the theme of "Ancient China, Colorful China, and Modern China" will offer French people a spiritual enjoyment of the traditional Chinese culture, ethnic and local culture in an all-round and deeper way. It will display to the French public a colorful and varied culture of China, a flourishing vista in which a hundred flowers are blossoming at the same time.

西方艺术界和公众对20世纪中国美术发展进程了解得十分不足，认为中国美术缺乏像西方现代艺术那样的文化价值，有的则将它笼统地视作为政治服务的艺术。而在文化年开幕当日揭幕的《东方既白——20世纪中国绘画展》，是20世纪中国的绘画成就首次在法国展示，它突出了一个鲜明的主题：中国的绘画主旋律与中国社会变革息息相关,具有鲜明的文化自主性,体现着另一种现代性。

The Western art circle and the public are short of understanding in the development of 20$^{th}$-century Chinese art, assuming that the Chinese art in that period has no comparable value as does its Western counterpart. Some even take it for an "art for politics sake". The "Dawning East—Exhibition of Chinese Fine Arts of the 20$^{th}$ Century" is the first time for Chinese arts to demonstrate their achievement in that period. The theme is terse and explicit: Chinese fine arts dance to the rhythm of the social development in the country, indicating the cultural independence that symbolizes another sort of modernity.

正如文化部长孙家正所说,中国文化年300多个文化展示项目将告诉人们,一个古老的中国如何跋涉过5000年的风雨沧桑,铸造出永铭史册的辉煌;一个多彩的中国,如何兼容并蓄,博采众长,描绘出百花齐放的绚丽画卷;一个现代的中国焕发出怎样的勃勃生机,继往开来,与时俱进。

The over 300 exhibits displayed in the Year of Chinese Culture tell the people, as Sun Jiazheng, Chinese Minister of Culture put it, how an ancient China has waded through the vicissitudes of 5000 years, creating a splendid culture in history. They also tell how a colorful China has painted a beautiful scroll of pictures by taking in what can be for its best and be compatible with them, and how a modern China full of go can open up something new by carrying on what's left over from the past to keep pace with the advance of the time.

正是这样的文化交流,带来了理解和沟通。中法文化年组委会法方主席昂格雷米十分感慨地说,筹办文化年本身就是交流的过程。中法双方思维有差异,工作方式也不尽相同,刚开始时双方都不太适应,但都怀有真诚的交流愿望,彼此开诚布公,双方就能建立起心灵上的交流,唱响合作的主旋律,许多困难迎刃而解。文化交流就是这样搭起了一架沟通和理解的桥梁。可以预计,未来的一年里,中国文化年必定带来双赢的结果:它将使中国文化充分而全面地展现自己的面貌,使法国公众视野开阔,更深刻地了解中国文化。中法合作将因文化交流而更上一层楼。

It is the very cultural exchanges that have brought about the understanding and communication, said Mr. Jean-PierreAngremy, French chairman with the Organizing Committee of Sino-French Year of Culture, and that the preparation itself is a kind of communication. It was not easy to work together at the beginning due to the differences in their ways of thinking and working. But with sincere desire to communicate, they finally overcame all the difficulties and built up good cooperation by wearing their heart on their sleeve. In this way they put up a bridge of understanding and communication for cultural exchanges. It is foreseeable that in the year to come, the Year of Chinese Culture would present a panoramic picture of Chinese Culture, enabling the French people to gain a better understanding of Chinese culture. As a result, the Sino-French cooperation in cultural exchanges will see a better day to come.

## 第三节　形合与意合

英语在发展的过程中，深受逻各斯中心主义的影响，以理性、逻辑性为尚，造成了英语非常注重形合，又称"显性衔接"的特点：常常借助各种连接手段（connectives），比如连词、介词、非限定性动词短语等，来表达语句之间的相互关系，句子结构严谨，逻辑关系清楚，如：I shall despair if you don't come.

汉语的情况则不一样。自汉晋以降，清谈兴起，理性失之于"个性"，士大夫们竞相追逐反逻辑、尚玄学的所谓名士风流，推崇"好读书，不求甚解，每有会意，便欣然忘食"。在这种审美旨趣下，久而久之，汉语形成了以意合为美的倾向，习惯用"隐性衔接"，即少用形式连接手段，注重逻辑顺序，通过借助词语或句子的隐含意义的逻辑联系来实现句子的连接。从句子整体来看，汉语语句结构松散、简洁，意涵富有"妙不可言"的"弹性"。试比较：a. 她怀孕了，嫁人了。b. 她嫁人了，怀孕了。

"形合（Hypotaxis）"与"意合（Parataxis）"是英汉两种语言的一个根本性差异，它不但源于两个民族不同的审美价值，而且也反过来不断强化、塑造两个民族的认知习惯，甚至在某种程度上影响了各自的国民性格。

对于当代国人来说，英语就是一个很好的载体，不但有助于开阔眼界，更能通过注重显性衔接的形合习惯和其他语法手段，使人在潜移默化中逻辑更明晰、思虑更缜密、表达更清晰、行为更理性。

从更广泛的意义上说，其实不止是英语，学习任何一门外语，都可以促使人在识别双语差异、解决思维模式冲突的过程中变得更聪明。《纽约时报》2012年3月18日登了篇题为"Why Bilinguals Are Smarter"的文章，文章指出：

*Being bilingual, it turns out, makes you smarter. It can have a profound effect on your brain, improving cognitive skills not related to language and even shielding against dementia in old age... there is ample evidence that in a bilingual's brain both language systems are active even when he is using only one language, thus creating situations in which one system obstructs the other. But this interference, researchers are finding out, isn't so* much a handicap as a blessing in disguise. It forces the brain to resolve internal conflict, giving the mind a workout that strengthens its cognitive muscles.

## 一、英语的形合衔接

英语造句通常用各种形式手段来连接词、语、分句或从句，注重显性接应，讲求结构完整，处处"以形显义"。这些衔接手段主要包括关系词、连接词、介词、非谓语动词等等。

### （一）关系词和连词

英语句子中的连接手段和形式不仅数量大，种类多，而且使用十分频繁，英语中的关系词包括关系代词、关系副词、连接代词和连接副词，如 who, whom, that, which 等，用来连接主句和定语从句、主语从句、宾语从句或表语从句。连词包括并列连词和从属连词，如 and, or, but, yet 及 when, while, as, since 等，用来连接词、词组、分句或状语从句。

[例1] One of the peculiarities of of the Eastern bazaar is *that* shopkeepers dealing in the same kind of goods do not scatter themselves over the bazaar, in order to avoid competition, *but* collect in the same area, *so that* purchasers can know where to find them, *and so that* they can form a closely knit guild against injustice or persecution.

中东集市的特点之一，是经营同类商品的店家，不是分散在集市各处以避免相互间的竞争，而是都集中在一块儿，既方便买主知道上哪儿找他们，也让他们自己可以结成紧密的联盟，保护自己不受欺侮和刁难。

该例原文中关系词和连词将主句和表语从句、状语从句等连成一体。译文并非拘泥于原文的连接手段，而是根据汉语的特性进行适当调整。译文因而地道、自然。

[例2] *And when* the evening mist clothes the riverside with poetry, *as* with a veil, *and* the poor buildings lose themselves in the dim sky, *and* the tall chimneys became campanili, *and* the warehouses are palaces in the night, *and* the whole city hangs in the heavens, *and* fairy-land is before us—then the wayfarer hastens home; the working man and the cultured one, the wise man and the one of pleasure, cease to understand, *as* they have ceased to see, and Nature, *who*, for once, has sung in tune, sings her exquisite song to the artist alone, her son and her master — her son *in that* he loves her, her master *in that* he knows her. (James Whistler  *Nature and Art*)

当傍晚富有诗意的迷雾象柔纱般地笼罩着河边，破旧的建筑消失在朦胧的天空，高高的烟囱变成一座座钟楼，大大小小的仓库恍如夜间的宫殿，整个城市悬在了空中，宛若仙境展现在我们眼前，那时候，路上的人们匆匆走路回家；劳动者和文化人，智者和浪子，因为他们熟视无睹，他们也就不能理解，而只在此时才开始歌唱的大自然便把自己微妙的歌唱给艺术家——她的儿子和她的主人；说他是儿子是因为他爱她，说他是主人是因为他理解她。（刘士聪  译）

原文句子比较长，但由于有 when，that，as，who，in that，and 等连接词贯穿全句，读来可谓脉络清楚。尤其是开头的六个 and，不仅将六个从句连接起来，为全句创造了十分优美平和的节奏和意境，而且产生了环境描写的渐增效果（cumulative effect），堪称神妙。

（二）介词（prepositions）

介词是英语中最活跃的词类之一，是连接词语或从句的重要手段。大体包括简单介词、合成介词、成语介词等。有些学者把英语称为"介词的语言"。

［例3］ Coming as she came, out of the mist into the dawn, she was like a spirit, like an intellectual presence. (John Masefield  *The Clipper*)
她一路驶来，出迷雾，入熹微，她好像一个魂灵，一个智慧女神。（刘士聪  译）

［例4］ The many colors *of* a rainbow range *from* red *on* the outside *to* violet *on* the inside.
彩虹有多种颜色，外圈红，内圈紫。

（三）非谓语动词

英语中的动词不定式、动名词和分词（现在分词和过去分词）称为非谓语动词，它们是英语中使用频繁的一种表达方式。在叙述一件事情时，汉语多用一连串的动词，各分句之间是并列的关系。英语一般只将其中的主要部分用谓语动词表达，其余的部分则经常使用非谓语动词来衔接，各小句之间在句法层次上多为主从关系。

[例5] She came trembling down to us, rising up high and plunging; showing the red lead below her water-line; then diving down till the smother bubbled over her hawseholes. (John Masefield *The Clipper*)

她飘然而至，时而随浪涌起，时而随浪而下，一会儿露出吃水线下面的测深铅锚，然后又潜入水中，让水雾淹没锚链孔。（刘士聪译）

该例中，英语原文中的*不定式短语* trembling 与 rising、plunging、showing 以及 diving 一样，都是"came"的伴随状语，属于主从结构，汉译并未照搬这种结构。

[例6] In terms of attitudes to creativity there seems to be a reversal of priorities: young Westerners making their boldest departures first and then gradually mastering the tradition; and young Chinese being almost inseparable from the tradition, but, over time, possibly evolving to a point equally original.

就对创造力的态度而言，优先次序似乎是颠倒了：西方的年轻人先是大胆地离经叛道，然后逐渐掌握传统，而中国的年轻人则几乎离不开传统，但是，随着时间的推移，他们也可能发展到具有同等创造力的境界。

该例英语原文使用了1个主句，1个现在分词短语，两者之间是主次结构，但在译成汉语时变成了并列的单句。

## 二、汉语的意合衔接

汉语句子重意合。与英语相比，汉语没有严格意义上的形态变化标志，没有显性的词类分别。汉语的句法关系则主要靠词序和隐含的语义关系来表达，它并不追求形式上的完整，而往往只求达意即可。比如：

[例7] 以正治国，以奇用兵。

Rule the state with transparent sincerity, but fight the war with treacherous secrecy.

[例8] 不要相信牧师的话——

上帝在他嘴上，
魔鬼在他心里。
Don't believe the preacher:
He has God on his lips
And Satan in his heart.

汉语主要有以下几种意合手段：

(一) 语序 (word order)

语序既包括单句中各个词的顺序，也包括复合句中主句和从句排列次序。词形变化与语序成正比。形态变化越多的语言，词序越灵活。汉语是典型的分析语，词汇缺乏形态变化，词语之间的关系经常要凭借词序的使用来表现出来。

汉语的许多主从复合句，很少用关联词，形式类似并列句，但是其分句意义却有主次。若从句前置，该从句本身就有"因为""如果""虽然""即便"等含义，一般不用关联词。据统计，汉语中三分之二的因果句不到必要时，不用关联词。比如，先"因"后"果"，几乎不用"因为"，属"常态"；先"果"后"因"，大多用因为，属"变态"。

相比较而言，英语主从的复合句中，从句位置灵活。表示原因、条件或时间的状语从句可以置于主句之前，也可置于其后，不影响其意义的表达、叙述、顺序很灵活。

［例9］其政闷闷，其民淳淳；
其政察察，其民缺缺。
If the government is lenient, the people will be simple.
If the government is severe, the people will feel a lack of freedom.

［例10］有缺点的战士终竟是战士，再完美的苍蝇也终竟不过是苍蝇。(鲁迅《战士与苍蝇》)
The fighter for all his blemishes is a fighter, while the most whole and perfect flies are only flies. (杨宪益 戴乃迭 译)

［例11］You might as well take a break, as you are exhausted.
你已经疲倦了，最好休息一下。

［例12］I hope you will give me the necessary help, as I am a perfect stranger.

我初来乍到，希望你能给我必要的帮助。

上面几个例子中，英语原文的原因状语从句既置于主句之后，也可以置于主句之前，都不会有任何突兀之感，奥秘就在于显性衔接。而汉语译文则按照汉语的常态，将原因状语从句、条件状语从句置于主句之前，也未用"因为""假如""当的时候"等显性衔接手段。

（二）排比、对偶、对照等句式（parallelism, antithesis, contrast, etc.）

这些句式词句整齐、匀称，往往不用关联词，译成英语时则需使用英语连接词，体现语句之间的逻辑关系：

［例13］百鬼多狰狞，上帝总无言。（贾平凹《我读何海霞》）

  Ghosts are hideously clamorous while God is silent. （刘士聪译）

［例14］君不见黄河之水天上来，

  奔流到海不复回！

  君不见高堂明镜悲白发，

  朝如青丝暮如雪！（李白《将进酒》）

  Don't you see the Yellow River pouring from heaven,

  Rushing to the sea, never to return?

  Don't you see, in the hall the mirror is saddened

  By the grey hair?

  Young and dark at dawn, but at dusk snowy! （朱纯深 译）

［例15］有的人活着

  他已经死了；

  有的人死了

  他还活着。

  有的人

  骑在人民头上："啊，我多伟大！"

  有的人

  俯下身子给人民当牛做马。（臧克家《有的人》）

  Some live,

  When they are already dead;

Others have died,
But are still alive.
Some
Ride on the backs of the people
and cry: "How grand am I!"
Others
Silently bend to draw the people's plough. (庞秉钧　闵福德　高尔登　译)

（三）紧缩句（compression）

紧缩句是由复合句压缩而成，即删去复合句中的一些词语，使语句紧凑，简洁明了。英语中并不存在这类语句。本质上，这类句式是紧凑的主从复合句，故而翻译成英语时通常需要补充连接词，译为主从复合句。

［例16］犹豫中妈妈还是打开了它。昨晚女儿的日记呈现于眼前："妈妈，您问是爱，不问是理解。"（孙雪梅《问与不问》）

After a few minutes' hesitation she eventually opened it to the entry of the night before. It reads: Mum, it's love that made you ask, but it would be considerate understanding if you hadn't. (陈文伯　译)

［例17］炒股炒成股东，炒房炒成房东，人生何处不悲催。

While coveting immediate returns from the stock market, one findshimself a loss-making share-holder; trying to make quick money from the housing market, one ends up an unwilling lease-holder. What a pathetic world!

［例18］欲寄君衣君不还，
不寄君衣君又寒。
寄与不寄间，
妾身千万难。（姚燧《凭栏人·寄征衣》）
I am afraid you'll not return home,
With my winter clothing to you.
I'm afraid you'll feel cold,
Without sending it to you.
I hesitate to say "yes" or "no",

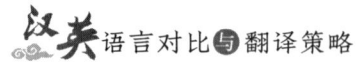

How difficult is to say so!（朱曼华 译）

### 三、英语形合与汉译意合的翻译转换

总之，英汉在语言学上最重要的一个区别就是形合和意合的不同。英语重形合，注重结构、形式，常常借助各种连接手段，比较严谨；汉语注重意合，注重功能、意义，常常不用或少用连接手段，因而比较简洁。

（一）英译汉

英译汉时，是从形合到意合的转换过程，难点在于如何化解原文的繁复，确保汉译的简洁，译者很多时候要省略衔接手段，使译文符合汉语的特点。

1. 省略关系词

［例19］You would think, when the child was born, there would be an end to troubles; and yet it is only the beginning of fresh anxieties; and when you have seen it through its teething and its education, and at last its marriage, alas!

一个小孩子生下来，你会想，麻烦事结束了；然而，那不过是新的烦恼刚刚开始。然后，你看他出牙了，上学了，最后，终于结婚了；天哪，事儿可真多啊！

上例中，英语语句通过连接词"when"和"and"实现了句子成分之间的衔接。不难看出，该句译成汉语时，这些词汇均省略不译，使译文具有汉语的意合特点。

［例20］Josiah Henson is but one name on a long list of courageous men and women who together forged the Underground Railroad, a secret web of escape routes and safe houses that they used to liberate slaves from the American South.

乔赛亚·亨森只是一长串男女勇士中的一个，这些勇士共同创建了"地下铁路"——一个由逃亡线路和可靠的人家组成的秘密网络，用以解放美国的南方黑奴。

该例中，原文的关系代词"who""that"将几个短句连接成了一个长句，译者则通过省略、还原的方式将其分成了几个结构完整的汉语短句。

2. 省略介词

［例21］Inadequate training for farmers and the low productivity of many farms place the majority of country dwellers in a disadvantageous position in their own countries.

农民缺乏训练,许多农场生产率很低,使得大多数农民在他们国家里处于贫穷的困境。

该例原文使用了5个介词和1个连词,表现出非常明显的形合特征,而汉语译文中只使用了1个介词"在"。

3. 介词译成动词。

[例 22] The car wound through the village and up a narrow valley, following a thaw-swollen stream.

汽车迂回盘旋,穿过村庄,翻越峡谷,沿着一条因解冻而涨水的小溪行驶。

英语原文使用介词,使句子成分联为一体,汉语译文则凭借语义联系,实现句子成分之间的衔接。

(二)汉译英

汉译英时,往往要先分析句子的功能、意义,才能确定句子的结构、形式,难点在于化去原文的模糊,确保英译的严谨。往往首先要梳理原文中重要的信息,使其成为英语主句或者主谓核心结构。原文中的次要信息则通过添加形式标记和连接词,变成英语的从句或者介词、非谓语动词引导的定语、状语等分支结构,从而使译文具有英语高度形式化和严密逻辑性的语言特征。

(1) 译成主从复合句,即通过补充关系代词、关系副词等,实现显性衔接。

[例 23] 我们并未太多的在报纸上电视上见过他,但京城消息传来,他还在活着,他还在作画。好了,活着画着,谁也不多提他,提他谁也心悸。(贾平凹《我读何海霞》)

We have not seen much of him on the TV or in the newspapers, but as rumor from Beijing has it he is still around. Around as he is, there has not been much mention of him, because the mere mention of his name makes one scared. (刘士聪 译)

(2) 添加并列连词。

[例 24] 燕子去了,有再来的时候;杨柳枯了,有再青的时候;桃花谢了,有再开的时候。但是,聪明的,你告诉我,我们的日子为什么一去不复返呢?(朱自清《匆匆》)

Swallows may have gone, but there is a time of return; willow trees may have died back, but there is a time of regreening; peach blossoms may have fallen, but they will bloom again. Now, you the wise, tell me, why should our days leave us, never to return? （张培基 译）

(3) 译成介词短语，即补充介词以实现显性衔接。

[例25] 已经不是很短的时间了，热闹的艺坛上，天才与小丑无法分清，不知浪潮翻过了多少回合，惊涛裂岸，沙石混沌。（贾平凹《我读何海霞》）

Over a long period of time, geniuses and "clowns" have been mixed up in the hectic realm of art, like rocks and sand mixed and driven by stormy waves along the shore. （刘士聪 译）

(4) 译成非谓语动词，即通过现在分词、过去分词、不定式等手段，将一连串处于并列结构的动词改为较为清楚的主次结构。

[例26] 面对着他的作品，我无法谈论某一方面的见解，谈出都失水准，行话全沦为小技，露出我一副村相了。（贾平凹《我读何海霞》）

I am not qualified to comment on any particular aspect of his works, for whatever I say would be short of professionalism, turning technical terms into frivolities, thus laying bare a layman's follies. （刘士聪 译）

(5) 译成特殊句型。

[例27] 人到醉时方觉醒，醒时难得醉时清。

It is not until you are drunk that you are sober, and you can hardly be as sober as when you are drunk.

(6) 综合运用以上几种手段，即综合使用关系代词、关系副词、介词、非谓语动词等，架构起主次分明、层次清晰的英语句子。有时候甚至可以通过增加副词（比如 however、thus）来实现句子之间的衔接。

[例28] 打开他的画册，我曾经独坐一个晌午又一个晌午，任在那创造的大自然里静定神游，作一回庄子，化一回蝴蝶。（贾平凹《我读何海霞》）

I remember sitting at home alone, for the whole of one morning after another, with his album open in front of me, my mind wondering about in the artistic natural world created by the artist, feeling as though I were Zhuangzi transformed into a butterfly fluttering around. （刘士聪　译）

[例29] 人是很有趣的，往往在接触一个人时首先看到的都是他或她的优点。开始吃头盘或冷碟的时候，印象很好。吃头两个主菜时，也是赞不绝口。愈吃愈趋于冷静，吃完了这顿宴席，缺点就都找出来了。

Human beings are interesting in that they tend to first see good in a new acquaintance. This is like dining in a restaurant. You will be not only favorably impressed with the first dish or cold dishes, but also profuse in praise of the first two courses. However, the more you have, the more sober you become until the dinner ends up with all the flaws exposed.

### 四、常态与变态（norm and deviation）

有"常态"，也就会有"变态"，英汉皆然。意合法在汉语里属"常态"，在英语里属"变态"。这类"变态"常见于一些简练的谚语、表达复合句内容的简单句等，如：

[例30] It is not uncommon, in the most pleasant of homes, to see pasted on the windows small notices announcing that the premises are under surveillance by this security force or that guard company.

即使是在最温馨的居家，也常常看得到窗上贴着小小的告示，称本宅由某家安全机构或某个保安公司负责监管。

[例31] 敌进我退，敌驻我扰，敌疲我打，敌退我追。

The enemy advances, we retreat; the enemy camps, we harass; the enemy tires, we attack; the enemy retreats, we pursue.

[例32] 写诗的人从海鸥身上找灵感

海鸥却忙于从浪花里找鱼（艾青《无题》）

A poet seeks inspiration in the seagulls.

The seagulls are busy seeking fish in the spindrift. （庞秉钧　闵福德　高尔登　译）

### 五、形合衔接的辩证法

毛荣贵教授在博文《〈背影〉两译，比读有益》中，以朱自清散文《背影》

的两个译本为例,探讨了形合意识对汉语意合语言翻译的影响,从辩证的角度来看,大致有以下几个方面:

(一) 善用形合,增强简洁性,提升英语味

[例33] 我们过了江,进了车站。我买票,他忙着照看行李。

V1: We entered the railway station after crossing the River. While I was at the booking office buying a ticket, father saw to my luggage.

V2: We crossed the Yangtze and arrived at the station, where I bought a ticket while he saw to my luggage.

比较之下,我们宁可读 V2,为什么?

(1) V1 不可谓不"忠",亦步亦趋地译成了两句,与 V2 相比,意合转化为形合的意识尚有一线之差,致使译文有了割裂之感。

(2) 再读 V2,发现译文紧缩为一句,系一"尾重"句。表达流畅,且英语味也浓郁。寻思之下,关键恐怕在 where 一词,这个关系副词的使用,令两句自然"壁合",紧接着又跟上一个 while,译文就获得了流畅感和英语味。

对比证明,英译添加了适当的 connective,构成形合句,译文英语味趋浓,而且句子遣词不是增加,而是有所减少。

(二) 结构性衔接词 vs 非结构性衔接词

[例34] 我北来后,他写了一信给我,信中说道,"我身体平安,惟膀子疼痛利害,举箸提笔,诸多不便,大约大去之期不远矣。"

V1: After I arrived in Beijing, he wrote me a letter, in which he said, " I'm all right except for a severe pain in my arm. I even have trouble using chopsticks or writing brushes. Perhaps it won't be long now before I depart this life."

V2: After I came north he wrote to me: "My health is all right, only my arm aches so badly I find it hard to hold the pen. Probably the end is not far away."

两句的字数比是:45:34。让人感到意外的是,V2 所使用的 connective 仅两个:After/so。

这又是为什么呢?两译对比,尤其是对 so 的思考,茅塞顿开。

(1) 所谓 connective,可根据其作用,分为两类:一种是结构性的

(structural connective)，另一种是非结构性的（non-structural connective）。结构性的 connective 既折射句子内部逻辑关系，又是句子的框架性构件，"支撑"起英语句子，可谓"一箭双雕"。

而非结构性的 connective 不是句子的逻辑标记，仅是行文的纽带，承接上下文，如：

After I arrived in Beijing, he wrote me a letter, in which he said...

After I came north he wrote to me...

（2）V1 使用的 connectives "前呼后拥"，如：after/in which/except for/or/before 等。但是，connectives 用得太多，或者用得不到位，读来仍然摆脱不了"牵丝攀藤"的感觉。其中的 in which 即非结构性 connective，不反映逻辑关系，承上启下而已。使用了这样的 connective，未必能简化表达，与 V2 中的冒号相比，V1 的 in which he said 就显得啰唆，徒增了行文的字数。

（3）结构性的 connective，化隐含的逻辑关系为明示的逻辑关系，假如依靠别的文字来描述或传达同样的逻辑关系，自然会多费笔墨。如上例 V2 中的 so，即属于结构性的 connective。So 虽不起眼，作用却大。So 不仅使"惟膀子疼痛利害，举箸提笔，诸多不便"一句中隐含的因果关系"浮出水面"，令读者易懂，而且使句子结构豁然。而 V1 中的 I even have trouble using chopsticks or writing brushes 独立成句，逻辑上产生割裂感，"前不着村，后不着店"一般。

由此可见，汉英翻译，对英语重形合、汉语重意合的规律只有朦胧印象或泛泛了解是远远不够的。光凭语感使用 connective，也未必能够达到简化表达的目的。只有对汉语原句作一番逻辑梳理，并亮出结构性的 connective，译文才会显出简洁、清楚的优势。

[例 35] 我读到此处，在晶莹的泪光中，又看见那肥胖的，青布棉袍，黑布马褂的背影。唉！我不知何时再能与他相见！

V1：Through the glistening tears which these words had brought to my eyes I again saw the back of father's corpulent form in the dark blue cotton-padded cloth long gown and the black cloth mandarin jacket. Oh, how I long to see him again! (43 个单词)

V2：When I read this, through a mist of tears I saw his blue cotton-padded gown and black jacket once more as his burly figure walked away from me. Shall we ever meet again?

（33个单词）

（1）"看见那肥胖的，青布棉袍，黑布马褂的背影"应该如何理解？其中隐藏着怎样的逻辑关系？这是一个需要结合上文细加推敲的问题。其"逻辑"背景是：当父亲离我而去的时候，我看见那肥胖的，青布棉袍，黑布马褂的背影。这个"逻辑"背景是全文之"眼"。汉语是意合的语言，"当父亲离我而去的时候"不必言明，此意已经很自然地溶入字里行间，读者足以意会。但是，在英译时，译者就必须遵从英语表达习惯，应该化隐为显，变无为有。

（2）遗憾的是，V1显然没有注意到这一点，而是作了直译：I again saw the back of father…句中的动宾搭配（saw/back），基本沿袭了汉语原句的动宾结构（看见/背影）。

（3）V2抛弃了原句的动宾结构，而是另立新的动宾搭配：saw / his blue cotton-padded gown and black jacket。这样就腾出了使用connective的空间，译笔多有创意！果然，紧接着出现了一个as（注：这是典型的结构性connective），非常清晰和有层次感地传递了"背影"出现的时间。as his burly figure walked away from me 在原句里寻找不到相对应的字眼，却能在上文里寻找到此译的背景。

（4）由as引导的从句，贯通了上下文，并成功点题，把父亲的"背影"给译活了，这比单纯地写I again saw the back of father—更让人喝彩：第一，从静态与动态处理的角度来看，译文I again saw the back of father—是一个过于冗长的静态表达，是死板的、平面的、孤立的，而译文I saw his blue cotton-padded gown and black jacket once more as his burly figure walked away from me 则是鲜活的、立体的、贯通上文的；第二，从形合与意合处理的角度来看，V2的as使其叙事脉络不再孤立晦涩，而是由隐到显，清楚明了地贯通了上下文；第三，从修辞的角度来看，V2用as将一个较长的偏正结构改为两个长度接近的小句，节奏更为平衡。

这个例子进一步说明，恰当使用结构性connective，大有妙处，不但可以节约篇幅，还可以明晰逻辑，合理调节句子节奏，避免头重脚轻根底浅的"大头"结构。

（三）过犹不及

一个有趣的现象是，在汉英翻译中，或是单纯的英语作文中，有的学习者知道了英语是形合语言，不管有没有必要，就甩开膀子大用特用形合手段，尤其是"which""that"等句子，真是漫天飞舞，颇有不上不成席之感。

[例 36] 过铁道时，他先将橘子散放在地上，自己慢慢爬下，再抱起橘子走。

  V1：In crossing the railway track, he first put the tangerines on the ground, climbed down slowly and then picked them up again.

  V2：He put these on the platform before climbing slowly down to cross the lines, which he did after picking the fruit up.

汉译英时需要有强烈的形合意合意识，要善用 connectives，但是，多用未必就好。以上的 V1 就根据汉语原句中的几个连续发生的动作（散放/爬下/抱起等），根据先后顺序，一一译出（put/climbed down/picked them up），条理清晰，层层递进。短短一句，V2 连续使用了几个 connectives（before/which/after 等），颇有点让读者眼花缭乱。尤其是句末的 which he did after picking the fruit up，令读者如入迷宫，一下子难以醒悟：这个 which 到底指代上文何词？经过琢磨，方能领悟，这个 which 是指 climbing slowly down to cross the lines。before 和 after 的使用，更是把本来一气呵成的几个动作搞得颠三倒四，突然增加了读者理解的困难。因多用了 connectives 而使译文由简单变得复杂，由流畅变得曲折，这可以说是一个典型的译例。

[例 37] 到南京时，有朋友约去游逛，勾留了一日；第二日上午便须渡江到浦口，下午上车北去。

  V1：I spent the first day in Nanjing strolling about with some friends at their invitation, and was ferrying across the Yangtze River to Pukou the next morning and thence taking a train for Beijing on the afternoon of the same day.（41 个单词）

  V2：A friend kept me in Nanjing for a day to see sights, and the next morning I was to cross the Yangtze to Pukou to take the afternoon train to the north.（32 个单词）

（1）对照阅读之下，一个强烈的视觉冲击是：原文简约，而 V1 竟如此拖沓！难道英语表达就应如此冗杂？（2）看了 V2，答案出来了：afternoon 用作形容词，置于 train 之前，如此以一当九——afternoon（train）= a train（for Beijing）on the afternoon of the same day——，意思丝毫未改，而且更"信"。这个例子说明，很多时候，慎用介词等形合手段，借鉴新闻英语中常见的扩展的简单句，即改采名词定语（或插入语、同位语、补语等），不仅可以避免

connective 的啰嗦累赘，还可以增加选项，减少句式的重复。

# 【翻译欣赏】

Ladies and Gentlemen,

女士们、先生们：

To talk about the importance and effectiveness of the global human resource management, I would like to take Coca-Cola Company as a quintessential.

我想把可口可乐公司作为一个典范，来谈谈全球人力资源管理的重要性和有效性。

The Coca-Cola Company is one of the most successful multinational enterprises. With operations in close to 200 countries and nearly 80 percent of its operating income derived from business outside the United States, Coca-Cola is typically perceived as the quintessential global corporation. Coca-Cola, however, likes to think of itself as a "multi-local" company that just happens to be headquartered in Atlanta but could be headquartered anywhere that presents the Coca-Cola brand with a "local face" in every country where it does business. The philosophy is best summarized by the phrase "think globally, act locally", which captures the essence of Coca-Cola's cross-border management mentality. Coca-Cola grants national business the freedom to conduct operations in a manner appropriate to the market. At the same time, the company tries to establish a common mind-set that all its employees share.

可口可乐公司是最为成功的跨国企业之一。它的业务通达近 200 个国家，差不多 80% 的营业收入来自美国以外，常被视为跨国公司的典范。然而，该公司却把自己看成一家"多本土性"的公司，其总部设在美国亚特兰大只是偶然，其实可以设在世界上任何一个有其业务的地方。无论在哪儿，可口可乐品牌都是以"本土面目"出现。"全球思维 地方行为"，就是这种理念的最佳写照，因为它正好反映了可口可乐跨国管理的精神实质。可口可乐公司给予其各国分公司充分的自由，可以自主地以适合当地市场的方式开展业务经营，同时，又努力在全体员工中建立一种共同的思想理念。

Coca-Cola manages its global operations through 25 operating divisions that are organized under six regional groups: North America, European Union, Pacific Region, Eastern Europe/Middle East, Africa, and Latin

America. The corporate human resource management (HRM) function is charged with providing the glue that binds these various divisions and groups into the Coca-Cola family. The corporate HRM function achieves this in two main ways: (1) by propagating a common human resource philosophy within the company, and (2) by developing a group of internationally minded mid-level executives for future senior management responsibility.

可口可乐通过25个业务部门来管理其全球业务。这些业务部门受控于六个区域集团,即北美集团、欧盟集团、太平洋集团、东欧/中东集团、非洲集团、拉美集团。公司人力资源管理的职能在于提供一种凝聚力,把不同的部门和集团凝聚在可口可乐大家庭里。人力资源管理部门通过两种途径来达到这个目的:(1)在公司里宣传一种共同的人力资源理念;(2)培养一群具有国际化思维的中层经理,作为未来高级管理的后备人员。

The corporate HRM group sees its mission as one of developing and providing the underlying philosophy around which local businesses can develop their own human resource practices. For example, rather than have a standard salary policy for all its national operations, Coca-Cola has a common salary philosophy—the total compensation package should be competitive with the best companies in the local market. Twice a year the corporate HRM group also conducts a two-week HRM orientation session for the human resource staff from each of its 25 operating divisions. These sessions give an overview of the company's HRM philosophy and talk about how local businesses can translate that philosophy into human resource policies. Coca-Cola has found that information sharing is one of the great benefits of bringing HRM professionals together. For example, tools that have been developed in Brazil to deal with a specific HRM problem might also be useful in Australia. The sessions provide a medium through which HRM professionals can communicate and learn from each other, which facilitates the rapid transfer of innovative and valuable HRM tools from region to region.

公司人力资源管理层的全部人员把培养和提供基础理念作为己任。有了这样的基础理念,各地分公司就能够制定自己的人力资源管理办法。譬如,可口可乐不为某国的业务经营设定标准薪酬政策,而是确定一种普遍的薪酬理念,即总的薪酬福利应该能与当地市场上最优秀的公司一比高低。此外,公司的人力资源管理部每年为25家业务部门的人力资源管理人员举办两次为期两周的指导性会议。这些会议主要是回顾公司的人力资源管理理念,并讨论如何能够把这些理念变为各地方业务部门的人力资源政策。可口可乐已经发现,信息共享是把人力资源管理专业人士团结在一起的最佳办法之一。例如,在巴西为解决某个人力资源管理问题而开发的工具,拿到澳大利亚也许同样适用。这些指导性会议为人力资源管理专业人士提供了一种媒介,有助于他们互相沟通,也就促进了那些具有革新意义的、有价值的人力资源管理工具在各地迅速传播。

As much as possible, Coca-Cola tries to staff its operations with local personnel. To quote one senior executive: "We strive to have a limited number of international people in the field because generally local people are better equipped to do business at their home locations." However, expatriates are needed in the system for two main reasons. One is to fill a need for a specific set of skills that might not exist at a particular location. For example, when Coca-Cola started operations in Eastern Europe, it had to bring an expatriate from Chicago, who was of Polish descent, to fill the position of finance manager. The second reason for using an expatriate is to improve the employee's own skill base. Coca-Cola believes that because it is a global company, senior managers should have had international exposure.

可口可乐总是尽一切办法招募当地人员来从事业务部门的经营。这里引用一位高级经理的话,他说:"我们努力限制本行业的国际人员数量,因为一般来说本土人员更适合从事设在他们本地的业务。"然而,出于两方面的主要原因,该系统仍然需要聘用一些侨民。这样一方面是为了填补本土不具备的某些技术,例如,当可口可乐开始在东欧开展业务的时候,就曾经被迫从芝加哥调了一位波兰裔侨民,填补财务经理这一职位。使用侨民的另一个原因,则是为了提高该员工本人的技术水平。可口可乐认为,作为一家全球化公司,其高级经理理应接受国际历练。

The corporate HRM group has about 500 high-level managers involved in its "global service program". Coca-Cola characterizes these managers as people who have knowledge of their particular field, plus knowledge of the company, and who can do two things in an international location—add value by expertise they bring to each assignment and enhance their contribution to the company by having international experience. Of the 500 participants in the program, about 200 move each year. To ease the costs of transfer for these employees, Coca-Cola gives those in its global service program a U. S. — based compensation package. They are paid according to U. S. benchmarks, as opposed to the benchmark prevailing in the country in which they are located. Thus, an Indian manager in this program who is working in Britain will be paid according to U. S. salary benchmarks—and not those prevailing in either India or Britain. An ultimate goal of this program is to build a cadre of internationally minded high-level managers from which the future senior managers of Coca-Cola will be drawn.

可口可乐的人力资源管理部主持了一个"全球服务项目",吸引了大约500名高层经理参与。公司认为这些人员不仅具有专业知识,同时也十分了解公司的情况,能在世界范围内做两件事情:一是通过自己的专门技术给每项任务增值;二是通过自己的国际经验提高对公司的贡献。在这500名"全球服务项目"经理中,有200名每年都在流动。为了照顾其流动的开销,公司给这500名"全球服务项目"经理制定了一项以美国为标准的薪酬包。他们的薪酬水准是参考美国的,而不是其所在国家或地方的薪酬水准。因此,一名参与该项目的印度经理,即使他在英国工作,其薪酬也是参照美国的,而不是依照印度的,也不是依照英国的。这个项目的最终目标,就是要培养一支具有国际化思维的高水平经理队伍,可口可乐未来的高级管理人员就从他们中间选拔。

The above is my observation of Coca-Cola's HRM. Thank you for your attention.

以上就是我对可口可乐公司人力资源管理的了解和认识。谢谢大家。

## 第四节　主次与流水

英语重形合，属于显性衔接，汉语重意合，是隐性衔接。英语和汉语之间这个根本性的差异，自然而然造成了英汉两种语言在句法结构上呈现出主次结构与流水结构的不同格局。先来看一个实例：

[例1] 二十岁的暑假，在家乡的大街上偶遇自己的暗恋对象，听说他考上了研究生，被他的进步所打击，心如刀绞，想到这辈子终于不能出色得让他看我一眼，不禁怆然泪下。三十岁之后，到处打听哪里可以花钱买个 MBA。

A：At 20, during a summer holiday I encountered my beloved one on the street of my hometown. I heard he was admitted to be a graduate. I was struck by his advance. I couldn't help shedding tears in my extreme grief. I thought that for this life I could never achieve much to let him see me in a new light. After 30, I inquire everywhere to purchase an MBA certificate.

B：At the age of twenty, I ran into the young man who I loved in private in the street of my hometown. Upon hearing that he had been enrolled as a graduate, I was virtually dealt a heavy blow, feeling, tears in my eyes, painfully that I could never be good enough to win his favor. After thirty, I busy myself here and there, inquiring where I could buy an MBA diploma.（扁担结构，平衡美，节奏感）

汉语原文结构简化，读来有如行云流水，绝无拖沓、盘错之感。英译 A 虽也结构简单，读来却并无流畅之感，反而觉得啰唆不堪；英译 B 虽然句子结构复杂，读来反而流畅，更有英语味，层次丰富，结构平衡。

### 一、英语复合句

英语由于"形合"衔接手段的运用，句子结构多为复合句，犹如"参天大树，树叶横生"，一般称之为"树形结构"，表现出三个方面的特征：①体量巨大，句子长而复杂。句子中的每一个成分，均可有修饰语（定语、状语、同位语、补语等），每个修饰语都可以很长。句中的修饰语还可被另一个修饰语所修饰。此外，修饰语的位置也非常灵活，可以出现在被修饰语的前后。②有一个总揽全局的主干结构。英语句子中，主语+谓语这一主干结构相当突出，能够控制、协调全句结构，起着全句结构轴心的作用。③层次关系清楚分明。在表达复杂的思想时，修饰性短语和主谓核心结构，主句和从句之间，往往借助大量反映逻辑形式关系的关系词、连词、介词、非谓语动词等进行空间搭架，其层次关系，尤其是句子结构的主次关系是显性的、清楚分明的。

[例2] As the boat slid across the river, Parker watched helplessly as the pursuers closed in around the men he was forced to leave behind.
小船徐徐驶向对岸，帕克眼睁睁地看着追捕者把他被迫留下的两个人团团围住。

[例3] Instead of liberating us, technology has enslaved us. Innovations are occurring at a bewildering rate. And as each invention arrives, it eats further into our time.
技术发展没有把我们解放出来，而是使我们成为奴隶。新技术纷至沓来，令人目不暇接。每一项新发明问世，就进一步吞噬我们的光阴。

[例4] All at once, in the thatch house across the clearing behind us came the sound of a recorder, playing a tune that twined over the village clearing, muted our talk on the bankside, and wandered over the river, dissolving downstream.
突然，我们身后空地旁的茅屋里，传出了录音机的声音，一首乐曲在村子空地之上缭绕，减弱了我们在河畔谈话的声音，然后又传至河面，飘散在逝去的流水中。

## 二、汉语流水句

汉语则属于典型的"意合"语言，句子结构犹如"万顷碧波，层层推进"，一般称之为"波浪结构"或"流水句"，表现出三个与英语完全不同的特征：（1）句子短小精悍。正如连淑能所说，"汉语……以中短句居多，最佳长度为7至12字。……书面语虽也用长句，字数较多，结构较复杂，但常用标点把句子切开，与英语相比，还属短句。没有标点符号的一气呵成的类似英语的那种长句在汉语里是不正常的（例如本句）。"显得结构简化，读来松散、舒缓、轻松、活泼，无拖沓、盘错之感。（2）没有一个总揽全局的主干结构。与英语讲究聚集，全句有一个 clause 作为全句核心（nexus），以协调控制全句结构相反，汉语造句采用"流水记事法（chronicle style）"，常用片句（fragments）（包括悬垂结构）来逐层叙述思维的各个过程，显得流散，句子中基本没有起着全句结构轴心作用的主干结构。(3) 层次关系是隐性的。即便书面语，汉语虽也用长句，字数较多，结构较复杂，但也少用或不用主从结构（subordinate construction）。相反，汉语常用松散句，多用省略句、无主句，少用虚词，因此，修饰性短语与核心成分之间，单句与复句之间，复句与更大的单位句群之间，语义上或有层次，但句法结构上界限并不是截然分明的，而是在表面上呈流水状的同层结构。

〔例5〕他有个女儿，（　）在北京工作，（　）已经打电话去了，（　）听说明天就能回来。

He has a daughter, who works in Beijing. Someone has phoned her and it is said that she will be back tomorrow.

〔例6〕宴席上凡是能喝的，都醉倒了。住处还远应走路的，点上火燎唱着笑着回家了。奏乐帮忙的，下到厨房，用烧酒和大肉丸子肥腊肉肿了脖子，补偿疲劳，各自方便，或抱了大捆稻草，攥紧空谷仓房里去睡觉，或晃着火把，上油坊玩天九牌过夜去了，我自然也得有个落脚处。（沈从文《湘西散记·雪晴》）

All the drinkers at the feast were drunk now. It was time for those who lived at a distance to leave. Torches were lit and they started home singing and laughing. The musicians and other helpers went to the kitchen to make up for their fatigue with liquor, big meat balls and preserved fatty meat. All were free to do as they pleased. Some took a sheaf of straw into an empty barn to sleep; others went off flourishing torches to play dominoes all night in the oil-press. I naturally needed somewhere to stay too.

（杨宪益　戴乃迭　译）

〔例7〕一人已习悭术，犹谓未足，乃从悭师习其术。往见之，但用纸剪鱼，盛水一瓶，故名曰酒，为学悭贽礼。偶值悭师外出，惟妻在家，知其来学之意并所执贽仪，乃使一婢用空盏传出，曰："请茶。"实无茶也。又以两手作一圈，曰："请饼。"如是而已。学悭者既出，悭师乃归，其妻悉述其事以告。悭师作色曰："何乃费此厚款？"随用手作半圈样曰："只这半边饼，够打发他。"

There was a miser who, hearing about the reputation of a greater miser than himself, went to the other miser's home to become his disciple. As usual, he had to bring some present to his new master and brought with him a bowl of water with a piece of paper cut in the form of a fish. As the great miser happened to be away from home, his wife received him. Upon knowing the intention and present from the pupil, she said "thanks" and had her maid bring up an empty cup and asked him to have tea, which was nonexistent at all. After the pupil had pretended to enjoy tea, the wife again asked him to help himself to the cakes by drawing two circles in the air with her hand. In came the master miser when he saw his wife drawing two cakes, and he shouted to her, "What extravagance! You are giving two cakes away! A semicircle should do!"（林语堂译）

## 三、翻译策略

### （一）英译汉

英译汉成功的关键在于句型的正确转换，即把英语纷繁复杂的复合长句转换成汉语的流水句，也就是把英语中的一个一个"枝杈"转换成一层一层的"波浪"。尤其是要考虑到汉语短语与单句之间，单句与复句之间，复句与更大的单位句群之间，界限并不是截然分明的这一特点，尽量使汉语译文少用甚至不用连接词语，表面的句法结构上呈流水状的同层结构，但语意层次分明，做到不露痕迹的意合衔接。

具体而言，英语长句的汉译常常采用分解、拆离和重组等手段进行灵活处理。试比较下例中的译文 A 与译文 B：

[例8] In the doorway lay at least twelve umbrellas of all sizes and colors.
　　A：门口放着一堆雨伞，少说也有十二把，五颜六色，大小不一。
　　B：门口放着至少有十二把五颜六色、大小不一的雨伞。

又如：

[例9] The use of traveling is to regulate imagination by reality, and instead of thinking how things may be, to see them as they are.
　　旅行的作用是用现实来调整想象，不是去臆测，而是去亲历目睹

事物的真相。

[例10] The motorcar promised unimaginable levels of personal mobility. But now, traffic in cities moves more slowly than it did in the days of the horse-drawn carriage, and we waste our lives stuck in traffic jams.

汽车曾使我们希望个人出行会方便得让人难以想象。可如今,城市交通比马车时代还要缓慢,我们陷入交通堵塞,困在车内,徒然浪费生命。

[例11] Your social and economical transformation has been even more remarkable, moving from a closed command economic system to a driving, increasingly market-based and driven economy, generating two decades of unprecedented growth, giving people greater freedom to travel within and outside China, to vote in village election, to own a home, choose a job, attend a better school.

贵国在社会和经济领域取得了令人瞩目的变革,经济体制从封闭性、指令性向日显生机、日趋注重市场性转变,20年来出现了史无前例的增长,人民拥有更多的自由,他们可以出入国境、参加村委会选举、购房、择业,以及选择更好的学校。

(二) 汉译英

汉译英成功的关键也在于句型的正确转换。这一般包括两个步骤:①要从层次关系并不是截然分明的片句、流水句中确立一个总揽全局的主干结构;②在主干结构的基础上,灵活、恰当地选用各种的连接词、非谓语动词等表示从属关系的成分,重新架构起成主次分明、层次清晰的句法结构。这其实就是长句翻译法中的一项技法——重组法,只是汉译英中的重组更是难上加难,而且应用也更广泛。

[例12] 医以生人,庸工以之杀人;兵以杀人,圣人以之生人。(张潮《幽梦影》)

Medicine is for saving life, but in the hands of quacks can kill people. Soldiers are for killing people, but in the hands of wise rulers, can save people's lives. (林语堂 译)

汉语原文中,"庸工""圣人"本是两个完整的散句的主语,在英译中却能够融入到了另外的句子的附属成分中,增加了层次分明的英语味,其成功关键,就在于通过使用恰当的连接词,终于将其"浓缩",做到了"无缝衔接"。

[例 13] 境内西湖如镜,知峰凝翠,洞壑幽深,风光绮丽。

> Hangzhou's West Lake is like a mirror, embellished all around with green hills and deep caves of enchanting beauty.

在上例中,汉语原文由四个分句组成,或者说有 4 层"波浪"组成。英语译文除了把"境内西湖如镜"译成主句外,其余的都是修饰成分,或者说都是"枝杈",而 of enchanting beauty 用来修饰 green hills and deep caves。若译员不注意英汉语句结构之间的转换,将原文译成"West Lake in Hangzhou is like a mirror. All around the lake tower the green hill, and in the hills one can find deep caves. Hangzhou's scenery is beautiful.",译文将十分蹩脚。试揣摩下列几个例子中的句法结构组织与转换:

[例 14] 汉有举孝,唐有孝悌力田科,清末也还有孝廉方正,都能换到官做。父恩谕之于先,皇恩施之于后,然而割股的人物,究属寥寥。足可证明中国的旧学说旧手段,实在从古以来,并无良效,无非使坏人增长些虚伪,好人无端的多受些人我都无利益的痛苦罢了。(鲁迅《我们现在怎样做父亲》)

> In the Han and Tang dynasties and at the end of the Ching dynasty, we had systems whereby filial sons could become officials. Thus in addition to parental exhortation there was state encouragement; yet even so there were very few limb-cutters. This proves that from ancient times till now the old ideas and old ways have achieved very little, simply making the bad more hypocritical and causing more useless suffering to the good. (杨宪益 戴乃迭 译)

[例 15] 文人讲武事,大都纸上谈兵;武将论文章,半属道听途说。(张潮《幽梦影》)

> A literary man discussing wars and battles is mostly an armchair strategist; a military man who discusses literature relies on rumors picked up from hearsay. (林语堂 译)

[例 16] 天目山林深人少,古树掩映,清泉石上流,雾生半山腰,如仙境一般。

> Mt. Tianmu, densely forested and sparsely populated, is like a

fairyland, where clear streams flow along the valleys and heavy mists envelop halfway up the mountain.

[例17] 偶尔某户人家弟兄内讧，夫妻斗殴，整条街道便会骚动起来，人们往来奔走，相告相劝，如同一河受惊的群鸭，半天不得平息。
If brothers fell out or husband and wife came to blows, the whole place was in a turmoil as all rushed to intercede, like a flock of startled duck, not coming to rest until after a long time.

[例18] 泉涸，鱼相与处于陆，相呴以湿，相濡以沫，不如相忘于江湖。与其誉尧而非桀也，不如两忘而化其道。（庄子《大宗师》）
When the pond dries up and the fishes are left upon the dry ground, rather than leave them to moisten each other with their damp and spittle, it would be far better to let them forget themselves in their native rivers and lakes. And rather than praise Yao and blame Chieh, it would be better to forget about both good and evil and lose oneself in Tao. （林语堂　译）

以上各例，汉语原文中的单句均译成一个英语从句或从属的修饰语。这样，汉语中的"波浪"便成了英语中的"枝杈"。

需要指出，在句子长度方面，真正重要的其实是适切性与多样性，而不是句子的平均长度。英汉修辞学都主张长短句交替、单复句相间。过分使用长句或短句都会产生单调感。句子的长短取决于作者和读者的年龄、教育程度、阅读经验、写作的题材、文体、强调以及句式变换的需要等因素。

句式的繁或简，与文体也很有关系，汉英皆然。一般说来，长句严密、周详、细致，宜于阐述复杂的观点，抒发细腻的感情，描述具体的细节，常见于书面语，尤其是政论文、科技论文、公文或小说的叙述与描写。短句简洁、明快、活泼、有力，宜于叙述事物，说明情况，抒发感情，对比强调，常见于口语，尤其是日常会话、辩论、演讲、台词、杂文、广播稿、儿童文学或小说里的人物对话。汉英互译时应注意繁简句式与文体的这种关系。

## 【翻译欣赏】

谢谢主席先生！今天能有这样的机会来与大家共同探讨跨国公司的管理问题，我感到很高兴。在这里，我想以我公司的长期合作伙伴壳牌石油公司作为案例，向大家介绍它的相关管理问题，希望对各位有所启发。

Thank you, Mr. Chairman. I am privileged to be here today to share with you my opinion about the management of a multi-national company. In the following I'd like to introduce the relevant management of Shell International, our long-term partner, and hope that it will shed a light in your future work.

壳牌国际公司是一家全球性石油公司，联合总部设在英国伦敦与荷兰海牙。该公司雇佣10多万人，其中约5500人曾作为侨民在国外生活和工作过至少一次。壳牌公司雇佣的侨民形形色色，有70多种民族身份，分散在100多个国家。公司早已认识到，作为一家全球性公司，其成功的关键在于它拥有一支具有国际流动性的作业队伍。然而，到了20世纪90年代初，壳牌公司发现为海外的岗位招聘要员要比以前更困难。为了弄清原因，公司于1993年采访了200多名侨民雇员以及他们的配偶，以此确定他们最为关心的问题。采访得来的数据被用来做成一份调查表，分发给17000名在职和已退的侨民雇员、侨民的配偶以及那些拒绝海外工作任务的雇员。

Shell International is a global petroleum company with joint headquarters in both London and Hague in the Netherlands. The company employs over 100,000 people, approximately 5,500 of whom are at least one time living and working as expatriates. The expatriates at Shell are a very diverse group, made up of over 70 nationalities and located in more than 100 countries. Shell has long recognized that as a global corporation, the international mobility of its work force is essential to its success. By the early 1990s, however, Shell was finding it harder to recruit key personnel for foreign positions. To discover why, the company in 1993 interviewed more than 200 expatriate employees and their spouses to determine their biggest concerns. The data were then used to construct a survey that was sent to 17,000 current and former expatriate employees, expatriates' spouses, and employees who had declined international assignments.

对这份调查表的回应率高达70%，清楚地表明了许多雇员对调查内容很重视。根据调查结果，影响雇员接受海外工作任务的因素有5个，按主次排列分别是：（1）离别了正在上中学的孩子（英国与荷兰的侨民在国外工作的时候，其孩子都在本国上寄宿学校）；（2）牺牲了配偶的事业和就业；（3）调动时无法与配偶打招呼和商量；（4）对于调动无法提供足够的信息和协助；（5）健康方面的问题。这些问题的潜台词是移居国外的基本单元是家庭而不是个人，壳牌公司当时需要做更多的事情才能认识清楚这一点。

The survey registered a phenomenal 70% response rate, clearly indicating that many employees thought this was an important issue. According to the survey, five issues had the greatest impact on the willingness of an employee to accept an international assignment. In order of importance, these were: (1) separation from children during their secondary education ( the children of British and Dutch expatriates were often sent to boarding schools in their home countries while their parents worked abroad), (2) harm done to a spouse's career and employment, (3) a failure to recognize and involve a spouse in the relocation decision, (4) inadequate information and assistance regarding relocation, and (5) health issues. The underlying message was that the family is the basic unit of expatriation, not the individual, and Shell needed to do more to recognize this.

壳牌公司于1994年推行了一系列方案，致力于部分解决这些问题。为了帮助解决孩子的教育问题，公司在侨民较集中的雇员所在地建立了小学；至于中学教育，则与地方学校合作，往往是给地方学校拨款以帮助它们提高教学水平。公司还提供教育辅助项目以帮助侨民把孩子送往东道国的私立学校就读。1994年以前，公司仅仅为员工的孩子在本国上寄宿学校支付费用。

In 1994, Shell implemented a number of programs designed to address some of these problems. To help with the education of children, Shell built elementary schools for Shell employees where there was a heavy concentration of expatriates. As for secondary school education, it worked with local schools, often providing grants, to help them upgrade their educational offerings. It also offered an education supplement to help expatriates send their children to private schools in the host country (before 1994, it would pay only for a child's boarding school education in its home country).

帮助员工的配偶解决工作问题倒是一个更为难的事情。据调查，随着家人到壳牌公司来工作，配偶中有一半的人能在调动前找到工作。而一旦这些人被当作侨民分配到海外工作时，配偶中只有12%的人能找到工作，33%的人希望有份工作。壳牌公司为此设立了一个配偶就业中心来解决这个问题。在员工接受海外工作期间或之后，该中心可以为他们的配偶提供就业咨询或帮助他们寻找就业机会。壳牌公司还提供补贴高达80%的职业培训费、进修费或考试鉴定费；为每次海外工作所补贴的金额也高达4,400美元。

Helping spouses with their careers is a more vexing problem. According to the survey data, half of the spouses accompanying Shell staff on assignment were employed until the transfer. When expatriated, only 12 percent were able to secure employment, while a further 33％ wished to be employed. Shell set a spouse employment center to address the problem. The center provides career counseling and assistance in locating employment opportunities both during and immediately after an international assignment. The company also agrees to reimburse up to 80 ％ of the costs of vocational training, further education, or re-accreditation, up to ＄4, 400 per assignment.

壳牌公司建立了一个称为"前哨"的全球信息与咨询网络，为那些希望到海外谋职的家庭提供服务。该网络把总部设在海牙，现已在30多个国家运营了40多个信息中心。该网络的成员由壳牌员工的配偶组成，并得到壳牌公司的全力支持。至1998年，它已经帮助过1000多对夫妇做好到海外工作前的准备。中心向人们推荐和介绍学校、医疗设施，提供住房咨询以及关于就业、学习、个体经营和志愿者劳动等方面的最新信息。

谢谢大家！

Shell also set up a global information and advice network known as "The Outpost" to provide support for families contemplating a foreign position. The Outpost has its headquarters in Hague and now runs 40 information centers in more than 30 countries. Staffed by spouses and fully supported by Shell, this network had by 1998 helped more than 1, 000 couples prepare for placements overseas. The center recommends schools and medical facilities and provides housing advice and up-to-date information on employment, study, self-employment, and volunteer work.

Thank you!

## 第五节　首重与尾重

语言学家卡普兰（Robert Kaplan）的研究表明，西方人是直线型思维模式，东方人则是螺旋型思维模式，如下图：

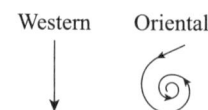

这种思维模式上的差异，对于汉英语言结构产生了很大的影响。

### 一、英语的尾重倾向

在直线型思维的影响下，英语句子的信息重心通常在前端，形成从一般到具体，从概括到举例，从整体到个体，从观点到案例的信息分布，这就要求把语法结构较复杂的定语、状语等用于补充信息的修饰成分置于被修饰语之后，很多时候也就是居于句子尾端。由于这些修饰成分字数较多、结构上又可以不断延展下去，客观上形成了状似孔雀尾的句子结构，这就是英语语序的安排中的一条重要原则——末端重量原则，也就是说，句子结构必须避免头重脚轻，句子的谓语部分应比主语部分更长一些，使句子结构平衡。为了方便起见，人们把这种结构形象地称为"孔雀尾"结构。

［例1］ It is comforting to realize that other species besides our own can stand back and assess the world around them, even if their horizons are more limited than ours.

想到除了我们人类，尚有其他物种，即便它们的视野比我们还狭小，却也能退后一步，清醒地审视周围的世界，不由令人深感宽慰。

［例2］ Did he lie to the American people when he said " I never had sex with that woman"?

当他说"我从来没有与那个女人发生性关系"时，他是否在对美国人民撒谎?

［例3］ We might as well get a feel for the fringes and hollows in which life is lived, for the Amazon basin, which covers half a continent, and for the life that—there, like anywhere else—is always and necessarily lived in detail: on the tributaries, in the riverside villages, sucking this particular white-fleshed guava in this particular pattern of shade.

我们不妨去感受一下有生命生活其间的远方水乡山谷,去感受覆盖了半个大陆的亚马逊河流域,去感受那样一种生活——在那里,一如在别的地方——那种必定总是琐碎的生活:在各条支流上,在临水的村落里,在有着独特形状的阴凉处吮吸着有白色浆果的独特的番石榴。

## 二、汉语的首重现象

汉语是螺旋型思维的语言,习惯从侧面迂回,或者旁敲侧击铺垫暗示,其信息分布为出先偏后正,由次到主,先摆事实后讲道理,宛如画龙点睛一般将重心置于句尾。从句法成分上来说,定语、状语等修饰语一般置于被修饰语之前,而且字数较多,在客观上呈现出前端重量的特点。人们把这种结构称为"狮子头",与英语的"孔雀尾"适成对照。

[例4] 中国是四大文明古国之一,地大物博,拥有茂密的森林,壮丽的山河,如利剑直插云霄的高峰,雄伟壮丽的瀑布,秀丽的湖泊及富有中华文化光辉的名胜古迹,令世界人民神往。

China, one of the four countries in the world with the oldest civilization, filled the world with longing with a vast territory and abundant resources, dense forests and majestic rivers and mountains where peaks pierce the clouds like so many gargantuan swords, magnificent waterfalls and beautiful lakes, and historical remains underlining her glorious past.

[例5] 因为亲戚们不是同一拨来的。他们往往分期分批,无计划、无组织,即兴而来,乘兴而去,令人无法预测,不可捉摸。(徐坤《亲戚们》)

The reason for these numerous trips is because relatives do not arrive in a batch but arrive singly, randomly, coming and going at their whim, totally beyond prediction and defying conjecture. (朱虹 译)

[例6] 于是在一片"识时务者为俊杰""浪子回头金不换""人文精神又回来了"的啧啧赞叹声中,亲戚们来往走动得更勤了。(徐坤《亲戚们》)

And so relatives come and go even more frequently to the tune of "the superior person is he (she) who knows the times," "the profligate returned is worth his (her) weight in gold," and "the spirit of humanity is revived" and so on. (朱虹 译)

当然,汉语作为意合语言,在句子的结构安排上要灵活一些,在"前端重量"现象突出的同时,也有相当多的句子采用句尾开放格局,并不会显得突兀。换言之,英语对于"孔雀尾"的执着,是要超过汉语对于"狮子头"的偏好的。

[例7] 亲戚们无论怎样做都是有道理的,因为他们是我们的亲戚们。他们总在提醒我们什么叫作血浓于水。他们总在提拎着耳根子对我们叮咛告诫:亲戚们的传统,不是说反就反了的。(徐坤《亲戚们》)

Relatives, like customers, are always right, just by the fact they are relatives. They are by their existence live reminders that blood is thicker than water. They are continually dinning this warning into our ears: the tradition of relatives cannot be overturned at will. (朱虹 译)

[例8] 为了不使自己不忠不孝的劣迹进一步发展成为醒世恒言,我们开始把从前留下的坏印象一点一点地努力往回拨反。下一轮亲戚来时我们比以前更殷勤,更周到,出手更阔绰,笑脸更相迎,更把身子艰难的蜷进夜晚的沙发里,蜷出一坨坨冻虾形的孝顺和贤明。(徐坤《亲戚们》)

Determined not to be go-down-in-history as pernicious examples of offenders against family virtues, we desperately tried to revive our past good records in hosting relatives. To the next batch of relatives, we presented ourselves as more solicitous than ever. We went to even greater expenses, greeted them with broader smiles and curled ourselves onto the sofa at night like frozen shrimps, the picture of family virtue and hospitality. (朱虹 译)

## 三、英语尾重句的汉译

### (一) 英语尾重句译成汉语前端开放句

1. 定语与谓语换位

在一些英语句子中,因为主语的定语较长,而谓语部分较短,为了避免头重脚轻,往往把主语的定语放在谓语部分之后。而在英译汉时,这部分定语可以译成其他成分,其位置也宜加以调整,可能置于句首,即主语之前。

[例9] Thus began by far the gravest crisis in the troubled 32 - year history of commercial atomic power.

麻烦不断的原子能商业利用历史上最严重的一次危机就这么开始了。

[例10] Accounts are given of huge mountains sinking, of former plains heaves aloft, of fires flashing out amid the ruin.

高山沉陷,平原凸起,火焰喷射,周围是一片废墟,这些都有记载。

2. 从句与主句换位

很多英语复合句常把概括性的信息放在主句,字数较多、结构庞大的细节信息放在从句,避免头重脚轻,呈现尾端开放的格局。但汉语短句多,结构不庞杂,也就没有句首过于复杂导致头重脚轻的问题,因此可以把概括性的信息置于句尾,形成流水句格局,显得句式流畅。

[例11] It might likewise deserve our most serious considerations how far, in a well-regulated city, those humorists are to be tolerated, who, not contented with the traditional cries of their forefathers, have invented particular songs and tunes of their own: such as was, not many years since, the pastry-man, commonly known by the name of the Colly-Molly-Puff; and such as is at this day the vendor of powder and wash-balls, who, if I am rightly informed, goes under the name of Powder-Wat.

还有些人——譬如说,不几年以前大家叫做"松软——可口——蓬蓬酥"的卖点心小贩,以及现在(如果我没有弄错的话)通称为"香粉沃特"的脂粉货郎,不以他们祖祖辈辈流传下来的叫卖为满足,还特别编出自己的歌曲来,以吟唱代替叫卖。在一个管理完善的城市里,对于这些市廛奇人究竟应该宽容到何种程度,也值得我们认真考虑。

[例12] There is a difference when listening to the *Chin* under a pine tree, to a flute in the moonlight, to a waterfall along a stream, and a Buddhist service up in the mountains. (张潮《幽梦影》)

松下听琴,月下听萧,涧边听瀑布,山中听梵呗,觉耳中别有不同。(林语堂 译)

3. 宾、补换位

众所周知,在英语复合宾语中,正常语序是"宾"前"补"后。不过,当宾语较长或带有较长的修饰语而补足语又短时,两者的语序就颠倒,构成尾重句。但在汉译文中,宾、补结构均可置于句首,即主语之前。

[例13] We shall regard as a personal favor any help you give to Mr Chadwick during his stay in your country.

查维克先生在贵国逗留期间,你们所给他的任何帮助我们将感同身受。

[例14] It is not uncommon, in the most pleasant of homes, to see pasted on the windows small notices announcing that the premises are under surveillance by this security force or that guard company.

一个司空见惯的现象是,即使在最温馨的居家,也可以看到窗上贴着小小的告示,称本宅处在某安全机构或保安公司的监控之下。

4. it 作形式主语

英语中如果主语太长,为避免头重脚轻,可以使用 it 作形式主语,将真正的主语移到后面,其结果使句子结构匀称,被后移的主语成为意义重心。不过,英译汉时,英语实际主语的汉语译文常常放在句首。

[例15] It gives me great pleasure to be able to come to Bangkok, the City of Angels, for the APEC CEO Summit.

今天,有机会来到被称为"天使之城"的曼谷,参加亚太经合组织工商领导人峰会,我感到十分高兴。

[例16] It is a strange thought, but I believe a correct one, that twenty or thirty pages of ideas and information would be capable of turning the present-day world upside down, or even destroying.

二三十页的观点和情报竟能把当今世界搞得天翻地覆,甚至把它毁灭，这是个奇怪的想法，但我相信这是个正确的想法。

5. 倒装结构

倒装句在英语中是常见的句法手段，其意义在于避免头重脚轻。这些倒装部分译作汉语时，可能置于句首，也可能置于句尾。

［例17］Also a good case in point is that China independently developed its atomic and hydrogen bombs and man-made satellite.

中国独立自主地研发"两弹一星"也证明了这一点。（或：一个突出的例子是，中国独立自主地研发了"两弹一星"。）

［例18］Is not a Patron, my lord, one who looks with unconcern on a man struggling for life in the water, and, when he has reached ground, encumbers him with help? The notice which you have been pleased to take of my labours, had it been early, had been kind; but it has been delayed till I am indifferent, and cannot enjoy it... （Samuel Johnson　*To Lord Chesterfield*）

伯爵阁下：见人挣扎于水中则默默然袖手旁观，见人安然登岸则遽遽乎殷勤相助，此非恩主之为人乎？阁下于拙著之锦注，若在昔年，诚不失为美意；惜于其姗姗来迟，今仆已兴味索然，难以欣赏……（黄继忠　译）

（二）英语尾重句译成汉语尾端开放句

但是，相对于英语句式往往严格遵循末端重量原则而言，汉语的"重量原则"要灵活得多，既可以句首开放，也可以句尾开放。换言之，在翻译中，尤其是口译中，译员也常常采用句尾开放的汉语句式，即采用"顺译法"。

［例19］Forasmuch, therefore, as persons of this rank are seldom men of genius or capacity I think it would be very proper that some men of good sense and sound judgement should preside over these public cries, who should permit none to lift up their voices in our streets that have not tunable throats, and are not only able to overcome the noise of the crowd, and the rattling of coaches, but also to vend their respective merchandises in apt phrases, and in the most distinct and agreeable sounds.　（Joseph Addison　*On the Cries of London*）

准此，既然在这个阶层里天才能人甚少，一切公共叫卖之声应该统归明理善断之士主管，嗓音不美者不得在街头大喊大叫，叫卖声不仅要压倒人声喧哗、车声轧轧，而且要使用恰当词句将各自贩卖的货色加以说明，发音也要清晰、悦耳。（刘炳善　译）

［例20］In the principle of religion and morality, Miss Sedley will be found worthy of an establishment which has been honoured by the presence of The Great Lexicographer, and the patronage of the admirable Mrs. Chapone. （William Thackeray *Vanity Fair*）

赛特粒小姐对于宗教道德的见解非常正确，不亏为本校的学生（本校曾蒙伟大的词汇学家参观，又承杰出的夏博恩夫人多方资助）。（杨必　译）

［例21］Buried under ground were bodies of plants and animals which were transformed into petroleum during the course of hundreds of millions of years.

埋在地下的是动植物的遗骸，经过亿年之后，已变成了石油。

［例22］In recent years, it has become increasingly popular for large corporations to form their own venture capital subsidiaries or investment vehicles.

近年来，一个日益普遍的现象是大公司组建了自己的风险资本子公司或投资工具。

## 四、汉语首重句的英译

汉语中的首重句，即所谓首端开放，结论在后的"网收状"类句子，在英译时通常要遵循英语的尾重原则对句子结构进行改动，将结论部分提前；或者也可以采用分译法，前后两部分分开翻译。

### （一）结论部分提前

［例23］长睫毛下一双欲眠、似醉、含笑、带梦的大眼睛，圆满的上嘴唇好像鼓着在跟爱人使性子。（钱钟书《围城》）

Under her long eyelashes was a pair of sleepy, seemingly drunken, dreamy, big smiling eyes; her full, round upper lip seemed to be angrily pouting at a lover. （凯利　茅国权　译）

［例24］为月忧云，为书忧蠹，为花忧风雨，为才子佳人忧命薄，真是菩

萨心肠。(张潮《幽梦影》)

It shows the heart of merciful Buddha to worry about clouds with the moon, about moths with books, about winds and rains with flowers, and to sympathize with beautiful women and brilliant poets about their harsh fate. (林语堂 译)

［例25］固然，我们的烧饼油条豆浆，永远吃不厌，但是看看街边炸油条打烧饼的师傅，他的装束，他的浑身上下，他的一切设备，谁敢去光顾！

Sure, we have sesame seed cakes, deep-fried dough sticks and soybean milk with which we never feel bored, but who is willing to eat these things when seeing the vendors making them on the sidewalks with all their dirty apparel and utensils?

［例26］尽管嘴上说友谊，对运动员来说重要的仍然是成绩。得第一名获金牌，第四名什么也拿不到。任何想获奥运冠军的人都得中断学业，牺牲自己业余时间。这一点常常是观众没有看到的。因此，运动员要求得到物质奖励是可以理解的。

Despite lip service paid to friendship, what matters to athletes is success. Whoever comes first wins a gold medal but anyone who comes fourth gets nothing. What the spectators sometimes fail to notice is that anyone who wants to become an Olympic champion has to break off his studies and has little spare time. It is understandable that athletes want some tangible reward.

(二) 分译

［例27］这次到台湾访问交流，虽然行程匆匆，但是，看了不少地方，访了旧友，交了新知，大家走到一起，谈论的一个重要话题就是中华民族在21世纪的强盛。

The current visit to Taiwan for exchange, brief and cursory as it is, has enabled us to see many places, to visit old friends while making new acquaintances. An important topic for discussing at our gatherings was the prosperity of Chinese nation in the 21st century.

［例28］狂赌救国，纵欲成仙，袖手杀敌，造谣买田，倘有人要续编《龙

文鞭影》的，我以为不妨加上这四句。（鲁迅《中国的奇想》）

Wild gambling saves the state,

And lust will bring you immortality;

With folded hands you kill your enemy,

By spreading rumours you win prosperity.

If anyone wants to compile another book of famous rhymes ancient and modern, he might, I think, include the four lines. （杨宪益　戴乃迭　译）

【翻译欣赏】

改革开放胆子要大一些，要敢于试验。冒一定的风险是必要的。不冒点风险，办什么事都有百分之百的把握，万无一失，谁敢说这样的话？一开始就自以为是，认为百分之百正确，没那回事。我从来就没那么认为。每年领导层都要总结经验，对的就坚持，不对的就丢掉或赶快改，新问题出来加紧解决，无论打仗还是搞改革，都经不起慢腾腾的决策。在很多情况下，都需要冒险试一试，然后一边前进一边改正自己的错误。恐怕再有三十年的时间，我们才会在各方面形成一套更加成熟，更加定型的制度。在这个制度下的方针，政策，也将更加定型化。

We must be courageous enough to venture on experiments as far as reforms are concerned. A certain account of risk-taking is necessary. *Who dares to claim* that he is 100 percent sure of success right from the beginning and without taking any risks? There is no such thing as certainty. I have never had such notions as thinking I'm 100 percent correct. Every year, leaders should review what they have done so as to hold to what works and discard what does not, or take immediate corrective steps. We should lose no time in tackling them whenever new problems arise. No one can afford the luxury of slow decision-making, when it involves fighting a battle or making a reform. In many cases, you have to take a chance, and correct your mistakes as you go along. I'm afraid that it may take another 30 years to establish a set of more mature and more consistent system in all fields of endeavor, under which all policies will be more consistent, too.

# 第一节　汉英音韵修辞对比与翻译

语言是思维的载体，依附于有声的外壳。很早以来，人们就发现了语言的音乐性质。范家材先生在《英文修辞》一书中说，"有时，在写作中，我感到遣词造句犹如谱写音乐。这种音乐性对我的吸引，远远超过词语本身。"邵志洪教授指出，音韵修辞手段利用各种音响特征巧妙和谐、有规则的配合，使声音高低有序、节奏分明、长短适度、优美悦耳，以达到语言鲜明、生动、形象的效果。

英语和汉语在音韵表达方法上有各自的特点。

汉语和英语在音节构成上存在着很大差异。英语音位的结合比较自由，英语单词多是多音节，音节结构的类型要比汉语音节结构的类型多，构成方式相当复杂，其辅音在构成音节时大多既可以出现在元音前，又可以出现在元音后，还会有大量的辅音连缀。而汉语基本由单音节构成，构成方法非常单纯：前声后韵，声调则附着在整个音节上。

从词句发音的衔接方式上看，汉、英语在发音和听感上都有明显的区别。汉语最清晰的单位是音节，而英语的音节有明显的元辅音拼合过程。所以汉语属于断奏音；就是说，连续发出的各个音之间有间断。而英语却是属于连奏音，就是说，连续出现的音圆滑而无间断。英语是以重音计时的，每一语句虽然是重音和轻音交错出现，但仍以重读音节为基础，为主体。汉语是以音节计时的，音节（字）的数目是韵律的基础。

## 一、汉英语拟声词的对比

拟声词又叫象声词，是用于模拟各种声响的词，其特点是丰富形象，极大地增强了语言的多样性和生动性，可以说是语言宝库中的璀璨明珠。汉英语言中的拟声词在造词理据及修辞功效上是基本一致的；同时，由于它们在语音系统、词汇形态和句法功能上存在很大差异，也成为翻译中的一个难点。

1. 语音形式对比

（1）相似的语音形式。

由于拟声词是对自然声音的模拟，因此不同语言里的拟声词可能出现语音重合的现象。有时对同一声音的模拟，汉英语中会采用相似的语音形式。

例如:

［例1］鸽子咕咕叫。The pigeon coos.

（2）相异的语音形式。

然而,拟声词的词汇形式也存在着某种程度的任意性或约定俗成,它们必须适应于特定语言的语音系统,而不是直接地模仿它们所代表的那些个声音。各种语言音系结构、词汇形态各不相同,各民族对同一声音的听觉感知和模拟习惯也不尽一致,再加上语言的任意性（arbitrariness）属性,不同语言中的拟声词在语音形式上就可能出现种种差别,甚至大相径庭。因此,拟声大都只是大体上像某种现实的声音,有的比较接近,有的不过大体表现出声音的简单轮廓或部分轮廓,有的则相去甚远。

［例2］The bird twitters. 鸟儿叽叽喳喳欢叫着。

其次,在汉英语中,声音与拟声词并非都是一一对应的关系。一个拟声词可能是对若干种不同声音的模拟,而一种声音也可能用若干不同的拟声词来描绘。例如:murmur 可用来描述人的咕哝声、喊喳声,微风的沙沙声,流水的淙淙声,蜜蜂的嗡嗡声等。

［例3］There appeared a *murmur* of delight in the audience.
　　　　观众中出现了欢乐的*喊喊喳喳声*。

［例4］The *murmur* of a distant brook highlighted the tranquility and peacefulness of the fortified mountain village.
　　　　远处小溪传来*汩汩的流水声*,更加突显了山寨的恬谧与安宁。

［例5］It was raining softly, a steady drizzling *murmur*.
　　　　绵绵细雨,*淅淅沥沥*地下个不停。

相比较而言,英语拟声词比汉语丰富一些。这与两种语言在词汇及文字形态上的差异有密切的关系。英语的拼音文字使其在创造拟声词方面具有更多的自由。但是,汉语的基本拟声词逼真度较高些,至少不会像英语那样用同一个词来模拟好几种声音,如 rustle 用来模拟"唰""哗啦""刷拉""瑟瑟""飒飒"几种声音,而 rumble 可以表示"轰隆""咕隆""咕噜"这三种声音。

2. 句法功能对比

英汉语中,拟声词的使用都很复杂,但如下两点较为明显。其一,英语的拟声词可以用作动词（包括限定式和非限定式）和名词（作介词宾语构成短语作状语等）;其二,汉语基本拟声词直接作状语或与"……的一声"连用作状语修饰动词。

英语拟声词都有明确的词类归属,除了少数只作名词或只作动词外,绝大

# 第四章
## 汉英修辞对比与翻译

修辞（figures of speech）可以增加语言的生动性、形象性和趣味性，是一个极富文学意味的范畴，故本章内容借鉴文学文体翻译的"三美论"，从音美、意美、形美的角度，划为音韵修辞、语义修辞、结构修辞三节，分别展开探讨。

多数既是名词也是动词，在句中可用作主语、宾语和谓语，直接用作状语的不多。实际上，"英语拟声词有明显的动词化倾向"。实例如下：

[例6] The baby is *babbling* out its first speech sounds.

小宝宝正在*呀呀*学语。

[例7] The crowd began to *hiss and boo* them for their unsportsmanlike sluggishness, but they kept on directing serves into the net and making simple errors like hitting the shuttlecock wide as if nothing had happened.

对于这种缺乏运动员道德的消极比赛行为，人群中开始响起了*"嘘嘘""呸呸"*的喝倒彩声，但她们不为所动，继续频频出现下网和出界的低级错误，好像没事人一样。

[例8] The war is actually begun. The next gale that sweeps from the north will bring to our ears the *clash* of resounding arms!

战争实际上已经开始！从北方席卷而来的又一次风暴即将带来震耳回响的*隆隆炮声*。

对于汉语拟声词的词类归属及语法地位，目前看法尚不明确，归纳起来大致有三种：(1) 拟声词与感叹词合为一类，统称"拟声词"，只能算虚词；(2) 拟声词和感叹词合起来统称"拟声词"，但归入实词；(3) 拟声词属形容词，归入实词。总的看来，汉语拟声词多半带有形容词性质，最常担任的句子成分是状语、定语和补语。也可作谓语，但往往带有临时性质。

[例9] 她的心儿啊，扑通扑通直跳。

Her heart went *pit-a-pat*.

[例10] 子弹嗖嗖地飞过他的头顶。

The bullets *whizzed* over his head.

[例11] 林中秋风飒飒。

The autumn wind is *soughing* in the trees.

## 二、拟声词的翻译

由于汉英拟声词之间存在的差异，在翻译过程中必须注意两者的转换，尤其是语音形式和句法功能两个方面的转换。

1. 语音形式的转换

(1) 直译。

英汉语中发音相近的拟声词，不妨直接翻译。如：

[例12] Wine-cups and chopsticks were laid out, and a delicious sizzling sound came from the chafing dish.

杯筷陈设在各人面前，暖锅里发出滋滋的有味的声音。

[例13] Alice giggled.

爱丽丝咯咯笑着。

[例14] "我愿意既不谎人，也不遭打。那么，老师，我得怎么说呢?"

"那么，你得说：'啊呀！这孩子呵！您瞧！多么……。啊唷！哈哈！Hehe! he, hehehehe!'"（鲁迅《立论》）

"I don't want to tell a lie, and neither do I want to be beaten. Then what should I do, sir?"

"Well, just say, 'Ai-ya, this child! Just look! Oh, my! Hah! Hehe! He, Hehehehe!'"（张培基 译）

(2) 改译。

从上面的对比看出，汉英拟声词的语音形式有很大差别。因此，翻译拟声词要熟悉译入语中对该声音的模拟习惯。如果没有与其一致或类似的语音形式，就应注意两种语言之间对应的拟声词的转换。例如：

[例15] Then foxes barked in the hills and deer silently crossed the fields, half hidden in the mists of the fall mornings.

那时侯，狐狸在小丘上嘶嚎，野鹿隐蔽在秋天的晨雾里悄悄地越过田野。

[例16] 后窗的玻璃上丁丁地响，还有许多小飞虫乱撞。

A pit-a-pat sounds from the glass of the back window, where insects are dashing themselves against the pane.

[例17] 是谁多事种芭蕉?

早也潇潇，

晚也潇潇。（蒋坦《秋灯琐忆》）

What busybody planted this sapling?

Morning tapping,

Evening rapping!（林语堂 译）

(3) 创译。

拟声造词是人类最古老的造词方法，而且至今仍在沿用这种构词方法造出新词。汉语的某些拟声词，英语中没有对应的拟声词，翻译时需要按照发音规律创造新的拟声词。

[例18] "呃啾"的一声响,爱姑知道是七大人打喷嚏了,但不由得转过脸去看。

"Ah-tchew!" Though Ai-ku knew it was only Seventh Master sneezing, she could not help turning to look at him.

[例19] 关关雎鸠,

在河之洲。

窈窕淑女,

君子好逑。(《诗经·国风·周南·关雎》)

Kwan kwan go the ospreys.

On the islet in the river,

The modest, retiring, virtuous, young lady:

For our prince a good mate she. (James Legge 译)

2. 句法功能的转换

由以上对比看出,拟声词在句法功能方面也存在很大差异,因此在翻译时要注意句法功能是否需要转换。

(1) 直译即保留拟声词在原文中的句法功能。在以下例子中原句法功能得到了保留。

[例20] 呜!呜、呜、呜……(独立成分)

汽笛叫声突然从那边远远的河身的弯曲地方传来了。

*Toot! Toot-toot-toot...*（独立成分）

Far up the bend in the canal a boat whistle broke the silence.

[例21] 听见狼嚎你可以握紧棍子

但毒蛇是没有声音的(宾补)(艾青《无题》)

You can grip the club when you hear the wolf *howl*.

But the serpent is silent. (宾补) (庞秉钧 闵福德 高尔登 译)

[例22] 一个蚊子哼哼哼,

两只苍蝇嗡嗡嗡。(谓语)

A mosquito hums and hums,

Two flies drone and drone. (谓语)

[例23] 战士战死了的时候,苍蝇们所首先发现的是他的缺点和伤痕,嘬着,营营地叫着,以为得意,以为比死了的战士更英雄。(状语)(鲁迅《战士和苍蝇》)

When a fighter has fallen in battle, the first thing flies notice is his blemishes and wounds. They suck them, *humming*, very pleased to think that they are greater heroes than the fallen warrior.（状语）（杨宪益 戴乃迭 译）

[例 24] The cricket's chirp and the patter of rain come to me through the dark,（主语）

like the rustle of dreams from my past youth. （Tagore *Stray Birds*）

蟋蟀的啁啾，夜雨的淅沥，穿越黑暗传至我耳边，（主语）

仿佛我逝去的青春来到我的梦境中。（徐翰林 译）

（2）转译即拟声词的句法功能有所改变。在许多情况下，拟声词在翻译时都需要进行句法功能的转换。通常作状语的拟声词转换为谓语或现在分词；作定语的转换成主语或宾语；而原来充当独立成分的则可根据需要转换为英语中常见的谓语、主语或宾语。

[例 25] The apple trees were coming into bloom but no bees *droned* among the blossoms, so there was no pollination and there would be no fruit.（谓语）

苹果树鲜花摇曳，但因为没有了嗡嗡嗡的蜜蜂在花间飞舞授粉，所以果实也就无从谈起。（定语）

[例 26] She *squelched* barefoot through the mud.（谓语）

她光着脚吧唧吧唧地在泥地里走。（状语）

[例 27] 哗啦啦一声巨响，一颗大树倒了下来.（状语）

A large tree toppled to the ground with a mighty *crash*.（介词宾语）

[例 28] 叮当的铃声响了，卖冰淇淋的车子来了。（定语）

The *jingle* of bells announced the arrival of the ice-cream truck.（主语）

（3）零译。拟声词在翻译过程中还会出现"零位转换"的情况，即原文使用了拟声词，而译文则转化成非拟声词。

[例 29] OUCH! Our Sale Prices Hurt Us…Not You!

挥泪甩卖！价格让我心痛……让您心动！

[例 30] Water bubbled up through the sand.

水透过泥沙冒了出来。

[例31] 怕只怕三杯下肚，豪情大发，嘟嘟嘟，来个瓶底朝天，而且一顿喝不上便情绪不高，颇有怨言，甚至会到处去找酒喝。（陆文夫《快乐的死亡》）

The trouble is after three cups of alcohol he will get wild and unrestrained and end in gulping down a whole bottle. One meal without liquor will upset him and set him complaining and searching around for drink. （张培基　译）

[例32] 关关雎鸠，

在河之洲。

窈窕淑女，

君子好逑。（《诗经·国风·周南·关雎》）

Merrily the ospreys cry,

On the islet in the stream.

Gentle and graceful is the girl,

A fit wife for the gentleman. （杨宪益　戴乃迭　译）

[例33] 她得不到爱情就嘤嘤地啜泣。

把涩的痛苦和酸的泪水

一滴滴的装入我的心里……（痖弦《瓶》）

Rejected, she wept bitter, heartbroken tears

And poured them, drop by drop,

Into my heart... （庞秉钧　闵福德　高尔登　译）

(4) 增译。原文没有拟声词，而译文可以酌情加上，以增强表达效果。试分析体会以下各例译文中增加的拟声词的效果。

[例34] The kids were crying loudly.

孩子们哇哇大哭。

[例35] Others came to fish the streams, which flowed clear and cold out of the hills and contained shady pools where trout lay.

山石之间，溪水潺潺流动，涓涓细流浸过一汪汪荫凉的浅池，冰凉而清澈，池中鳟鱼自在嬉游，引得一些人专程来此溪边垂钓。

[例36] 去罢，苍蝇们！虽然生着翅子，还能营营，总不会超过战士的。你们这些虫豸们！（鲁迅《战士和苍蝇》）

Buzz off, flies! You may have wings and you may be able to hum, but you will never surpass a fighter, you insects! （杨宪益

戴乃迭　译）

[例37] "你的本事不过这一点点，"我这样想着，觉得胆子更大了。我用轻蔑的眼光看它，我顿脚，我对它吐出骂语。（巴金《狗》）

"Aha, he's now used up all his tricks!" said I to myself, feeling much more emboldened. I stared at him scornfully, stamped my feet and shouted vicious abuse.（张培基　译）

[例38] 猫向你献媚

她瞅着你碗里的鱼（艾青《无题》）

The cat purrs,

And eyes fish on your plate.（庞秉钧　闵福德　高尔登　译）

综上所述，拟声词生动形象，不仅在文学作品中多见，而且在口语中更是大量使用。在翻译中根据情况准确恰当地运用拟声词能够取得很好的修辞效果，增加译文的感染力和表现力。

### 三、押韵

#### （一）英语的押韵

英语诗文的押韵，有全韵与半韵之分。

1. 全韵（Full rhyme）

全韵即严格的押韵，其要求是：（1）韵要押在重读音节上，其元音应相同，如 today/away；（2）元音前的辅音应不同，如 why/sigh；（3）如果元音之后有辅音，应相同，如 hate/late；（4）重读音节之后如有轻读音节，也应相同，如 powers/flowers。

[例39] A hedge between keeps friendship green.
　　　　君子之交淡如水。

[例40] You do the crime, you got to do the time.
　　　　天网恢恢，疏而不漏。

2. 半韵（Half rhyme）

半韵即半谐音，部分押韵，包括头韵、谐元韵、谐辅韵、元辅音结合押韵。

（1）头韵（Alliteration）。

英语中的 alliteration 用来指 "The repetition of usually initial consonant sounds in two or more neighbouring words or syllables"，即重复两个或更多相

邻词语或音节开头的辅音。如：

［例41］Scientists See Planet outside Solar System.
　　　　天文学家观察到天外有天。

［例42］Spare the rod and spoil the child.
　　　　黄荆棍下出好人。

然而，alliteration 并不仅仅限于"开头辅音的重复"，它至少还可以是以下的情形：

①开头元音的重复。

［例43］Apt alliteration of artful aid
　　　　头韵的巧妙帮助

②字母的重复。

［例44］His heavy-shotted hammock-shroud　　他弹痕累累的吊床样桅索
　　　　Drops in his vast and wandering grave.　　堕入他广阔而漫游的坟柩。

尽管 shotted 和 shroud 两个词中的 h 前有 s 字母，发音也分别发〔ʃ〕，但仍然与发〔h〕的 heavy 和 hammock 一样，计为四处全部押字母 h 的头韵。

③alliteration 的音节可以有不同的发音，如：

［例45］This changed conviction into certainty.
　　　　这使得我们所深信不疑的事变成了现实。

当然，作为音韵修辞手段，主要是需要语音的重复来达到音响效果的。那些只有字母相同但发音不一致的情况有时并不被认为是 alliteration，而仅仅被称为"eye alliteration"。

（2）谐元韵（Assonance）。

范家材先生在《英文修辞》中指出："谐元韵是一种重要的选音方式，一般在重读音节上重复某些相同或相似的元音，使语句具有节奏感和诗意，从而增强表现力、感染力。"《牛津现代高级英汉双解词典》将 Assonance 解释为，"agreement between stressed vowels in two words, but not in the following consonants"，即"两字间只有重读的元音相同，而其后之辅音不相同"。如：

［例46］From out waste places comes a cry,
　　　　And murmurs from the dying sun.
　　　　一阵泣涕从外面荒地传来，
　　　　垂死的太阳杂音低迷。

[例 47] But even though Job's style could be demoralizing, it could also be oddly inspiring.

但尽管乔布斯的作风可以令人泄气,说来奇怪,也可以令人鼓舞。

(3) 谐辅韵（Consonance）。

范家材先生在《英文修辞》中,有如下定义:"谐辅韵,即词尾或重读音节中辅音重复。"以美国作家爱伦·坡的两行诗文为例:

[例 48] And the *silken*, *sad*, *uncertain rustling* of each purple curtain
Thrilled me—*filled* me with *fantastic* terrors never *felt before*.

前一句有四个"s"的辅音,仿佛听到窗帘掀动的悉索作声,后一句有四个"f"辅音,依稀听到一个受惊而哆嗦口吃的话音"f-f—f-fear",惟妙惟肖地烘托出了诡异的气氛感应。

再看一个例子。

[例 49] At this point, certainly, falling in love and getting married may be less a matter of choice than a *stroke* of wild great *luck*.

（二）汉语的押韵

1. 双声

汉语中的双声指的是两个词的声母相同,如:斑驳、惆怅、参差、踟蹰、璀璨、踌躇、尴尬、光怪陆离、辉煌、拮据、慷慨、坎坷、玲珑、淋漓、褴褛、伶俐、袅娜、忸怩、崎岖、忐忑、颓唐、挣扎等。

2. 叠韵

汉语中的叠韵指两个词的韵母相同。韵母有单韵母和复韵母两类。如果是单韵母,叠音单韵母必须相同。如:迷离、睥睨、呜呼、驱除。复韵母的韵腹有的相同,有的相近,但韵尾必须相同。如:荡漾、烂漫、酩酊、徘徊、蹒跚、彷徨、咆哮、缠绵、缥缈、宛转、汹涌、窈窕,它们的韵尾相同,韵腹也相同;又如缤纷、崔嵬、峥嵘、玲珑、憧憬、呻吟,它们的韵尾相同,但韵腹不同,只是相近。

3. 双声、叠韵与 alliteration、assonance 之差异

双声叠韵和 alliteration, assonance 之间,除了上述定义上的差异,还有以下几个方面的区别:

(1) 英语 alliteration 和 assonance 以词为构成单位,汉语双声叠韵却以字为构成单位,汉语的字只相当于英语词中的音节。所谓"双声""叠韵"是指

两个字的声音关系所形成的音响效果,而 alliteration 和 assonance 则不仅限于两个词之间,它们往往还出现在三个甚至更多的词之间。

[例50] Magnetic, Magnificent Meryl

美貌动人,美名高筑——美瑞尔

[例51] *Hair loss can be triggered by drugs, disease and diet.*

脱发可能由药物、疾病和食物所引起。

(2) 汉语双声叠韵必须是两个同声或同韵的字紧靠在一起,至于这两个字是否同属一个词或词组则不受限制。一旦隔开使用,就会失去连绵的音响效果。刘勰在《文心雕龙·声律》中归纳了这一局限性,指出:"双声隔字而每舛,叠韵杂句而必睽。"双声词和叠韵词作为整体来运用是美的,如果强行分割、分隔,中间插入一些别的成分,就会不和谐了。然而,alliteration 和 assonance 几乎在所有情况下都是由其他音节分隔开来的。

[例52] 那轻,那娉婷,你是

*鲜妍*百花的*冠冕*你戴着,

你是天真,庄严,你是*夜夜*的*月圆*。

雪化后那篇鹅黄,你像;

新鲜初放芽的绿,你是;

柔嫩喜悦水光浮动着你梦期待中白莲。

你是一树一树的花开,

是燕在梁间呢喃,

——你是爱,是暖,

是希望,你是人间的四月天!

So light, so graceful, were you!

Everywhere was grace and beautiful

That 100-flower-crown you wore was of the royal.

Really were you

Naive, dignified, you seem the full moon

That shines every night through my window.

After snow melt, you seem to be in light yellow;

And also you were freshly green, tender and joyful

As water light fluctuating in a dream,

You long for a white lotus blooming to you.

You seemed to be trees with blossoms or some swallows.

My porch was with your twittering, love and warmth for you.
You were my human April-day; you were my hope!
（林薇因《你是人间的四月天》朱曼华  译）

[例 53] Fat people will gab, giggle, guffaw, gyrate, and gossip. They are generous, giving, and gallant. They are gluttonous and goodly and great. (Susan Britt Jordan  *That lean and Hungry Look*)

胖子喜欢闲聊、傻乐、狂笑、欢蹦乱跳、转来转去、爱传小道消息。他们慷慨、大方、豪爽。他们贪吃、漂亮、伟大。（刘士聪  马会娟  译）

（3）双声叠韵在古汉语中具有特殊的修辞作用，因为古汉语中一个节拍由两个音节构成，大多数词都是单音节。因此使用双声叠韵能创造和谐悦耳的音乐美。从历史上看，汉语双声叠韵盛于六朝。宋朝倡导清新明快的文风，双声叠韵逐渐失势。如今双声的作用主要构成双音节词。

[例 54] 她是有 　　　　　　She was such a girl：
　　　丁香一样的颜色，　In lilac-like color,
　　　丁香一样的芬芳，　With lilac-like smell,
　　　丁香一样的忧愁，　She behaves in the lilac-like gloomy style.
　　　在雨中哀怨，　　　She was sad in raining,
　　　哀怨又彷徨；　　　Walking back and forth, walking...
　　　她彷徨在这寂寥的雨巷。Walking down the lonely lane.
（戴望舒《雨巷》朱曼华  译）

alliteration 发轫于诗歌，其渊源比尾韵（end-rhyme）还要古老。在中古英语的诗歌中，由于没有尾韵，alliteration 独领风骚几百年。随着时间的推移、诗歌形式的发展，才产生了尾韵和不同的格律，从而使 alliteration 降到了次要地位，但仍然在诗歌、散文、谚语、标题，几乎所有的各类文体中都有广泛的应用，有时甚至到了痴迷的地步。

[例 55]

*Super Savings in the Skies*

　　Airlines say "Happy New Year" with a rousing round of price rollbacks.

　　The spark for the latest skirmish is People Express, the fastest-growing airline in the annals of aviation. Economists admire Donald Burr and People Express for bringing tough competition to a once clubby and complacent industry. People Express's low prices have kept its profits slim, and many Wall Street investors shun its stocks. And critics of the airline's Spartan service have dubbed the carrier People Distress. However, controllers in the tower of Chicago's O'Hare International continue to guide People pilots through busy takeoffs and touchdowns. From Boston to Houston to Newark, a panoply of People passengers produce both grins and grimaces as they learn to fly without frills. Love it or loathes it, almost everyone agrees that People Express has turned the airline industry topsy-turvy.

（三）尾韵

汉语和英语一样，往往在诗行的末尾使用押韵（现代的自由诗也有不押韵的）。主要的不同之处在于，汉语是押最后一个字的韵母，英语则是最后一个音节。

［例56］ If you can't be a pine on the top of a hill,
如果你做不成山顶上的乔松，
Be a scrub in the valley—but be
就做山谷里的小灌木，
The best little scrub by the side of the rill;
但要做溪流边最茁壮的小灌丛——
Be a bush if you can't be a tree.
如果你做不成大树。

If you can't be a bush be a bit of the grass,
如果你做不成灌木，就做草，
And some highway happier make;
把大路点缀得更欢愉！
If you can't be a muskie then just be a bass—
如果做湖里的大梭鱼办不到，
But the liveliest bass in the lake!
那就做最活跃的小鲈鱼！

(DouglasMalloch, *Be the Best of Whatever You Are* 黄杲炘 译)

[例57] 那河畔的金柳，　　It's riverside with the golden willow,
　　　　是夕阳中的新娘；　That's a bride of the setting sun in glow.
　　　　波光里的艳影，　　Under the water, all colorful shadows,
　　　　在我的心头荡漾。　In my mind and heart, seem to sparkle.

　　　　软泥上的青荇，　　The green grass grow up in soft mire.
　　　　油油的在水底招摇；Oily in the water bottom swagger.
　　　　在康桥的柔波里，　In the gentle waves of the river,
　　　　我甘心做一条水草！To be a piece of grass, I prefer!
（徐志摩《再别康桥》朱曼华　译）

（四）押韵的翻译

1. "大体押韵"

翻译家朱曼华在《中国历代诗词英译集锦》中提出，"我欣赏'大体整齐押韵'的提法，把读起来口型相似、听起来有韵律实感，但写起来并非同韵的两个词也视为近似押韵的一种模式"。这个观点对音韵的范畴作了扩展，对于音韵等艺术信息在译文中的再创造，具有很强的实用意义，为诸多翻译名家在实践中采用，是一种行之有效的方法。

[例58] 对酒当歌，To sing a song with a cup of *wine*,
　　　　人生几何？I ask is it how long a *life*?
　　　　譬如朝露，It's like the morning rolling *dews*,
　　　　去日苦多。The past days were full of *bitterness*.

　　　　慨当以慷，Let indignation transfer sigh *vehement*,
　　　　忧思难忘。The possible worry should not be *forgot*.
　　　　何以解忧，How to release your grief *strong*?
　　　　唯有杜康。It's an only way to drink *Dukang*.

　　　　青青子衿，It's your green *skirt*,
　　　　悠悠我心。That'll leisurely beat my *heart*.
　　　　但为君故，You are my true reason,

沉吟至今。I recite a lyric time and again.

（曹操《短歌行》朱曼华　译）

[例59] 在天愿作比翼鸟，

　　　　在地愿为连理枝。

　　　　天长地久有时尽，

　　　　此恨绵绵无绝期！

Be a pair of lovebirds, wing to wing, flying in the skyline *end*,

Be a pair of sprigs, side by side, growing in the same *land*.

The endless heaven or earth may be inevitably changeable,

The unending lovesick grief or sorrow will be eternally stable.

（白居易《长恨歌》朱曼华　译）

[例60] 枯藤老树昏鸦，

　　　　小桥流水人家，

　　　　古道西风瘦马。

　　　　夕阳西下，

　　　　断肠人在天涯。

The withered vine around an old tree with the raven at dusk;

Near a resident family a small bridge across a gurgling creek;

On an old road an old thin horse is against the west wind.

The setting sun is inclining westward,

My heart broken love is at the skyline's end.

（马致远《天净沙·秋思》朱曼华　译）

2. 押韵的翻译策略

（1）原地转换。

押韵作为一种语言音乐化的手段，是音韵美的一个重要方面。适当地使用押韵，能够增强语言的感染力，从而具有声律上的听觉美。所以翻译时，也应尽可能地将这种音美传达出来，比方说，某一具体的双声/叠韵与 alliteration/assonance 在音韵效果上有比较大的相似性，因此在原来的位置上完整地进行对应转换；汉语和英语中诗行的尾韵也基本上可以进行对应的再创。

[例61] Sweet, Smart & Sassy.

　　　　蜜、美、迷。

[例62] 三十岁之后，看见破旧肮脏的的士都心烦。

After thirty, a mere sight of a shabby and sordid taxi may sicken me.

[例63] Ah! Love, could you and I with Him conspire
To grasp this sorry Scheme of Things entire,
Would no we shatter it to its bits—and then
Remould it nearer to the Heart's Desire!
啊，我爱！愿咱与命运商讨，
抓住这万物的糟糕图稿！
怎不把这世界捣成碎片？
好按我们的心愿再抟再造！
（Edward Fitzgerald, *Rubaiyat* 柏丽 译）

[例64] 多情自古伤离别，
更那堪，
冷落清秋节！
今宵酒醒何处？
杨柳岸，
晓风残月。
此去经年，
应是良辰好景虚设。
便纵有千种风情，
更与何人说！
Farewell full of lovesickness since ancient time,
Especially it's on the autumn festival under moonlight.
Where would I be when I awoke from wine tonight?
It's the poplar willow-shore of the riverside,
Where the breeze blew and the crescent bright.
My long trip would fail to enjoy the scenic sight.
Even if the romantic events were myriad in mind,
No one could understand why I sigh.
（柳永《雨霖铃》朱曼华 译）

(2) 句内补偿。

但是，英语押韵以词为构成单位，汉语双声叠韵却以字为构成单位，汉语的字只相当于英语词中的音节。如果执着于把某一具体的韵脚在原来的位置上完整地转换，就会面临很大的难度。因此，如果这种转换不拘泥于该韵脚所在的具体位置，而只在它所处的句子中，就会使得押韵的声音效果在整体上传达成为可能，例如：

[例65] 两岸的豆麦和河底的水草所发散出来的清香，夹杂在水气中扑面的吹来；月色便朦胧在这水气里。（鲁迅《社戏》）

The scent of beans, wheat and river-weeds wafted towards us through the mist, and the moonlight shone faintly through it. （杨宪益、戴乃迭 译）

[例66] 松林中射来零乱的风灯，都成了满天星宿。（冰心《雨雪时候的星辰》）

*Lights* from hurricane *lamps* flickering about in the pine forest created the *scene of a star-studded sky*. （张培基 译）

[例67] ……天黑时，我躺在床上，他便伶伶俐俐地从我身上跨过，从我脚边飞去了。（朱自清《匆匆》）

In the evening, when I lied on my bed, it nimbly strides over my body and *flits past my feet*. （张培基 译）

（3）句外补偿。

有时，原文押韵所在处无法合适地互相转换，那么，可以在可能并适当的情况下在文章其他地方增加押韵，就是采用一种弥补的方法来进行转换。例如：

[例68] 月光是隔了树照过来的。高处丛生的灌木，落下参差的斑驳的黑影，峭楞楞如鬼一般；弯弯的杨柳的稀疏的倩影，像是画在荷叶上。（朱自清《荷塘月色》）

Moonlight was glowing from behind the trees, and the dense *shrubs* above cast down *gloomy ghostlike shadows* of varying lengths and *shades* of colour. But the beautiful *sparse shadows* of the arching willows were like a picture etched on the lotus leaves. （王椒升 译）

[例69] 我就邀他同坐，但他似乎略略踌躇之后，方才坐下来。我起先很以为奇，接着便有些悲伤，而且不快了。（鲁迅《在酒楼上》）

I invited him to join me, but he seemed to hesitate before doing so. This struck me as strange, then I felt rather hurt and annoyed. （杨宪益 戴乃迭 译）

[例70] 连夜雨雪，一点星光都看不见。

It had been snowing all night, not a single star in sight.

(4) 异律补偿。

对于押韵声音效果的弥补并不限于这几种修辞手段本身的使用,译者也可以采用其他的音韵修辞方式或者能够产生音律效果的手段,比如谐音双关、平行结构等。

［例71］ Intel Inside.
给电脑一颗奔腾的"芯"。

［例72］ It changed our well water to wonderful water.
变井水为净水。

［例73］ Wraptures: Hang up your hat and hit the headlines this summer with an eye-catching scarf!
丝巾头饰,裹出魅力:收起夏日凉帽,带上靓丽丝巾,引领最新时尚。

［例74］ No pain, no palm; no thorns, no throne; no gall, no glory; no cross, no crown.
不经艰难,哪有胜利;不经磨砺,怎得天下;不经劳苦,哪有荣耀;不经挫折,何谈桂冠。

(5) 零转换。

押韵同样存在着零位转换的情况。这包括两种情形:

①原文没有使用类似的音韵修辞手段,而译文中则可创造性地增添使用某种形式的押韵以增添文采或者弥补原文其他形式的修辞手段之美。

［例75］ The few birds seen anywhere were moribund; they trembled violently and could not fly.
他们后院喂鸟的食具显得凄然萧索,偶然在什么地方看到几只鸟都是病恹恹的,哆哆嗦嗦,飞也飞不动。

［例76］ 在缓缓的转动之中,莫名其妙地一阵阵空虚,突然间对一切感到索然无味。
In the slow rotating, an indescribable emptiness, all of a sudden, seizes me, and I find everything dull and dry.

［例77］ 它可能是一条现代的乌衣巷,家家有自己的一本哀乐帐,一部兴衰史,可是重门叠户,讳莫如深,夕阳影里,野草闲花,燕子低飞,寻觅旧家。(柯灵《巷》)
It may be a modern piece of Wu Yi Xiang, a special residential

area of nobility in the Jin Dynasty southeast of today's Nanjing, where each family, secluded behind closed doors, has its own covered-up *story* of joys and *sorrows*, and rise and decline. When the *sun* is *setting*, *swallows* will *fly* low over wild *flowers* and grass on their way to their nests. (张培基 译)

②有时候，这种声音效果不必传达或者无法传达，译文中可以将其省略，而且有时过多的声音的重复也是没有必要的。

[例78] 淡黑的起伏的连山，*仿佛*是*踊跃*的铁的兽脊似的，都远远地向船尾跑去了，但我却还以为般慢。（鲁迅《社戏》）

Distant gray hills, undulating *like* the backs of some *leaping* iron beasts, seemed to be racing past the stern of our boat; but I still felt our progress was slow. （杨宪益、戴乃迭 译）

在上例中，"仿佛"和"踊跃"这些双声或叠韵词就没有进行转换，其声音效果也没有在附近得到弥补。译文中的"like"和"leaping"虽然有alliteration之相，但一来数量较少，只有两个单词，二来其间相隔较远，并不具有突出的音韵效果。

即便是在诗文写作中，都有越来越多的人反对因韵害义，鼓励自然晓畅的免韵创作。苏轼《念奴娇·赤壁怀古》里"大江东去，浪淘尽，千古风流人物"那样，放弃严格的音韵协调，选择在开篇改采拗怒的曲风，反而开创出激越高亢的豪放派风格。

同样，在英文世界中，不用押韵，只使用音步作为格律规范的，也是不乏其人：

[例41] But, *soft*, what *light* through *yon*der *win*dow *breaks*?
It *is* the *east*, and *Jul*iet *is* the *sun*.
*Arise*, fair *sun*, and *kill* the *en*vious *moon*,
Who *is* alread*y* sick and *pale* with *grief*
That *thou* her *maid* art *far* more *fair* than *she*. （William Shakespeare, *Romeo and Juliet*）

轻声！那边窗子里亮起来的是什么光？那就是东方，朱丽叶就是太阳！起来吧，美丽的太阳！赶走那嫉妒的月亮，她因为她的女弟子比她美得多，已经气得面色惨白了。（朱生豪 译）

上例采用英语的五步抑扬格，十音节，五音步（每十音节为一行，每两个音节为一音步，）斜体的重读音节与非斜体的轻读音节交替吟诵，虽然是素韵，

167

但天然之音自成韵律，读来也有一种"玲玲如振玉，累累如贯珠"的效果。朱生豪先生的译文甚至都没有采用诗行的格式，而是纯用白话翻译，但准确反映了原作的内容，也有一番自然流畅、浓烈热切的意致。

这表明，在多元化的现代世界，"殷勤花下同携手，更尽杯中酒"固然谐顺缠绵，和婉悦耳，但放下谐婉的执念，搁置诸多清规戒律，改采自然达意的语言，也有其自身的吸引力。这一认识，对于翻译实践也有参考意义，至少无需为此过于介怀，更不用处处强求再现原文音韵上的谐顺了。

## 【翻译赏析】

The January wind has a hundred voices. It can scream, it can bellow, it can whisper, and it can sing a lullaby. It can roar through the leafless oaks and shout down the hillside, and it can murmur in the white pines rooted among the granite ledges where lichen makes strange hieroglyphics. It can whistle down a chimney and set the hearth-flames to dancing. On a sunny day it can pause in a sheltered spot and breathe a promise of spring and violets. In the cold of a lonely night it can rattle the sash and stay there muttering of ice and snowbanks and deep-frozen ponds.

一月的风儿，奏响千种号角，诉说万般风情。它时而尖叫，划破长空；时而怒吼，响彻宇宙；时而耳畔细语，似也千百种蜜意；时而哼着小曲儿，又如慈母般柔情。山坡上的橡树林，树叶凋落，风儿嚎啸过处，仿若猛虎下山，威风振振。银松林里，白露茫茫；花岗崖上，绿苔青青。赏略着茫茫林间美景，玩味着斑斑灵异石画，风儿一路轻声而过，路过村庄，钻进烟囱，为炉里火焰的翩翩舞姿，奏响串串哨音。白天，阳光明媚，过阴凉处，也会逗留片刻，飘洒春天将至的气息，预示紫罗兰芬芳的花香。夜晚，寒气逼人，也觉人间孤苦寂寞，摇曳窗棂，吱吱作响，恍似在咕哝着提醒人们，大地已然一片冰雪世界。

## 第二节　汉英语义修辞对比与翻译

### 一、比喻

#### （一）明喻与 simile 的对比

1. 明喻与 simile 的定义基本一致

明喻，是通过比喻词将具有某种共同特征的两种不同事物连接起来的修辞手法，常用的比喻词有"像、仿佛、宛如、恰似"等。

［例1］老鼠对猫从来都是敬而远之的，就像朝露在旭日升起来就要消散一样。

The mouse has ever fled the approach of the cat, as the morning mist flees before the sun.

［例2］我虽无缘亲见此画，但我觉得名画有若美人，美人而有所属，不免是件憾事。（冯亦代《向日葵》）

I had never had the good luck to see the original but, to me, a masterpiece is like a beauty and when the beauty is claimed by someone else you feel deprived of your access to her.（刘士聪　温秀颖　译）

英语中 simile 定义为 "an expression that describes something by comparing it with something else"，常用的结构有 "like" "as" "A is to B what C is to D" "no more/less... than..." "compare ... to... /remind... of..." "be something of..." "and" 等。

［例3］Life is like a dogsled team. If you ain't the lead dog, the scenery never changes.

生活就好比是一支狗拉雪橇队。你如果不是领头犬，那你的视野永远是一成不变。

［例4］As always, faith is something of an irrational leap in the dark, a gift of God.

信仰总是黑暗中某些非理性的飞跃，是上帝的礼物。

从以上定义可以看出，明喻与 simile 格式基本相同，都使用"像、仿佛"（as、like）等词连接。

2. 汉英语言对明喻/simile 中的新颖性有不同要求

（1）英语中提倡使用 novel simile，反对使用 trite simile。

英语中有许多现成的 simile。这些 simile 包罗万象，涉及宗教、人生、历史传统、动物植物、天文地理等各个方面，可以说是社会历史的一面镜子。但仔细观察一下当代英语中，trite simile 被认为缺乏感情色彩，即缺乏美学信息，因此通常避免使用，如：

[例5] He is as cool as a cucumber.

[例6] He drinks like a fish.

相反，当代英语作家更加倾向于选择使用 novel simile（新颖的明喻），避免使用信手可拈的 trite simile（老一套的明喻）。试体会下面两例中的新颖形象：

[例7] The ride was actually over in six and a half minutes, and I had no choice but to hobble like an off-balance giraffe on my one flat, one four-inch high arrangement.

开车不过六分半钟，而下车时我不得不一翘一翘活像一头失去平衡的长颈鹿，一只脚平底踏地，另一只脚踩着十厘米的高跟鞋。

[例8] A person without a sense of humour is like a wagon without springs—jolted by every pebble in the road.

缺乏幽默感的人，就像没有弹簧的货车，一路上每一块卵石都会让你颠簸得够呛。

（2）汉语修辞中也提倡"新鲜美"，但却不像英语中那样一概而论地反对使用 trite simile。

大量的熟语性的，特别是一些四字格的成语，在当代汉语中，一些熟语性明喻语言代码被认为形式精练，内容丰富，极富于表现力，即不乏美学信息，因此仍然充满活力，运用普遍。

[例9] 稍老一辈的中国文人，皆知弘一法师其人其事，李叔同先生博涉文学、音乐、绘画，尤擅书法。早年演剧，反串"茶花女"。他东渡日本留学，翩翩浊世佳公子，称得上一代风流的了。想必出国前已成家事，所以归国之日，携一日本女子回府，原配夫人闹得个烟尘陡乱。据说李先生就是因为调停乏术，万念俱灰，快速看破红尘。孑身潜往杭州灵隐寺剃度受戒。（木心《圆光》）

[例 10] 于是想小国寡民。于是想采菊篱下。于是想欧洲乡间的风景如画,澄静如洗。于是想闭紧房门拉严窗帘,喧嚣的世界与己无关。(斯妤《躁动的平静》)

(二) 隐喻与 metaphor 的对比

1. "metaphor"的含义比"隐喻"广泛

从修辞格层面上看,汉语"隐喻"主要是用来指一种修辞格,它不使用比喻词,常用"是、成了、成为"等连接本体和喻体,是一种隐藏的比喻,属于比喻的一种。例如:

[例 11] 卑鄙是卑鄙者的通行证,
高尚是高尚者的墓志铭。(北岛《回答》)
Baseness is a passport for the base,
Honor an epitaph for the honorable.(庞秉钧　闵福德　高尔登译)

就一般意义而言,英语中的 metaphor 与汉语的隐喻基本一致,即在比拟两个不同类的事物时,把本体和喻体合二为一,变抽象和未知为具体和亲切,激发读者的想象力,使事物栩栩如生。

[例 12] The town lay in the midst of a checkerboard of prosperous farms, with fields of grain and hillsides of orchards where, in spring, white clouds of bloom drifted above the green fields.
小镇坐落在星罗棋布的农场中央,遍地都是庄稼,满山都是果园,处处都是一片欣欣向荣的富足景色。春天,花儿绽放如片片云朵,在绿色的田野上飘荡。

[例 13] A schedule defends from chaos and whim. It is a net for catching days. It is a scaffolding on which a worker can stand and labor with both hands at sections of time.
计划可以避免混乱和一时冲动。那是一张捕捉光阴的网。那是一个工人可以站立的脚手架,踩着它,工人可以在各个时间段用双手干活。

广义的 metaphor 是运用最广泛、最频繁的修辞方式,与人们的交际生活有着密切的关系。P. Newmark 把"metaphor"定义为"any figurative expression: the transferred sense of a physical word; the personification of an abstraction; the application of a word or collocation to what it does not literally denote, i. e., to describe one thing in terms of another." 可见只有第三类用法中的"例如"部分才属于汉语中"隐喻"的内容。Encyclopedia Americana (《美国百科全书》) 把"metaphor"分为九大类。

  epithet（绰号）如：Evan the Butcher, The Great Emancipator Lincoln, PIGS, HOMES.

  eponym（名祖）如：Buffet Rule, post-Mao era, Elizabethan.

  hyperbole（夸张）如：tons and tons of love.

  metonymy（转喻）如：Envy has no holidays.

  oxymoron（矛盾修饰）如：true lies.

  paradox（似非而是）如：more haste, less speed.

  personification（拟人）如：Flowers danced about the lawn.

  pun（双关）如：Seven days without water make one weak.

  synecdoche（提喻）如：Who would shake a hand with comrades' blood?

其中只有第一和第二类与汉语中的"隐喻"相一致。故"隐喻"和"metaphor"并非完全等值的概念，"metaphor"的含义比"隐喻"广泛得多。

2. 英汉 metaphor 的释义可能有差异

比较隐喻和 metaphor，可以看到有的 metaphor 可以根据词语的基本意义、显著特征、状况或比喻说法等进行释义的，英汉很多时候都是相容的。如：

[例 14] We're here to get the city out of our lungs.

    我们来到这里，就是要把城市从肺里赶出去。

[例 15] You have become an aristocrat.

    你现在可是贵族了哈。

但当有的 metaphor 可以根据习惯说法、感觉、前后搭配关系以及转喻或提喻等方面进行释义时，许多 metaphor 在汉英语中是不相容的。如：

[例 16] The cat laughed and talked loudly.

    这个包藏祸心的女人大声说笑着。

用"cat"指代包藏祸心的女人，而汉语中猫没有这样的联想意义，所以如果直译为"猫"，意思就发生很大改变。再如，汉语中常用"龙"代指迅猛勇敢的人，但英语中"dragon"是一种凶恶的动物，含贬义。在翻译时，这些因素都应考虑在内。

### (三) 比喻的翻译

汉英语中在比喻修辞格的运用上非常接近，这体现了人类思维的共性，即用比喻时所选用的两种事物的相同点或是相似点作比，而且所用的比喻方式（figure of speech）、喻体（vehicle）、本体（tenor）和喻义（reference）、喻词（the comparative word）都相同。但是，完全对应的比喻在整个汉英语言比喻中所占的比例不大，很多比喻是基本不对应或是完全不对应的。

比喻翻译的困难在于，某种形象和某种意义（以联想意义为基础的比喻意义，即语用意义）的结合往往是约定俗成的。这种结合的可能性在各种语言里不尽相同，因此译者必须在保留源语形象、转换源语形象或者舍弃源语形象而只传达喻义这三者之间做出选择。

1. 直译法

当某形象和喻义的结合在源语和译语中是共同的，或者源语形象承载的喻义不难被译语读者看出时，译者如果直译原文，可以收到事半功倍的效果。

[例17] I have dreamed in my life, dreams that have stayed with me ever after, and changed my ideas; they have gone through and through me, like wine through water, and altered the color of my mind.

生活中我有过梦想，那些一直伴随着我，改变了我的观念的梦想；如同酒虑自水，它们在我心头过滤，并改变了我思想的色泽。

[例18] A mind all logic is like a knife all blade.
It makes the hand bleed that uses it. （Rabindranath Tagore, *Stray Birds*）
满是理智的思想，犹如一柄全是锋刃的刀，
让挥舞它的手鲜血直流。

[例19] 自私与贪婪相结合
会孵出许多损害别人的毒蛇。（艾青《无题》）
Selfishness wedded to greed
Will sire many venomous snakes. （庞秉钧　闵福德　高尔登译）

[例20] 我的心灵是一只古老的瓶；
只装泪水，不装笑涡。

只装痛苦，不装爱情。（痖弦《瓶》）

My heart is an antique vase,

Fit for tears, not smiles,

For suffering, not love. （庞秉钧　闵福德　高尔登　译）

［例21］曲曲折折的荷塘上面，弥望的是田田的叶子。叶子出水很高，像亭亭的舞女的裙。

As far as eye could see, the pool with its winding margin was covered with trim leaves, which rose high out of the water like the flared skirts of dancing girls.

以上例子中，源语中比喻的形象和喻义与译语是共同的，或者这种形象所承载的喻义显而易见，因此可以采用直译法，既保留了源语形象，使译文在内容上和修辞上与原文保持一致或者基本保持一致，又可以使译文的比喻形象新颖生动。

当然，直译并不排斥字词的润饰调整。上面最后一例中"像亭亭的舞女的裙"在直译形象的同时，加了"flared"一词，可谓妙笔生花，形神俱佳。

2. 替换法

如果源语词语形象所承载的喻义在译语里习惯上由另外一个形象承载，而这个形象与源语文化之间又没有冲突的话，可以视具体上下文采用归化手段，用译语形象替换源语形象。

［例22］A young woman was coming toward me, her figure long and slim. Her golden hair lay back in curls from her delicate ears; her eyes were blue as flowers.

一位年轻的姑娘向我走来，她身材颀长，亭亭玉立。一头卷曲的金发披在秀美的耳后；碧蓝的眼睛如清晨的花瓣儿一般清澈美丽。

［例23］这人原先胆子小，干啥也是脚踩两只船。

This man had formerly been a coward, *a fence-sitter*.

"her eyes were blue as flowers"如果直译成"眼睛像花儿一样蓝"，对汉语读者来说是有一点难以领略的。但改为"如清晨的花瓣儿一般清澈美丽"就很好理解了。

有时候，汉英两种语言运用比喻的习惯不同，有时比喻中的同一个形象在两种语言中可能引起不同的联想，所以翻译时不能直接采用，而要改换原比喻性词语所用的形象，用英语中含有类似意义的比喻性词语，如：

[例 24] Don't be scared, chickens!
别害怕，胆小鬼！

另外，翻译实践中还有这样一个现象，有时候把译入语形象与源语形象之间只是略作改动，就能带来更上一层楼的美妙效果。试看下例中"仿佛是好水果"的翻译：

[例 25] 天生着一般女人要花钱费时、调脂和粉来仿造的好脸色，新鲜得使人见了忘掉口渴而又觉嘴馋，仿佛是好水果。（钱钟书《围城》）

One look at her fresh and natural complexion, which most girls would have to spend time and money to imitate, was enough to make one drool and forget his thirst, as though her skin were a tasty cherry.

3. 零译法

当源语形象和喻义的结合关系对译语来说很陌生，难以移入译文，或者源语形象在上下文里不太重要时，可采用概略化释义的方法只译出喻义。

[例 26] 只见他两个眼睛肿的桃儿一般，满面泪光。（曹雪芹、高鹗《红楼梦》）

Her eyes were *swollen*; her face was bathed in tears. （杨宪益、戴乃迭 译）

由上可见，当原文比喻的形象在译文中难以再现或不合乎译文语言习惯时，需要舍去原文比喻性词语所用的形象，保留原比喻的含义，舍形求意，采用意译法。

4. 注释法

除此之外，译者还可以采用加注的办法来处理一些比喻，如下例：

[例 27] "难道这也是痴丫头，也象颦儿来葬花不成？"因又暗自笑道："若真葬花，可谓'东施效颦'了，不但不为新奇，而且更为可厌。"（曹雪芹《红楼梦》）

"Can this be another absurd maid coming to bury flowers like Taiyu?" he wondered in some amusement. "If so, she is Tung Shih imitating Hsi Shih, who is not original but rather tiresome."

*Hsi Shih was a famous beauty in the ancient Kingdom of Yue. Tung Shih was an ugly girl who tried to imitate her* ways.（杨宪益　戴乃迭　译）

"东施效颦"具有浓厚的汉语文化背景，对于译语读者来说很陌生。因此译文采用了直译加注的办法，译出喻义，同时用注释的方法就涉及的文化背景作了说明。

［例28］Lawyers and woodpeckers have mighty long bills.

律师和啄木鸟一样，账单厉害，鸟喙特强。

＊原文 Lawyers and woodpeckers have mighty long bills 中的"bill"系双关语，表示"账单、鸟喙"，指啄木鸟鸟喙强大，不停啄食，和律师的账单异曲同工，予取予求。

需要注意的是，以上方法并不互相排斥，在翻译实践中，往往需要综合使用，比如：

［例29］Yesterday is history, tomorrow is a mystery, but today is a gift. That is why it is called the present.

昨日种种昨日死，明日之事不可期，把握现在莫等待，所以我们要活在当下。

上例译文以拟人性质的"昨日死"来翻译"history"，用的是替换法，而"mystery"与"gift"的翻译则属于零译法。

总之，在任何情况下，比喻的翻译都是应当保证传意的，不然交际的根本目的就没有达到。当然，对于比喻这种修辞手段，形象也是很重要的，只要有可能，译者就应设法传递源语的形象，或者代之以译语读者较能接受的另一个形象作为补偿。不过在喻义和形象不能两全时，译者应毫不犹豫地舍形象，保喻义，而不应因过分强调源语形象的字面指称意义而造成喻义的丢失。

## 二、双关与 pun

### （一）双关与 pun 的对比

1. 双关与 pun 的一般分类

（1）pun 与双关并非完全对应的修辞格。双关是用一个语词同时关顾着两种不同事物的修辞方式，就是有意识地使同一个词或同一句话，在同一个上下文中，兼有两层意思。也就是说，双关只是有一个词语去关涉两种意义，即"一"语双关。双关可以分谐音双关和语义双关两种。谐音双关"利用同音、近音、音似的条件"构成，例如：

［例1］9岁小学生的爆汗作文——《纠结》：我和钟秋洁分手了，现在在

等郭晴婕，但实际上我特喜欢方韩佳，好想方韩佳……不过她姐姐方淑佳更美，我更喜欢……但我内心一直最爱步尚雪，我多么想永远和她在一起，当然还有她的姐姐步尚班……

［例2］小沙弥问正在打坐的老僧："师父，何处有慈悲？"～老僧抬起右手，指了指门外，闭目不发一言。小沙弥顿悟了：原来世间众生万物，无论是达官贵人，贩夫走卒，还是花鸟虫鱼，一草一木，处处皆有慈悲啊。老僧看小沙弥站那里不动，便说："门外桌子上，白色的那个就是瓷杯！"

语义双关"利用词的多义现象"构成，例如：

［例3］两个五毛结婚了，他们以为可以永远在一块，谁知道通货膨胀了，他们现在是一块二。

［例4］夜正长，路也正长，我不如忘却，不说的好吧。

（2）而英语修辞学家通常把 pun 区分为三类：syllepsis（兼用双关），paronomasia（谐音双关），antanaclasis（换义双关）。

syllepsis 利用一词多义形成双关，不重复使用双关词，与汉语中的语义双关对应。如：

［例5］Money doesn't grow on trees,
But it blossoms at our branches.
钱不能长在树上，
在我们"行"就行。

paronomasia 相当于汉语中的"谐音双关"，此种双关语在英汉语中也完全对应。如：

［例6］Yeah! She wins!
耶！（叶）赢了！

（"Yeah! She wins!"与 2012 伦敦奥运上中国游泳运动员叶诗文的姓名读音相似，这个谐音可以说是对这位备受质疑的天才运动员的力挺。）

Antanaclasis 包含重复意义不同的同一个词或者词的同一个形式或发音，即可以利用两个甚至两个以上同音词或近音词形成"二语双关"。这类 pun 以重复为特征，重复的可以是同音词或近音词，也可以说是多义词或同形异义词，把两个词语、两个意义并列摆出，其概念更宽。这种 pun 是汉语双关所不包括的。如：

［例7］Reckless drivers can't be wreckless drivers.

上例中的 reckless 和 wreckless 都构成了 pun，但这两例中的两层意思都

明白地显露出来了,并非汉语双关中两层意思是一明一暗的。再看两例:

[例8] I never saw a saw saw a saw.

[例9] If a can can can a can, can the can can a can with the can?

2. 双关与 pun 的独特类型

(1) 通常所谓的"双关"是指具有双重含义或关涉两种事物,然而实际上,双关所包含着的意思不一定就是两层,完全可以是三层甚至三层以上。例如:

[例10] 莲子心中苦,梨儿腹中酸。(金圣叹)

这一对联有这样三层意思:莲子芯味道苦,梨儿内味道酸;莲子(儿子乳名)内心凄苦,梨儿(儿子乳名)腹中悲酸;怜(谐音)子心中凄苦,离(谐音)儿腹中悲酸。

(2) 同汉语双关一样,英语 pun 既可以是双关(dual meanings),也可以是多关(multiple meanings)。各种辞典的释义中 pun 都不限于关涉两种事物,而是关涉不同的事物。从词源上探究,不管 pun 还是 paronomasia,也都没有 two 或 double 的语义成分。因此英语辞格 pun 并不限于双关的内涵,可能三关四关。例如:

[例11] "It was Walker, my sweet pet," replied Mowcher, "and he came of a long line of Walkers, that I inherit all the Hookey estates from!"

"他叫华尔克,我的可爱的宝贝,"毛奇尔小姐回答道,"他是多少代传下来的华尔克子孙,我从这个家族继承了所有的弧吉遗产。"

Hookey estates 有多重含义:它指弧吉家族遗产、祖传的撒谎本领、钩鼻子的面部特征以及 Mowcher 的习惯:说话时举起手指点着自己的鼻子。

(3) 汉语中也有一类独特的双关:析字双关。这是基于汉语独特的文字形态而产生的。例如:

[例12] 何处合成愁?离人心上秋。纵芭蕉不语也飕飕。(析字双关)

[例13] 迢迢兼程唯见雨,无缘冷月会明空。(析字双关,"明空"既指明朗的天空,也指旅行目的地的代表性人物武则天)

(二)双关与 Pun 的翻译

双关与 pun 虽然修辞作用相似,但由于两种语言的语音不同,两种语言的多义词也很难找到绝对对应的,所以一般认为双关语是不可译的。但实际上,双关语只是翻译障碍很大,难以直译,如果仔细琢磨,还是有可能找到办法的。双关语的翻译策略基本上有直译、创译、零译、补偿四种情况。

1. 直译

［例14］Everybody is crazy about Linsanity.

人人都为林来疯发狂。

2. 创译

(1) 双关语译为双关语:将原文双关语的一部分予以保留,另一部分则加以某种改造,类型可以与原文双关相同,也可以不同。

［例15］The professor tapped on his desk and shouted:"Young men, Order!"——The entire class yelled:"Beer!"（语义双关）

A:教授敲击桌子喊道:年轻人,请安静!——学生:啤酒。

［英语的order含歧义:请安静;点(菜),要(饮料)］

B:教授敲击桌子喊道:年轻人,吆喝什么呢!——学生:啤酒。（谐音双关）

［例16］What flowers does everyone have? —Tulips.（谐音双关）

A:人人都有的花是什么花?——郁金香。

B:人人都有的花是什么花?——泪花。（语义双关）

［例17］M:What kind of money do you like?

W:Matrimony.（谐音双关）

男:你喜欢什么钱,欧元还是美元?

女:良缘。（谐音双关）

(2) 另外创造一个双关语:重新创造一个不同类型的双关语,以传递出原文双关语的效果。

［例18］我叫黄西,黄瓜的黄,西瓜的西。

My name is Joe Wong. But to most people my name is known as "Who?". "Hu" actually is my mother's maid name.

［例19］你是萍——凭什么打我儿子!

Why, you are my—mighty with your fists?

［例20］I was going to make myself a belt made out of watches, but then I realized it would be a waist of time.（a waste of time 谐音）

我用一串镜子做了条腰带,发现它是一个照腰镜。

［例21］Q:What did the volcano say to his wife?

A:I lava you.

问：火山对它媳妇说什么？

答：我喜欢你的熔岩（容颜）。

[例22]译文中的"熔岩（容颜）"显然是借鉴了英语的独特双关类型Antanaclasis（换义双关），可以说是有效丰富了汉语的表达。

（3）创造一个类双关语（punoid）：译文用某些带有文字游戏性质的修辞手法，例如近音重复、所指含糊、反语、仿说等，形成某种类似双关语的表述，以求再造原文的效果。

[例23] All power corrupts, but we need the electricity.

州官随意放火，百姓仍须点灯。

[例24]朱焕然：岳母！

程夫人：贤婿！

朱焕然：再"咸"，我就吃不得了。

ZHU：Esteemed Mother!

MADAM：Esteemed Son!

ZHU：There is enough steam to cook my goose!

[例25]程雪雁：你说什么呀？郎君？

朱焕然：郎君？我真狼狈了。

XUEYAN：What did you say, Duckie-poo?

ZHU：Duckie-poo? How about just plain "dead duck"?

（4）非双关语译成双关语。原文并不具有双关语的特征，译文无中生有地创造出一个双关语。

[例26] Think different.

不同凡"想"

3. 零译

（1）双关语译为非双关语：以非双关语的方式传达原文双关语的一层或两层意思。

[例27]东边日出西边雨，道是无晴却有晴。（刘禹锡《竹枝词》）

The west is veiled in rain,

The east basks in sunshine,

My beloved is as deep in love

As the day is fine. （许渊冲 译）

上例中，原文的"晴"表面上是指天气阴晴的"晴"，实际上是指"感情、爱情"。该双关语在翻译时未能保留，在原双关处只译出了表层意思，然后又增添"*the day is fine*"和"*deep in love*"来表达原文里双关的两层意思。再看两个例子：

［例 28］Goodbuy Winter! 100% Cotton Knitwear $49.95.
换季贱卖！100%纯棉针织服装，仅售$49.95。（双关零译）

［例 29］宜春———一座叫春的城市
Yichun—the spring city

（2）照抄原文：把原文双关语原封不动地搬到译文里，同时借助编辑手段，在注释、译序等地方解释原文的双关语或者提供另一种译法，等等。

［例 30］My campaign slogan is: "Who cares?"
我的竞选口号是："Who cares（谁管你啊）?"（注：因为说话者的胡姓渊源，与 who 是谐音双关，所以这里也有"让我来关心你们，管你们"的意思。）

（3）双关语译为零：删去包含双关语的一段文字。

4. 补偿

把双关语译为非双关语，但自己制造平行结构、拈连、异叙等其他修辞手段作为补偿。例如：

［例 31］We must all *hang* together, or we shall all *hang* separately.
我们必须共同上战场，否则就得分别上刑场。（Cf：如果我们不能紧紧团结一致，那就必然分散地走上绞刑台。）

［例 32］Ask for More. No cigarette gives me More taste. I'm More satisfied.
再多来点摩尔吧！是它，给予我独特的品位。摩尔香烟，我更喜欢。

## 三、拈连/异叙与 zeugma/syllepsis

（一）拈连/异叙与 zeugma/syllepsis 的比较

1. 定义

①拈连，就是当把甲、乙两件并提的时候，为了提高表达效果，故意把只适用于甲事物的词也用于乙事物，而在一般情况下乙事物是不能用这个词的。例如：

［例 1］淅淅沥沥的秋雨敲打着窗户，也敲打着我的心。

［例 2］农民生活这么苦，你们这些当官的还剥削他们，你们的心瞎了，

难道眼也瞎了?

上面两例中,"敲打"与"窗户"是正常搭配,但与"心"就是变格搭配。同样,"眼"与"瞎"是正常搭配,但与"心"与"瞎"则是变格搭配。

许多汉语修辞著作并未把"异叙"专门列为一种修辞格。但是拈连确实与下述情况不同:

〔例3〕邹吉蒲道:"再不要说起!而今人情薄了,这米做出来的酒汁都是薄的!"

〔例4〕太阳照得人身暖,毛主席的思想光辉照得咱心里亮。

上面两例中,前一个"薄"意为"冷漠寡情",后一个"薄"是指"淡而无味";前一个"照"意为"照耀",后一个"照"则为"指引"。两例中的两个搭配都属于正常搭配。由此可见拈连与异叙的不同:异叙虽然也同样是用一个词分别与两个(或更多的)词搭配,但它是利用一词多义的特点在与不同的词搭配时表现出词义上的变化,因此这些搭配都是正常搭配,这与拈连中有一个或多个搭配是变格搭配的情况不同。

②英语中 zeugma 和 syllepsis 在表现形式上也都是指在同一句子里一个关键词可以与两个或两个以上词语搭配的修辞手段,但在 syllepsis 中所有这些搭配在句法规则和语义上都是正确的,并产生不同的字面意义和比喻意义,而在 zeugma 中,关键词与其中一个词构成的搭配是非规范的变格的,但它巧妙地借助与前一个词的正常搭配,运用到后一个词身上,不但不牵强,反而具有很强的表现力。例如:

〔例5〕After winning his own freedom from slavery, Henson secretly helped hundreds of other slaves to escape north to Canada—and liberty.

上例中,"escape to Canada"是合乎逻辑的正常搭配,"escape to liberty"则是变格搭配。

〔例6〕Give neither counsel nor salt till you are asked for it.

上例中,"give"分别与"counsel"和"salt"两个词构成正常搭配。

2. 结构模式

(1) 在结构模式上,拈连和异叙中的搭配常见的有:

①一个动词与两个或多个宾语搭配。

〔例7〕破晓,病房,嗡嗡作响的空调,握着父亲的手,也握着我们父子之间一生沉默的互动。(宋明亮《最深的交流》)

②两个主语与一个谓语搭配。

[例8] 劝君今夜须沉醉，尊前莫话明朝事。珍重主人心，酒深情亦深。（韦庄《菩萨蛮·劝君今夜须沉醉》）

③一个形容词与两个或多个名词搭配。

[例9] 百姓固然怕"流寇"，也很怕"流官"。（鲁迅《谈金圣叹》）

（2）zeugma 和 syllepsis 中的搭配常见的有：

①一个动词与两个或更多的宾语搭配。

[例10] The general lost the town and his head.

②两个主语与一个谓语搭配。

[例11] Ten minutes later, the coffee and Commander Dana of Naval Intelligence arrived simultaneously.

③一个形容词与两个或多个名词搭配。

[例12] Yesterday he had a blue heart and coat.

④一个介词与两个或多个名词搭配。

[例13] Miss Bo rose from the table considerably agitated, and went straight home in a flood of tears and a sedan chair.

由此可见，拈连和异叙与 zeugma 和 syllepsis 在结构上大体相同，只是 zeugma 和 syllepsis 的第四种类型，即利用介词构成的 zeugma 和 syllepsis 在汉语中较少见。原因在于，汉语中的介词用法比较少，就语法功能和词汇意义的范围和变化来说，汉语介词都不如英语介词那么活跃。

在表现形式上，拈连和异叙有紧缩式与松散式两种。紧缩式指拈连和异叙的前项、后项及关键词都浓缩在一个单句中；而松散式则不拘泥于一个句了之中，有时呈排比句式出现，有时则散现在一个段落中。另外，拈连和异叙的关键词往往要重复一遍，甚至根据表达的需要多次重复，这是它们结构模式的一个重要特点。zeugma 和 syllepsis 则比较紧凑，多出现在一个单句中，关键词一般只出现一次。

（二）拈连/异叙和 zeugma/syllepsis 的翻译

既然英语中的 zeugma 和 syllepsis 与拈连和异叙颇为相似，那么可以直译时就直译。但因英、汉两种语言在表达方式上有很大差别，所以在许多情况下又不得不进行变通处理。总的来说，拈连和异叙可以有以下四种翻译方法：

（1）汉语中拈连/异叙译成英语中的 zeugma/syllepsis，或者相反，以挽留原文的韵味。

[例14] 他喝的不是酒，喝的是伤感。

He is drinking wine and sorrow.

［例15］几件小摆设，每一件代表着一个故事，珍藏着它们就像珍藏着一份美好的回忆。

There are several small souvenirs, each with a story behind it, which I treasure as so many happy memories.

［例16］At noon Mrs. Turpin would get out of bed and humor, put on kimono, airs, and the water to boil for coffee.

中午时分，特宾夫人从床上起来，心情不好，穿上和服，端着水，也端着"架子"去煮咖啡。

(2) 照原句直译，以保留原句的行文风格。这里所说的"照原句直译"，并非是语义上的直译，而是指把原句中的语言形式尤其是结构模式"复制"过来。

［例17］Take nothing but pictures, leave nothing but footprints, kill nothing but time.

除了记忆，不带走一草一木；除了脚印，不留下些许痕迹；除了光阴，不捕捉任何猎物。

［例18］胸中小不平，可以酒消之；世间大不平，非剑不能消也。（张潮《幽梦影》）

A small injustice can be drowned by a cup of wine; a great injustice can be drowned only by the sword. （林语堂 译）

［例19］兰圃的门锁了

却锁不住香味（艾青《无题》）

The gate of the orchid garden is locked,

But not its fragrance. （庞秉钧 闵福德 高尔登 译）

(3) 创译。将原文的"排比""对偶"或类似英语押头韵等其他类型的修辞格，甚至一般搭配，译为拈连/异叙或者 zeugma/syllepsis；或者反其道而行之，将拈连/异叙或者 zeugma/syllepsis 译成"排比""对偶"或类似英语押头韵等其他类型的修辞格，以使意义上互不相关的词语在形式上得以某种搭连。

［例20］Don't deny it, but don't be defined by it. Be twice as good, and you can make it.

（面对歧视怎么办？）不要把它否定，不要被它锁定。力争双倍优胜，你一定会成功。

［例21］朋友们怀念着他伟大的灵魂，眼里流着泪，万分悲痛地前往他的

墓地。

Commemorating the great soul, the friends of his went to the grave yard with weeping eyes and hearts.

［例22］你可以哭泣，但不可以泄气

You may shed tears, but not yield to tears.

［例23］程夫人：事到如今，有什么长策无有？

朱焕然：这会儿，甭说长策，我连个短策都没有了。

MADAM: Now have you an inspiration?

ZHU: An inspiration? No, just a lot of perspiration!

(4) 意译。在难以再现原文修辞之美的的情况下，灵活处理，果断抛开修辞手法，只译出基本含义。

［例24］... when I and my sorrows are dust.

等到我的尸骨化为飞灰，我的哀愁也随风散去时……

［例25］She lost her heart and necklace at a ball.

在一次舞会上，她倾心爱上了一个人，但却丢失了她的项链。

［例26］满心"婆理"而满口"公理"的绅士们的名言暂且置之不论不议之列，即使真心人所大叫的公理，在现今的中国，也还不能救助好人，甚至于反而保护坏人。（鲁迅《论"费厄泼赖"应该缓行》）

We need not trouble ourselves just now with the aphorisms of those gentlemen who hav *justice on their lips but self-interest in their hearts*. Even the justice so loudly demanded by honest folk cannot help good people in China today, but may actually protect the bad instead.（杨宪益　戴乃迭　译）

## 【翻译欣赏】

沿着荷塘，是一条曲折的小煤屑路。这是一条幽僻的路；白天也少人走，夜晚更加寂寞。荷塘四面，长着许多树，蓊蓊郁郁的。路的一旁，是些杨柳，和一些不知道名字的树。没有月光的晚上，这路上阴森森的，有些怕人。今晚却很好，虽然月光也还是淡淡的。

A path paved with coal-dust zigzags along the lotus pond, so secluded as to be little frequented in the daytime, to say nothing of its loneliness at night. Around the pond grows a profusion of luxuriant trees. On oneside of the path are some willows and other plants whose names are unknown to me. On moonless night, the place has a gloomy, somewhat forbidding appearance. But on this particular evening, it had a cheerful outlook, though the moon was pale.

  曲曲折折的荷塘上面，弥望的是田田的叶子。叶子出水很高，像亭亭的舞女的裙。层层的叶子中间，零星地点缀着些白花，有袅娜地开着的，有羞涩地打着朵儿的；正如一粒粒的明珠，又如碧天里的星星，又如刚出浴的美人。微风过处，送来缕缕清香，仿佛远处高楼上渺茫的歌声似的。这时候叶子与花也有一丝的颤动，像闪电般，霎时传过荷塘的那边去了。叶子本是肩并肩密密地挨着，这便宛然有了一道凝碧的波痕。叶子底下是脉脉的流水，遮住了，不能见一些颜色；而叶子却更见风致了。

  On the uneven surface of the pond, all one could see was a mass of leaves, all interlaced and shooting high above the water like the skirts of slim dancing girls. The leaves were dotted in between the layers with white flowers, some blooming gracefully, still in bud. They were like bright pearls and stars in an azure sky. Their subtle fragrance was wafted by the passing breeze, in whiffs airy as he notes of a song coming faintly from some distant flower. There was a tremor on leaf and flower, which, with the suddenness of lightning, soon drifted to the far end of the pond. The leaves, jostling and overlapping, produced as it were, a wave of deep green. Under the leaves, softly hidden from view, water was rippling even its color was not discernible so that the leaves looked more enchanting.

  月光如流水一般，静静地泻在这一片叶子和花上。薄薄的青雾浮起在荷塘里。叶子和花仿佛在牛乳中洗过一样；又像笼着轻纱的梦。虽然是满月，天上却有一层淡淡的云，所以不能朗照；但我以为这恰是到了好处——酣眠固不可少，小睡也别有风味的。月光是隔了树照过来的，高处丛生的灌木，落下参差的斑驳的黑影，峭楞楞如鬼一般；弯弯的杨柳的稀疏的倩影，却又像是画在荷叶上。塘中的月色并不均匀；但光与影有着和谐的旋律，如梵婀玲上奏着的名曲。

  Moonlight was flowing quietly like a stream down to the leaves and flowers. A light mist overspread the lotus pond. Leaf and flower seemed washed in milk. It was a full moon, but a pale cloud hanging over head made it lose some of its brilliance. Moonlight was glowing from behind the trees, and the dense shrubs above cast down gloomy ghostlike shadows of varying lengths and shades of colour. But the beautiful sparse shadows of the arching willows were like a picture etched on the lotus leaves. Uneven as was the moonlight over the pond, there was a harmony between light and shade, rhythmic as a well-known melody played on the violin.

（节选自朱自清《荷塘月色》王椒升 译）

## 第三节　汉英结构修辞对比与翻译

### 一、对偶与 antithesis

（一）对偶与 antithesis 的对比

对偶是指用两个句法相似、字数相等、意义对称的词组或句子来表达相反、相似或相关意思的一种修辞方式，在诗词曲赋等韵文中称为对仗。对偶从意义上讲前后两部分密切关联，凝练集中，有很强的概括力；从形式上看，前后两部分整齐均匀、音节和谐、具有两两相对的戒律感。严格的对偶还讲究平仄，充分利用汉语的声调。

Antithesis 用两个词组或句子成对排列，特点是含义相反、指向相异、字数接近、结构相同、节奏紧凑、听觉铿锵、出其不意突然转折，凭借对称句式逼出词义的反弹。这种修辞手段便于突出矛盾，表现一个整体的两个不同侧面，相反相成，从而表达一个深层的题旨，也有利于通过鲜明的对照，在读者脑海中迅速建立兴奋灶，产生欲知究竟的兴趣。

作为各自语言中重要结构修辞手段之一，对偶和 antithesis 都具有音韵和谐、整齐匀称之美，看起来整齐醒目，听起来铿锵悦耳，读起来朗朗上口，便于记忆、传诵，为人们喜闻乐见。两者之间有着基本一致的对应。但是，两者无论在构成机制还是在修辞特色上都存在很大差异。

1. 语义关系对比

首先，从定义和前后语言单位的语义关系来看，对偶是用字数相等、句法相似的两句，成双成对排列成功的辞格。它可以表达相关、相似或相反的意思。antithesis 是 "those sentence patterns which balance opposing thoughts by placing them in similar or parallel structures or positions"，是一种揭出互相对立的现象，使它们相应相衬，以达到加强文势的效果的修辞格。

①构成对偶的前后两个语言单位除了可表达相反的意思之外，还可以表达相关或相似的意思。因此，对偶在内容上常常被分为三类。

A："由两个意思相反或相对的短语或句子构成"的为反对，如：

[例1] 岁月无多人易老，乾坤虽大愁难著。（吴潜《满江红·豫章滕王

阁》）

［例2］花树得晴红欲染，远山过雨青如滴。（吴潜《满江红·金陵乌衣园》）

B."上句和下句在意思上相似、相近、相补或相衬"的对偶为正对，如：

［例3］明月别枝惊鹊，清风半夜鸣蝉。

［例4］楼头残梦五更钟，花外离愁三月雨。
窗间斜月两眉愁，帘外落花双泪堕。

C."由两个在内容上有承接、递进、因果等关系的短语或句子组成，意思是前后连贯的"对偶为串对，也叫连对、流水对，如：

［例5］行到水穷处，坐看云起时。（王维《终南别业》）

［例6］人类一思考，上帝就发笑。

②而 antithesis 是有意把两个意思相反的词或观点（contrasting words or ideas）置于相同或相似的句法结构中。语义形成对立对照是构成 antithesis 的基本要求，因此从内部机制上看，antithesis 最多只能与对偶中的一种即"反对"相等同，而包括在对偶中为数众多的正对和串对则是 antithesis 所不能概括的。这是对偶与 antithesis 的本质区别之一。

［例7］Art is long, life is short.

［例8］Men always want to be a woman's first love—women like to be a man's last romance.

2. 结构形式对比

从结构形式来看，antithesis 与对偶也存在相当大的差异。由于汉字基本由单音节构成，构成方法非常单纯：前声后韵，声调则附着在整个音节上；同时汉语在词句发音的衔接方式上属于断奏音，连续发出的各个音之间有间断，这就导致汉语具有便于作成对偶的特性。从古至今，对偶就是汉语民族所喜闻乐见的。Antithesis 虽然也经常以结构相同或相似的平衡句的形式出现，但它对于形式工整对称的要求远不如汉语对偶那么严格。

（1）连接词。

来看下面两例 antithesis：

［例9］Her eyes were shining brilliantly, but her face lost its color within twenty seconds.

［例10］The joys of parents are secret, and so are their griefs and fears; they cannot utter the one, nor they will not utter the other.

"Her eyes were shining brilliantly" 与 "her face lost its color" 这一

antithesis 的前后句用了"but"衔接。"cannot utter the one"与"will not utter the other"这一 antithesis 则使用"nor"作为衔接。实际上，antithesis 的前后语言单位之间存在各种各样的连接方式，如连接平行结构的 and，than，or 等等。还可采用介词或准介词，甚至还取谓语动词为平衡柱来达到这种平衡对称。这样就造成许多 antithesis 的前后语言单位字数不等，甚至相差甚远。

这一差异也充分体现了英汉语在衔接上的不同。英语重形合，结构严谨，常使用各种各样的连接手段；而汉语重意合，结构松散，常通过语义获得前后文的衔接。对偶主要通过互文见义的方式帮助意义凝聚。

（2）重复。

antithesis 的平衡或平行的结构中可以存在完全相同的词语，有时还借助字词的重复来突出重点。而对偶上下句之间往往会回避字词的重复。antithesis 有时也会省略平行结构中的重复词语以达成使句子简洁有力这一效果，导致平行结构字数的不相等，而这违反了形成对偶的基本要求，即"词类相当、结构相同"，上下联字数必须基本相等。总之，antithesis 中形成对照的往往只是平衡句中表达对立思想的部分，这一点两个意义相反的单词就可以做到。因此 antithesis 中可以出现重复的字词，有时甚至借此来突出重点，加强效果，比如：

［例11］ If there is an irresistible force, there can be no immovable object.
If there is an immovable object, there can be no irresistible force.

［例12］ To err is human, to forgive, divine.

［例13］ Small minds are concerned with the extraordinary, great minds with the ordinary.

而对偶句要求大部分字词都对应，古典诗词中的对偶句甚至要求字字相对、平仄相谐。且不说古汉语中对偶对重复的严格避忌，现代汉语中也很少重复用词用字，尤其是名词、动词等实词。即使是相对于"严式对偶"的所谓"宽式对偶"，重复的也仅限于虚词或个别的关键性实词，比如：

［例14］ 风急天高猿啸哀，渚清沙白鸟飞回。
无边落木萧萧下，不尽长江滚滚来。
万里悲秋常作客，百年多病独登台。
艰难苦恨繁霜鬓，潦倒新停浊酒杯。（杜甫《登高》）

［例15］ 女：从空中看上海，高楼耸立，鳞次栉比，楼宇和夜空相互映衬，挺拔了一座城市的高度。

男：从空中看上海，霓虹闪烁，华灯璀璨，灯火与星光交相辉映，照耀了一座城市的繁华。

女：这是一个不眠之夜，从今晚开始，激情的上海迎来世博历史上盛况空前的人类文明盛宴。

男：这是一个欢乐之夜，从今晚开始，发展的中国倾心合力铸造理想之城。

女：今夜上海在微笑，东方明珠广播电视塔卓然秀丽，她以得天独厚的壮势在向世界招手，在美好的夜色中绽放美好的表情。

男：今夜上海在自豪，年轻的环球金融中心高高耸立，她以960万平方公里第一高度的自豪眺望和期盼。

（3）句法单位。

antithesis的构成除平衡句外，还以其他平行或平衡结构，如平行或平衡的字词、短语或从句等形式出现，而对偶主要以句子为单位构成。对偶主要是以两句为单元构成，而antithesis可以是两个句子，也可以是一个句子内部存在着的平行结构。

［例16］When others go low, you go high.

［例17］You are what you give.

［例18］The only difference between the saint and the sinner is that every saint has a past and every sinner has a future.

［例19］It's better to be hated for what you are than to be loved for what you are not.

［例20］I'd rather be a failure at something I love than a success at something I hate.

［例21］Modern in touch, Chinese in feel.

［例22］There is no such thing as a moral or an immoral book. Books are well written, or badly written.

3. 音律对比

从音律上看，antithesis所具有的声律效果只是在客观上带来了语言简洁、声韵和谐的声律效果，而汉语中的对偶却把平仄相协的声律效果作为构成上的一个条件。古汉语的律诗和骈体文非常讲究平仄，比如律诗的四联中，中间两联的对偶要求语义要相当（也就是虚实相当），字调要相反（也就是平仄相反），所谓"一阴一阳谓之道"也。就算后来燕乐曲词兴起之后，虽然句式的错综变化不可胜穷,但遵从"奇偶相生、轻重相权"的八字法则,仍具有重要地位。

[例23] 柳丝长,春雨细。
惊塞雁,起城乌。
玉炉香,红蜡泪。
眉翠薄,鬓云残。(温庭筠《更漏子·柳丝长》)

[例24] 落花人独立,微雨燕双飞。(晏几道《临江仙》)

虽然英语格律也讲究音步(metrical feet),但是英语的特点决定了在antithesis方面,它的音律无法做到像汉语的对偶那种整齐和谐。汉语是单音节性的,在语法上是孤立型,没有词尾变化,而且汉字字体方正,使得对偶中前后的语言单位能够应对工整。英语是多音节语言,语法上富于形态变化,再加上用来拼写单词的字母数量也不同,antithesis 就很难取得对偶那种两两相对的效果。因此,antithesis不能完全等同于对偶。

[例25] Art is long, life is evanescent.

[例26] In the selection of a wife, as in a project of war, to err but once is to be undone forever.

## (二) 对偶与 antithesis 的翻译

对偶与 antithesis 一般都可以直译,只需要在个别地方略做调整,稍加润饰即可,如:

[例27] Freedom is never voluntarily given by the oppressor; it must be demanded by the oppressed.
自由从来不是压迫者主动给予的,而必须是被压迫者努力争来的。

汉语对偶的翻译就要麻烦一些。由于它上下句字数相等,而且往往平仄相对,具有很强的意义美、结构美和音韵美。因此,对偶翻译的基本要求是译文应尽可能地再现原文的意美、形美和音美,如:

[例28] 横眉冷对千夫指,
俯首甘为孺子牛。(鲁迅《自嘲》)
Fierce-browed, I coolly defy a thousand fingers;
Head-bowed, like a willing ox I serve the children.

译文相当好再现了原文的结构对等和声律效果。译文上下句分别使用"fierce-browed"和"head-bowed"两个表面结构相同的复合词置于句首,使得上下句结构有很强的平行感。虽然两词在内部构造上并非完全一致:"fierce"是形容词而"head"是名词,"brow"是名词而"bow"是动词,但两词都是以"-ed"结尾而在表面结构上有巧妙的相似,同时也忠实地再现了原文"横眉"和"俯首"之义。译文上下句中主句的结构也是大体相似的,只是上句中只用了"coolly"的单个副词作状语,而下句却不得不使用"like a willing ox"这个词组作状语,从而使上下句在字数上无法对等。这也是由原文的意义所决定的。

[例29] 墙上芦苇,头重脚轻根底浅;
　　　　山间竹笋,嘴尖皮厚腹中空。
　　　　The reed growing on the wall—top-heavy, thin-stemmed and shallow of root;
　　　　The bamboo shoot in the hills—sharp-tongued, thick-skinned and hollow inside.

译文较好地再现了原文的结构美和意义美。原文上下句开头的"墙上芦苇"和"山间竹笋"是完全相互平行的结构:字数相等并且词性一致,体现了汉语对偶的美感。译文用两个平行的、结构类似的"The reed growing on the wall"和"The bamboo shoot in the hills"基本再现原文的这种结构。然后,译文又使用"top-heavy"和"thin-stemmed"与"sharp-tongued"和"thick-skinned"分别构成平行的结构,尤其"thin-stemmed"与"thick-skinned"是完全相同的内部结构,因此译文在视觉上也体现较强的结构美。同时原文的意义也通过直译得以传达。

需要特别留意的是结构形式,包括以下三个方面:

(1) 由于汉语重意合,结构松散,而对偶是通过互文见义的方式帮助意义凝聚,这与英语重形合、结构严谨,常使用各种各样的连接手段有着明显的不同。因此对偶英译时,应注意到汉英语在这一点上的不同,在需要的时候增添连接手段,不能因为追求结构上的完全对等而忽略了结构的正确性。比如可以改采主从复合句的结构,添加使用连词。

[例30] 假作真时真亦假,
　　　　无为有处有还无。(曹雪芹、高鹗《红楼梦》)
　　　　When false is taken for true, true becomes false;
　　　　If non-being turns into being, being becomes non-being. (杨宪益　戴乃迭　译)

译文采用"When false is taken for true"和"If non-being turns into

being"两个状语从句以及结构相同的主句来传达原文对偶上下句的平行结构，很好地再现了原文的结构美。同时，原文对偶的意义也在译文中得到了忠实的体现。

（2）鉴于汉语中对偶的基本要求是上下句"词类相当、结构相同"，字数必须基本相等，而antithesis往往会省略平行结构中的重复词语以达成使句子简洁有力这一效果，汉语对偶句的英语译文不必使用与原文对偶完全相同的上下句并列结构，有时也可以采用简单句等别的句型，例如：

［例31］古为今用，洋为中用。

　　　　Make the old serve the present and the foreign serve China.

（3）有的对偶句的重复词语成为原句成功的关键因素，如果保留重复，在译语允许的条件下使用与原语相似的句式，则会收到更好的效果。例如：

［例32］风声雨声读书声声声入耳

家事国事天下事事事关心

A：We should listen with open ears to the sound of wind and rain and the reading voice as well；

We must not only concern ourselves with personal affairs but the affairs of the state and the world.

B：The sound of the wind, the sound of the rain, the sound of the study of books——all these sound enter the ear.

The affairs of family, the affairs of state, the affairs of all under heaven——all these affairs concern my mind. （Arthur H. Smith译）

比较两个译文我们可以发现，译文A基本上省略了原文上下句分别对"声"和"事"的重复，成功地再现了原文的思想内容，而原文在结构上的对称美和音韵上的节奏却没有得到很好的体现；译文B保留了重复，在译语允许的条件下使用了与原语相似的句式，因此在传达原文的音、形方面明显优于译文A，同时原文内容也得到了相对较好的凸显，更容易给人以深刻的印象。

综上所述，由于对偶的修辞效果主要体现在结构的视觉美以及听觉上的音律美，在翻译时要尤其注意结构上的处理，以尽可能地传达这两种效果。同时，也要注意汉英语在连接手段上的差异可能造成的原文和译文在转换时会出现的问题。

## 二、排比与 parallelism

### (一) 排比与 parallelism 的对比

汉语排比与英语 parallelism 有着相似的功用：用来说理，条理分明；用来抒情，感情洋溢；用来叙事写景，层次清楚、描写细腻、形象生动。汉语排比与英语 parallelism 既有相似之处，但也存在明显的区别。

1. 定义

parallelism 有广义与狭义之分。广义的 parallelism 指英语语言组织的一种重要形式。它以相同的语法形式排列表现意义相似的概念，一般出现在列举、系列和并列的结构中，通过 and，or，but，yet 等词衔接。它既是语法问题又是修辞问题，包括句子和篇章层面内几乎所有并列的语法结构。

[例1] In English, there are countless *situations*, *moods*, and *relationships* for which there is no single work.

[例2] They came not *to help*, but *to hinder* us.

[例3] The plan was opposed to not *by Frederick* but *by Maria*.

[例4] *The danger of the past was that men became slaves. The danger of the future is that men may become robots.* (Erich Fromm *The Sane Society*)

以上各例表现了从词到句子各个层面上的 parallelism，它们都是一种结构上的"平衡"。这种 parallelism 与汉语中的排比相去甚远。这类结构在写作类书中一般译为"平行结构"。它是一种重要的衔接手段，帮助语义连贯。

狭义的 parallelism 指作为修辞手段使用的 parallelism，要求有三个以上有公分母的词语元素。

[例5] Lawrence Powell weighed in *quietly on business issues*, *firmly on family concerns*, *and fiercely on medical matters*.

[例6] At the end of the day, the only questions I will ask myself are: Did I love enough? Did I laugh enough? Did I make a difference?

[例7] If you were a tree, cast a shade;
If you are a clear spring, nourish the land;
If you are a tall grass, add a green.

根据《现代汉语词典》，排比是一种"修辞方式，用一连串结构类似的句子成分或句子来表示强调和一层层的深入"。一般认为，与英语作为修辞手段的 parallelism 一样，汉语排比修辞结构的一组语句往往也包含三项或三项以上相关的内容。

[例8] 静物是凝固的美，动景是流动的美；直线是流畅的美，曲线是婉转的美；喧闹的城市是繁华的美，宁静的村庄是淡雅的美。生活中处处都有美，只要你有一双发现美的眼睛，有一颗感悟美的心灵。

[例9] 在沁凉如水的夏夜中，有牛郎织女的故事，才显得星光晶亮；在群山万壑中，有竹篱茅舍，才显得诗意盎然；在晨曦原野中，有拙重的老牛，才显得纯朴可爱。

[例10] 十六世纪末尾的时候，西班牙的文人塞万提斯做了一大部小说叫做《堂·吉诃德》，说这位吉先生，看武侠小说看呆了，硬要去学古代的游侠，穿一身破甲，骑一匹瘦马，带一个跟丁，游来游去，想斩妖服怪，除暴安良。（鲁迅《中华民国的新"堂·吉诃德"们》）

2. 句法结构对比

（1）关于排比的各个项目之间的关系。

排比的各个项目之间的关系，有的是并列的，有的是承接的，有的是递进的。但不论关系如何，各排比项总是处于并置状态（juxtaposition）。而 parallelism 的平行项并不一定处于并列关系。也可以处于从属关系。如：

[例11] If we do not *hang* together, we shall all *hang* separately.
我们如果不能共同上战场，就得分别上刑场。

[例12] When trouble comes in through the windows love goes out through the doors.
麻烦窗前入，爱情门外走。

以上两列中的 parallelism 都是分别处于主句和条件从句之中。这种处于主从关系的句法结构是汉语排比不允许的。英语 parallelism 各成分之间可用连词 and，or，but，yet 等连接，而汉语排比通常不用连词。

（2）关于重复。

汉语和英语之间的另一个区别性特征是：汉语喜欢重复用词，尤其是在排比中。重复的句子成分和句式可以体现一种铺排的语势美，有很强的渲染效果。英语 parallelism 要求有三个以上有公分母的词语元素，但同时又要兼顾英语力求避免重复词语的倾向。例如：

[例13] 天行有常，不为尧存，不为桀亡。应之以治则吉，应之以乱则

凶。*强本而节用，则天不能贫；养备而动时，则天不能病；修道而不贰，则天不能祸。*

［例 14］ To spend too much time in *studies* is sloth; to use *them* too much for ornament, is affectation; to make judgment wholly by *their* rules, is the humour of a scholar.

前例中都重复名词"天"；后例中第一句用名词 studies，第二、三句则用 them 或 their 代替。

但是，是否使用"共同词语"并不能用作区别排比和 parallelism 的绝对标准。根据《现代汉语》，一般说排比的各部分又常带有共同或相似的提示语。这种提示作用也可以只通过相同的结构表现出来。事实上，汉语排比有不带"共同词语"的，如：

［例 15］ 坐山看虎门，借刀杀人，引火吹风，做干岸儿，推倒油瓶不扶，都是全挂子的武艺。

而英语 parallelism 也有带"共同词语"的，如：

［例 16］ *With this faith, we will be able to* hew out of the mountain of despair a stone of hope. *With this faith, we will be able to* transform the jangling discords of our nation into a beautiful symphony of brotherhood. *With this faith, we will be able to* work *together*, to pray *together*, to struggle *together*, to go to jail *together*, to stand up for freedom *together*, knowing that we will be free one day.

由此可见，排比和 parallelism 之间似乎不存在"是否强调使用共同词语"这种区别。

此外，英语中将句子间隔反复也视为 parallelism。间隔反复是指相同词语或句子的间隔出现，这种包括了篇章层面的 parallelism 也是汉语排比没有的。

［例 17］ *I have a dream* that one day this nation will rise up and live out the true meaning of its creed: "We hold these truths to be self-evident, that all men are created equal."

*I have a dream* that one day on the red hills of Georgia, the sons of former slaves and the sons of former slave owners will be able to sit down together at the table of brotherhood.

*I have a dream* that one day even the state of Mississippi, a state sweltering with the heat of injustice, sweltering with the heat of oppression, will be transformed into an oasis of freedom and justice.

*I have a dream* that my four little children will one day live in a nation where they will not be judged by the color.

*I have a dream* today!

(3) 表面对称的 parallelism。

英语中还有一类表面对称的 parallelism，它只需要结构上的表面相似就能达到。例如：

［例 18］My paintings the visitors admired. My sculptures they disliked.

［例 29］My paintings the visitors admired. My sculptures irritated them.

前例中两个宾语都被前移到句首的主题位置加以强调。后例中的 My paintings 是宾语，而 My sculptures 却是主语。但是因为两者都处于句首的主位上，表面看仍然是平行对称的。然而，汉语排比不包括这类表面对称的句法结构。

（二）排比与 parallelism 的翻译

1. 直译

排比是一种极具表现力的修辞手段。它借助于铺排的结构增强语势，同时也增强了节奏感，因此具有形式上的美和音律上的美。大多数排比都是可以进行直译的。对含有重复成分的排比进行直译可以基本保留原文的形式美和声音美，同时也可以通过再现的重复使突出强调的效果得以保持，使原文的语势美得以传达。而对基本不含重复的排比更可以进行直译，既可保留原文的结构又不需担心重复问题。例如：

［例 20］所以心如槁木不如工愁多感，迷朦的醒不如热烈的梦，一口苦水胜于一盏白汤，一场痛哭胜于哀乐两忘。（叶圣陶《没有秋虫的地方》）

Therefore, being sentimental is better than staying apathetic, living in a dream is better than being awakened, drinking a bitter cup is better than a cup of insipid water, having a cry is better than being insensitive to both sorrow and happiness. （张培基译）

［例 21］告诉你吧，世界，Listen to me, world,
我——不——相——信！I do not believe!

如果你脚下有一千名挑战者，
If a thousand challengers lie beneath your feet
那就把我算作第一千零一名。
ThenI am Number One Thousand and One

我不相信天是蓝的；I don't believe the sky is blue;
我不相信雷的回声；I don't believe the thunder's roar;
我不相信梦是假的；I don't believe that dreams are false;
我不相信死无报应。I don't believe that death has no revenge.
（北岛《回答》庞秉钧　闵福德　高尔登　译）

上面两例中，原文的排比都通过直译得到了完整的转换。原文中的排比都是整个句式的排比，重复的成分很多。而译文对于这种重复予以了全部的保留，这样就使原文中的排比语势美在译文中也得到了充分的体现和保留。

[例22] 采采芣苢，薄言采之。Gathering plantain,
Here we go plucking it;
采采芣苢，薄言有之。Gathering plantain,
Here we go plucking it.
采采芣苢，薄言掇之。Gathering plantain,
Quick fingers strip it;
采采芣苢，薄言捋之。Gathering plantain,
By handfuls pull it.
采采芣苢，薄言袺之。Gathering plantain,
Here we fill skirts with it;
采采芣苢，薄言襭之。Gathering plantain,
Belt up full skirts!
（《诗经·芣苢》许渊冲　译）

在上例原文中，看起来很单调的重叠，却又有它特殊的效果：正是在不断重叠中，产生了简单明快、往复回环的音乐感。译文基本保留了这种效果。

2. 增添重复 vs 合并重复
（1）增添重复（英译汉）。

英语倾向于避免重复，省略重复的词语。即使在排比句中，也多用代词，特别是人称代词来做替换处理，而汉语则喜欢重复用词，尤其是在排比中，更加倾向于重复名称、人名或称谓。因此，在进行英语的 parallelism 的翻译时，

199

可以采用适当增加重复的办法来促成结构上的整饬之美。试比较下例中的两个译文：

[例23] The rich man believes he possesses his big house, his expensive clothes, his horses and servants and his bank accounts. He does not. He depends on them. He worries about them. They possess him. He is their slave.

A：有钱人认为他拥有大房子、昂贵的服饰、马匹、奴婢和银行存折。其实，他并没有真正拥有。他依靠这些财富，他为这些财富而忧心忡忡，是财富占有了他。他是财富的奴隶。

B：富人以为是他占有豪宅、华服、骏马、奴仆、银行存款。不，富人傍财而活，为财而忧，被财所占。富人，财之奴也。

[例24] We stole from ourselves, took and gave bribes, lied in the reports, in newspapers, from high podiums, wallowed in our lies, hung medals on one another. And all of this — from top to bottom and from bottom to top.

A：我们盗窃自己的资产，彼此行贿和受贿，无论在报纸、新闻还是讲台上，都谎话连篇，然后再沉湎在我们自己的谎言里，为彼此颁发勋章。这种情况——自上而下，自下而上——无处不如此。

B：我们监守自盗，我们行贿受贿，我们在报告中说谎、在新闻里说谎、在高高的讲台上说谎，我们一面沉溺于自己的谎言，一面为彼此佩戴奖章。而且所有人都在这么干——从上到下，从下到上。

(2) 合并重复（汉译英）。

如前所述，英语倾向于避免重复，省略重复的词语。有时排比项中包含的重复并不需要进行全部完整的传达，过多的重复会造成结构上的臃肿和冗余。因此在进行翻译汉语的排比句时，应注意在适当时候避免重复。这时可以采用对重复部分进行全部或部分合并的办法来避免结构上的重复，或者，也可以采用同义的结构来避免用词上的重复。

[例25] 卑鄙是卑鄙者的通行证，
高尚是高尚者的墓志铭。
看吧，在镀金的天空中，
飘满了死者弯曲的倒影。

Baseness is a passport for the base,

Honour an epitaph for the honourable.

See how the gilded sky teems

With the twisted shadows of the dead.

（北岛《回答》庞秉钧　闵福德　高尔登　译）

[例26] 于是……洗手的时候，日子从盆里过去；吃饭的时候，日子从饭碗里过去；默默时，便从凝然的双眼前过去。（朱自清《匆匆》）

Thus—the day *flows away* through the sink when I wash my hands, *wears off* in the bowl when I eat my meal, and *passes away* before my day-dreaming gaze as I reflect in silence. （朱纯深　译）

前例译文也把排比项"卑鄙是卑鄙者的通行证""高尚是高尚者的墓志铭"中的重复成分"是"合并，只用了一个"is"来搭配，避免了重复。后例中的三个排比项都重复了"过去"，译文则分别采用"flows away" "wears off" "passes away"三个同义词组对三个"过去"进行转换。这样译文中既构成了相似的、平行的句法结构，又避免了完全的重复。

## 【翻译赏析】

### 1

It begins when a feeling of stillness creeps into my consciousness. Everything has suddenly gone quiet. Birds do not chirp. Leaves do not rustle. Insects do not sing.

起初，有一种平静的感觉悄然爬上我的心头。世间万物，顿时沉寂。鸟儿不再啁啾，树叶不再作响，昆虫不再吟唱。

The air that has been hot all day becomes heavy. It hangs over the trees, presses the heads of the flowers to the ground, sits on my shoulders. With a vague feeling of uneasiness I move to the window. There, in the west, lies the answer—cloud has piled on cloud to form a ridge of mammoth white towers, rearing against blue sky.

整日灼热的空气变得格外沉闷，它笼罩着树木，逼迫花朵垂向地面，并坐压在我的双肩。怀着茫然的不安，我信步走到窗前。原来，答案就在西边天际：云层重重叠叠，就像一排嵯峨的白塔，高耸在蓝天之上。

Their piercing whiteness is of brief duration. Soon the marshmallow rims flatten to anvil tops, and the clouds reveal their darker nature. They impose themselves before the late-afternoon sun, and the day darkens early. Then a gust of wind whips the dust along the road, chill warning of what is to come.

云彩那夺目的白色,稍瞬即逝。顷刻间,葵花状的云边变得像铁砧一样平展,云层也露出了阴暗的本色。它们强行遮住西斜的红日,使天色早早地黑了下来。接着,劲风骤起,抽打着道路,漫天尘土飞扬,冷飕飕的,警示着即将发生的一切。

In the house a door shuts with a bang, curtains billow into the room. I rush to close the windows, empty the clothesline, secure the patio furnishings. Thunder begins to grumble in the distance.

砰的一声,风关上了一扇房门,窗帘随风扬起,向屋内翻飞。我急忙跑过去关上窗户,收下晾衣绳上的衣服,安顿好院子里的家什。此刻,远外开始响起了隆隆的雷声。

The first drops of rain are huge. They splat into and dust and imprint the windows with individual signatures. They plink on the vent pipe and plunk on the patio roof. Leaves shudder under their weight before rebounding, and the sidewalk wears a coatof shiny spots.

最初的雨点很大,扑扑地打在尘土里,在玻璃窗上留下了一个个印记。雨点如珠坠地,排气管道叮叮当当,院子顶棚噼噼啪啪,树叶也被砸得瑟瑟发抖,难以抬头。人行道披上了一层亮闪闪的水珠。

The rhythm accelerates; plink follows plunk faster until the sound is a roll of drums and the individual drops become an army marching over fields and rooftops. Now the first bolt of lightning stabs the earth. It is heaven's exclamation point. The storm is here!

雨加快了节奏,叮叮当当,噼噼啪啪,一阵紧似一阵,鼓点密集,终于连成一片。零星的雨点,汇成一支大军,铺天盖地,扑向田野,扑向屋顶。这时,一道闪电刺向大地——那是老天划出的惊叹号。暴风雨来了!

In spite of myself, I jump at the following crack of thunder. It rattles the windowpane and sends the dog scratching to get under the bed. The next bolt is even closer. It raises the hair on the back of my neck, and I take an involuntary step away from the window.

随即响起了一声霹雳,我身不由己地跳了起来,雷声震得窗玻璃格格作响,连狗都吓得三抓两爬地钻入床底。又是一闪,更近了,惊得我寒毛倒竖,不由得从窗边后退一步。

The rain now becomes a torrent, flung capriciously by a rising wind. Together they batter the trees and level the grasses. Water streams off roofs and out of rain spouts. It pounds against the window in such a steady wash that I am sightless. There is only water. How can so much fall so fast? How could the clouds have supported this vast weight? How can the earth endure beneath it?

暴雨倾盆而下,狂风助长雨势,雨柱飘忽不定。风雨交加,恣意猛击树木,淹没草地。雨水从房顶,从排水管奔流而下,如同瀑布,不停地瓢泼重击在窗户上,使我什么也看不清楚。眼前只有水。怎么有这么多雨水,怎么下得这么急?云层怎么承受得住如此巨大的雨水重量?大地又如何承受得了?

(Nancy Peterson,*Glories of the Storm*)

**2**

女:中央电视台

男:中央电视台

HOSTESS: This is CCTV.

HOST: This is CCTV.

女:各位观众,这里是中华人民共和国,上海市。

男:这里是第 41 届世界博览会的举办城市,中国上海。

HOSTESS: Dear Audience, here we are in Shanghai, the People's Republic of China.

HOST: Here we are in Shanghai, the hosting city of the 41st World Expo.

女:今晚我们将在上海世博园为您现场直播中国 2010 年上海世界博览会的开幕式盛况,盛况分为室内的庆典仪式、文艺演出,和室外的灯光焰火、喷泉表演。

男:今晚我们将在雍容磅礴、匠心独运的世博园区中,与您一同奏响城市让生活更美好的华美乐章。

HOSTESS: This evening we will broadcast live the grand opening of Shanghai World Expo 2010 at the Expo Park. The opening ceremony consists of the celebration ritual, artistic performances inside Shanghai Expo Cultural Center and the fireworks and lights and fountains show on the waterfront promenade, the Bund.

HOST: This evening we will enjoy the splendid gala themed "Better City, Better Life" together at this grand, elegant, and unique Expo Park.

女：从空中看上海，高楼耸立，鳞次栉比，楼宇和夜空相互映衬，挺拔了一座城市的高度。

男：从空中看上海，霓虹闪烁，华灯璀璨，灯火与星光交相辉映，照耀了一座城市的繁华。

HOSTESS: Seen from above, tall buildings and the night sky set off each other, which makes the skylines of Shanghai even more glamorous.

HOST: Seen from above, colorful lights interweave with the blinking stars, which gives Shanghai a more prosperous look.

女：这是一个不眠之夜，从今晚开始，激情的上海迎来世博历史上盛况空前的人类文明盛宴。

男：这是一个欢乐之夜，从今晚开始，发展的中国倾心合力铸造理想之城。

HOSTESS: This is a sleepless night. From this evening, a spectacular event of human civilization is going to be held in the beautiful city of Shanghai.

HOST: This is a joyous night. From this evening, an ideal city is going to be created with the joint effort of all people in the developing China.

女：今夜上海在微笑，东方明珠广播电视塔卓然秀丽，她以得天独厚的壮势在向世界招手，在美好的夜色中绽放美好的表情。

男：今夜上海在自豪，年轻的环球金融中心高高耸立，她以960万平方公里第一高度的自豪眺望和期盼。

HOSTESS: At this fabulous evening, Shanghai is smiling. The Oriental Pearl Tower is standing there waving her hands to the world with her unique charm.

HOST: At this pleasant evening, Shanghai is proud. The Global Finance Center is looking into the distance at her fullest height in China.

第五章

# 汉英语用对比与翻译

　　翻译并不仅仅是一种跨语言的文本转换过程，它同时也是一种跨文化的交际活动。因此，为了提高翻译质量，译者绝不可止步于"忠实+通顺"等语言层面的要求，更要跳出词、句、修辞等微观层面的框框，关注翻译的交际功能（functionality），明晰源语文化和译语文化在语用方面，尤其是在功能、目的方面的差异。这就是许多专业人士提倡的"忠实+通顺+功能"的要求。

　　在翻译的过程中，译者一定要坚决克服那种不做语用与文化等宏观层面的分析，一个猛扎子直接进入微观层面，结果往往迷失在逐字逐句翻译里的不良习惯。相反，译者应该谨记，翻译的第一步，应该是一个自上而下的策略选取过程（top-down decision process）。实践表明，译者如可进行宏观分析，善用功能对等（functional equivalence）等现代翻译理论，提高英汉语用功能差异意识，必能有效避免语用失误，准确、得体地开展翻译工作。

## 第一节　语用功能与翻译

词汇的翻译不仅仅与词汇的语义有关，而且还涉及词汇的文化特色、感情色彩及政治内涵等。译者应尽可能准确地把握词汇词义的内涵，做到与讲话者语体风格和有关词汇色彩和内涵的一致。

### 一、词汇的语用功能与翻译选词

（一）词汇的情感色彩与翻译选词

通常，一些词汇往往包含强烈的感情色彩，译者应尽量在译文中注意这些词汇色彩的传递。

［例1］恐怖主义行径激起了全世界人民的极大愤怒。

The atrocity of terrorists roused the people around the world to great indignation.

原文中"行径"和"愤怒"两个词含义非常强烈。译者选用了"atrocity"和"indignation"，而不使用"action"和"anger"从而将恐怖主义行径之恶劣，以及全世界人民对此深恶痛绝的程度表现出来。

［例2］"台湾独立"是绝不能允许的。

"Taiwan independence" is absolutely impermissible.

译文选用"impermissible"，强调"台湾不能独立"，这没有任何商量的余地，其语气十分强烈，与原文意义相符。原文若译成"Taiwan independence can never be allowed"，既不符合英语的表达方法，又不够强烈。

［例3］主权问题是不能谈判的。

The question of sovereignty is nonnegotiable.

如果译成"The question of sovereignty can not be negotiated"，原文非常强硬的语气就会被削弱，说话者的态度就会显得不那么坚决。

（二）词汇的政治色彩与翻译选词

在翻译实践中，我们不仅应注意词汇的文化色彩和情感色彩，而且应高度重视词汇的政治色彩或政治内涵，注意自身的政治立场和政治观点。

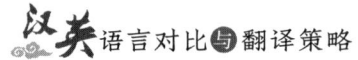

［例4］香港特别行政区将保持自由港和独立关税地区的地位。

The Hong Kong Special Administrative Region will keep the status of a free port and a separate customs territory.

一般说来，译员一听到"独立"这个词，就会立刻翻译成"independent"。倘若如此，听众会把香港理解成一个独立于中国的政治实体，这显然是错误的。译文选用"separate"翻译"独立"是非常恰当的。它既把原文中香港这一关税地区的独立性表达出来，又符合香港是中国一部分的这一政治概念。

［例5］Both President Bush and Secretary of State Powell have expressed their sincere regret over your missing pilot and aircraft. Please convey to the Chinese people and to the family of pilot Wang Wei that we are very sorry for their loss.

Although the full picture of what transpired is still unclear, according to our information, our severely crippled aircraft made an emergency landing after following international emergency procedures. We are very sorry the entering of China's airspace and the landing did not have verbal clearance, but very pleased the crew landed safely.

A：布什总统和鲍威尔国务卿对贵方的飞行员与飞机至今下落不明均表示了真挚的遗憾。请向中国人民和飞行员王伟的家人表示，我们对他们的损失深表歉意。

我们对美方飞机未经许可而进入中国领空和降落中方机场向中方深表歉意，并感谢中方为妥善安置美方机组人员所作的努力。

B：布什总统和鲍威尔国务卿对贵方的飞行员与飞机至今下落不明均表示了诚挚的遗憾。请向中国人民和飞行员王伟的家人表示，我们对他们的损失感到非常惋惜。

虽然事情发生的全部经过尚不明确，但根据我们的消息，我们的飞机受到严重损坏后遵照国际紧急程序做了紧急着陆。我们非常抱歉他们在进入中国领空和降落时没有得到口头许可，但我们很高兴他们安全着陆，也感谢中方为照顾我方机组人员所作的努力。

在美机撞毁我战斗机的事件中，我方要求美方作出"正式道歉"。美方坚持不肯用"apology"一词，而是以美国驻华大使在给时任中国外长的信中使用了两处含义模糊的"sorry"来应付。对此，中方将两处都译为"深表歉意",而且相应地将"Although the full picture of what transpired is still unclear... following international emergency procedures"略去未译以凸显美方的道义错失。但美国国务院却只将后一个"very sorry"译为"非常抱歉",而前一个"very sorry"则译为"非常惋惜"。美方之所以自己提供这么一个译文,大概是想要撇清其对导致王伟死亡的侦查及撞机事件应负的责任,回避中方的责难,以免妨碍其继续进行类似的侦查活动。换言之,政治语境对于翻译产生了关键性的影响。

（三）词汇的语体色彩与翻译选词

语言使用者在不同的场合下会采用不同形式的语言来表达同一种思想和信息。这些随交际情景不同而形成的各种语言形式就是语体,也称为语言变体。语体可以分为五种：庄严、正式、商议、随意、亲密。语体因交际地点、场合、交际事件和交际双方的地位和相互关系的不同而不同。在翻译中要想做到准确、达意,离不开对语体的正确把握。

[例6] 非常感谢您邀请敝人参加这次招待会,敝人的确过得十分愉快。

It was extremely gracious of you to have invited me to the reception, andI have bags of fun there.

该例原文语言比较正式。译文的前半句使用了"extremely gracious"体现出了原文的正式和严肃,但是后半句却使用了"bags of fun"这样的表达方法,显得十分随便。显然,译文的后半句不符合原文的语体,而且译文语体前后也不一致。因此,原文后半句可译为"and I did enjoy myself here"。

[例7] 现在,让我们为合作成功和持久友谊干杯！

Now allow me to propose a toast to our successful cooperation and to our long-lasting friendship, bottoms up.

该例原文是在一次正式宴会上,某领导结束正式发言后建议大家举杯时说的,译文的语体也应该是比较正式的。译文前半句中"propose a toast to"恰到好处地反映了这一语体,但是后半句中"bottom up"的选用并不妥当。"干杯"在汉语中使用极为广泛,可适用于各种语体,而"bottoms up"在英文中是名副其实的喝,是要将杯子倒过来证明喝掉了的那种,属于豪气的通俗语言,只能使用于非正式场合。而"cheers"则适用于各种场合,如果是正式的场合,其含义类似于"propose a toast",是比较正式的举杯祝贺,不一定真的要干。

[例8] 请江主席宣布99'昆明世界园艺博览会开幕。

I have the great honor to invite his Excellency, Jiang Zemin, President of the People's Republic of China, to announce the opening of the 99' International Horticultural Exposition in Kunming of China.

［例9］请李校长宣布99'校运会开幕

I'd like to ask President Li to declare the opening of the 99' College Sport Meet.

以上两例从语言形式来看没有太大的差别，都是"某人宣布……开幕"。但是这两句话所处的语境大不相同。前者的情景语境是重要国际博览会的开幕式，极其隆重和正式，而后者的情景语境只是某学校运动会的开幕式，属于普通场合。因此，两者的译文语体现出较大的差异。

总之，译员应根据具体情景语境，语言活动的内容和言语所要达到的目的进行语体预测和识别，并在译文中再现原文的语体。如果是领导发言，语体往往趋向庄重含蓄。带外宾参观或进行贸易谈判，语体应表现出正式严谨。多年的贸易伙伴交谈时语体则显得轻松活泼。翻译如若涉及特殊的场合题材，译员的语言应不同于普通口语。简言之，翻译措辞和造句应注意与语体风格保持一致。

## （四）情景语境与翻译选词

情景语境指语言交流的外部语境，它包括面部表情、姿势、身体的活动，在场的所有人，以及人们所处的环境。谈话双方由于地位高低的不同，亲疏远近的不同，所使用的语体和选词都会有很大的区别，这些区别随着场合的变异仍会有变。翻译工作本身的情景性非常强。翻译译员必须充分考虑到具体交际事件、交际场所的具体环境、交际双方的具体、交际双方之间的关系，以及听众的身份等因素，分析和理解话语的语用意义，即说话人的意图和话语的隐含意义，选择合适得体的词，准确传达讲话人的意图，控制好话语出口之后所要达到的效果。以1996年英语专八考试汉英翻译中的两个句子为例：

［例10］在这种场合，陌生人相识，如果是亚洲人，他们往往开口之前先毕恭毕敬地用双手把自己的名片呈递给对方，这好像是不可缺少的礼节。

　　A: When strangers meet on such occasions, an Asian tends to present his name card respectfully with both hands at the beginning of the conversation, which seems to be their normal etiquette.

  B: When strangers meet on such occasions, an Asian tends to present his name card respectfully with both hands before starting a conversation, which seems to be their normal etiquette.

［例11］然而，法国人一般却都不大主动地递名片，双方见面寒暄几句，甚至海阔天空地聊一番也就各自走开，只有当双方谈话投机，希望继续交往时，才会主动掏出名片。

  A: Instead, they will excuse themselves after exchanges of a few words of greetings or even after a rambling chat about everything under the sun. They offer cards only when they find each other agreeable and hope to further the relationship.

  B: Instead, they will simply walk away after exchanges of a few words of greetings or even after a casual chat. They offer cards only when they find they like each other and hope to further the relationship.

［例12］中，"开口之前"如果翻译成"before opening the mouth"，或者"before starting a conversation"，容易传递出一个滑稽的画面，而"at the beginning of the conversation"则契合了文中所说的情景语境。［例11］中，"各自走开"如果译成"they will simply walk away"，无异于传递出一个粗鲁的"社会性死亡"画面；而"they will excuse themselves"就不一样了，它不但完全表达了原意，还兼具声音、形象方面的画面感，与酒会里的情景语境完美匹配。

再比如，汉语"休息"一词的英语对应词为"to take a rest"或"to have a rest"，"to take a break"或"to have a break"等。在翻译过程中，译者应根据不同的情景语境，选用相应的对应词。

［例13］超市元旦不休息。

  The supermarket is open as usual on New Year's Day.

［例14］我们休息一会吧。

  We'd better take a break.

［例15］这一周我要休息3天。

  I'll have 3 days off in this week.

综上所述，翻译的选词以及顺畅达意都离不开英汉词汇语用功能的对比分析，包括对词汇色彩以及对情景语境的准确理解与把握。语用环境的理解和把握是确保翻译速度与质量，避免误译和错译的基础。因此，译者在翻译工作中应该牢记语用环境的重要作用，力求出色地完成翻译任务。

## 二、句子的语用功能对比与翻译

根据语用学原理，人们说话时常常实施三种行为：言内行为，言外行为和言后行为。言内行为是指说话行为本身，是通过说话表达一定字面意义。言外行为是通过"说话"这一动作所实施的一种行为，如提出建议、发布命令等，是通过字面意义表达说话人的意图。言后行为是指"说话"这一行为所产生的后果。其中，言外行为便是我们常说的语用功能，它通常分为阐述类、指令类、承诺类、表达类和宣告类等。言外行为或语用功能是人们运用语言进行交际时关注的焦点，因为任何交际都旨在传达说话人的交际意图。言内行为只是表达言外行为的手段，而言后行为则直接受言外行为的制约。事实上，只有透彻理解具体语句所实施的言外行为或其语用功能，方能成功地进行语言交际。因此，在英汉翻译实践中，译员应重视英汉词或语句语用功能的对比分析，尽可能在译文中体现原话的语用功能，确保高质量地完成翻译工作。

### （一）英汉套话语用功能对比与翻译

由于所属的文化不同，汉英两种语言各有一套被各自读者理解，在特定语境中具备语用意义的习惯表达方式。这些习惯表达对其读者常常是约定俗成、心照不宣的，具体表现为一些深受文化影响的"套话"的使用。在翻译中，由于深受母语汉语的影响，要么按汉语的语言结构套入译语中去，要么误用了英语的其他表达方式，其结果往往是使人们听起来觉得费解、别扭。

［例15］看你红光满面，真是高兴.
　　A：I'm so happy your face look so red.
　　B：You look so healthy and energetic.

英语中"Your face look so red"的语用功能为表示"不好意思，发窘"，而汉语原文"红光满面"表示"面色很好，精力充沛，身体健康"。两者的语用功能显然不对等。实际上，跟"红光满面"语用功能对应的译文就是"healthy and energetic"。

［例16］没事儿。
　　A：Never mind.
　　B：It's my pleasure.

在汉语中,当别人表示歉意或对不起时,可使用"没事儿"作答。另外,"没事儿"还可用于表示"不用谢"之义。而在英语中,"Never mind"仅用于对别人的道歉不介意。可见,"没事儿"和"Never mind"的语用功能并不完全对等。当"不要紧"表示"不用谢"时,可译作"It's my pleasure"等。在以下例子中,不同的译文可能适用于不同的语用场景:

[例17] 这是我应该做的。

  A:It's my duty to do so.

  B:With pleasure.

[例18] 平时不烧香,临时抱佛脚。

  A:Burn the incense everyday, no just in times of adversity.

  B:If you work hard everyday, it will not seem overwhelming.

[例19] 我尽量去……

  A:I'll do my best to...

  B:I'd like to, but...

[例20] 祝与会代表家庭幸福。

  A:I wish you a happy family.

  B:I wish the conference a great success and wish you good health and a happy stay.

[例21] 各位游客:你们好!首先请允许我借这个机会,代表我们旅游公司,也代表我们公司的全体员工,并以我个人的名义,对大家表示热忱的欢迎!

  A:Ladies and gentlemen, first of all, on behalf of my company, my Chinese colleagues and myself, I'd like to take this opportunity to extend a warm welcome to you!

  B:Ladies and gentlemen, good day! Please allow me, on behalf of our company, to extend a warm welcome to you!

[例22] 各位嘉宾,金秋送爽,丹桂飘香,各方宾客云集无锡。首先我个人代表美国共和党亚裔总党部以及在座的各位嘉宾,衷心感谢亚太总裁协会与无锡市人民政府盛情邀请和款待。也对本次峰会的召开表示衷心的祝贺!

  A:Ladies and gentlemen: The golden autumn is so cool with the gentle breeze, the fragrance of red osmanthus permeates the air, and guests from home and abroad gettogether at the city of Wuxi. First of all, on behalf of Asian American Republican National Federation, I'd like to extend my appreciation to Wuxi Municipal Government and Committee of Asia-Pacific CEOs Association for your warm welcome and gracious hospitality. And I would also like to express my congratulations to the successful opening of this summit.

B: Ladies and gentlemen: At this beautiful time of September, guests from home and abroad gettogether at the city of Wuxi. First of all, on behalf of Asian American Republican National Federation, I'd like to extend my appreciation to Wuxi Municipal Government and Committee of Asia-Pacific CEOs Association for your warm welcome and gracious hospitality. And I would also like to express my congratulations to the successful opening of this summit.

很多时候,照搬原语的套话还会进一步引起英汉语际转换的负迁移,比如在源语文化中用来示好的句子,经过字面翻译后,完全丧失了原有的语用功能,在译文受众那里引起消极的心理暗示或潜意识,甚至激发某种事与愿违的负面的观感。试比较以下几例中的译文,体会各个译文的语用效果:

[例23] 辛苦了。

A: You are tired.
B: Did you enjoy your trip?

[例24] 我随便讲几句吧。

A: I haven't prepared, so I will just say some words casually.
B: I'll be brief.

[例25] 今晚的菜不好,请多多原谅。

A: I'm sorry that the dinner is not very good. Please forgive us.
B: Thank you for coming. I hope you have enjoyed the feast this evening.

[例26] 此次华东之旅,行程十二天,线路较长,旅途比较辛苦,我们司陪将本着"宾客至上、服务第一"的宗旨,尽心尽力做好服务工作,同时也希望我们的工作能够得到各位游客的支持和配合,促进我们提高服务质量,从而使大家吃得满意,住得舒适,玩得愉快,走得顺利,乘兴而来,满意而归。

A: Our East China Tour will last 12 days. It is a quite long tour and it is quite tiring. The driver and I will, according to the principle of "customer foremost, service first", work closely and serve you in the best possible way. In the meantime, we also hope you can support us, cooperate with us, and help us improve the quality of our service, thus ensuring you a wonderful trip with satisfying eating, comfortable boarding, pleasant entertainment, smooth transportation.

B: Our East China Tour will last 12 days as a quite long tour and it calls for a good balance between sightseeing and relaxation. The driver and I are both here to work closely and serve you in the best possible way. We look forward to your support and cooperation. And we do hope that you will enjoy your trip all the way here and back home.

由于英汉语言文化的诸多差异，看似对应的英汉句的语用功能却往往有着本质的不同。正确理解并掌握这些语句语用功能的差异对于提高翻译质量显然具有重要的实际意义。

### (二) 英汉完整句语用功能对比与翻译

完整句即句子结构完整，没有省略任何句子成分的语句。在英汉语言中，使用完整句，可规范、严密地表达某一具体的思想或观点。然而，不同的是，在商务谈判中，滥用英语完整句，会给人不耐烦的印象。鉴于此，译员应注意英语完整句在特定场合下所具有的特殊语用功能或特殊含义，避免完整句使用所导致的语用失误。

[例27] 外方：I have tried to set out these thoughts about joint ventures generally. It is clear that joint ventures are not easy. Like marriages, they're not in the word of our prayer book to be entered upon ill-advisedly or lightly.

译员：我已经尽量概括地把我对合资企业的看法都讲出来了。很显然，建立合资企业不是件容易的事，正如婚姻一样，用圣经上的语言来说，不加考虑，草率行事是不对的。

中方：中国也一样，我们结婚之前必须要订婚。

译员：Same in China. Marriage is under an engagement.

外方：I mean business.

译员：我是认真的。

中方：我也是。

译员：I mean business.

外方：(shrugging) Another thing must be clear：any dispute of whatever nature arising out of or in any way relating to the contract or to its construction or fulfillment may be referred to arbitration?

译员：(耸肩) 还要明确一个问题：但凡是有关本合同的制定或执行本合同所发生的任何争议都可付诸仲裁解决吗？

中方：当然，所有争议都可通过仲裁解决。

译员：(slowly and clearly) Yes, of course, any dispute of whatever nature arising out of or in any way relating to the contract or to its construction or fulfillment may be referred to arbitration?

外方：(very angry) What do you mean by that? I don't think we could reach any agreements...

该例中，译员将中方最后一句话译作英语完整句，显得啰唆，给人的印象是中方有些不耐烦，或者中方在耍脾气。从语用学的角度分析，说话人（无意中）违反了语用学大师格赖斯（Paul Grice）提出的会话合作原则中的"量的准则（Maxim of Quantity）"，让听话人推导出本不该有的含义，谈判因此陷入僵局。实际上，译员只需将中方的最后一句话译成"Yes, you are right."即可。

[例28] 女儿推门进屋时，妈妈若无其事地在沙发上看电视。

"妈，我回来了"

"回来了。"

"对不起，今天有些晚。您还没睡？"

"没呢，噢，那个，那个男孩是谁呀？"（孙雪梅《问与不问》）

When the girl came in, the mother was watching TV, pretending nothing had happened.

"Mum, I'm back."

"Yeah."

"Sorry to be late. Still sitting up?"

"Yes. Oh, that... who's that boy?"（陈文伯　译）

上例中,"回来了"系重复对方的话,在汉语中很正常,但在英语中则用了"Yeah"来表示,以免引起听者不适。"您还没睡?""没呢"是一种寒暄,分别译成"Still sitting up?""Yes",符合当时的语境。如果照字面直译,难免破坏氛围。

因此,翻译工作者一定要留意个别完整句在不同场合的特定含义,尽量避免语用失误的产生。

(三)英汉修饰语语用功能对比与翻译

汉语里修饰语使用得较多,如顺利进行、胜利完成、热烈拥护、积极支持、努力做到、认真贯彻、广泛开展、严肃处理等。但翻译时,汉语中的修饰词不一定统统照译,应仔细推敲,决定如何处理。英译文修饰词过多会显得这些词语面临通货膨胀似的效力下降,原来想强调的反而削弱了。以历史典籍中的"效天符运立中体正至文圣武智勇仁慈俭勤孝敏宽定成皇帝"为例,如果每个形容词都一一翻译出来,会显得装腔作势,语用效果适得其反。

[例29] 进一步简化手续,及时地积极地从国外引进技术,并且认真组织科学技术人员和广大职工做好消化和推广工作。

We should further simplify procedures and take prompt and vigorous action to import urgently needed technology and earnestly organize scientists, technicians and the mass of workers to assimilate and popularize imported technology.

译者使用英语修饰词 further、simplify、prompt and vigorous、earnestly、the mass of 等,译文显得重复和累赘,不能有效传达原文意义。

此外,有些汉语修饰语的使用很自然,完全合乎汉语习惯。但这些修饰语若译成英语,效果往往适得其反。如参观某团体或公司时,中方代表总喜欢对来访的外国专家说:"请提出宝贵意见",如果这句话译为"Please give us your valuable opinions",相当一部分对中国文化不了解的外国访问者就有可能会感到为难,可能会想:"How do I know whether my opinions are valuable or not?",并认为在这种场合如果提了意见,就不够谦和。因为这无疑等于说"Yes, my opinions are valuable. Here they are.",因此,为了避嫌,他们干脆什么意见也不提了。其实,该句可译为:"We'll appreciate it if you could give us your opinions."

另外,"胜利召开"在汉语里本意是一种自豪的宣示,但若译为"successfully convened",则会使人感到召开前遇到过不少困难,最后才得以开成。而原文可能根本没有这种含义。"成功的会谈"也有相似情况：

[例30] 首先，我代表中国政府和人民，对布什总统的来访表示热烈欢迎。这是我与布什总统的第二次会晤。4个月前，我们在上海亚太经合组织会议期间进行了成功的会晤。在今天的会谈中，我与布什总统回顾了中美关系 30 年来的历程，深入讨论了双边关系和当前国际形势，达成了许多重要共识，取得了多方面的积极成果，我希望并相信，这次会晤对中美关系的改善和发展将产生积极的影响。

First of all, on behalf of the Chinese government and the Chinese people, I would like to express my warm welcome to President Bush's visit to China. This is my second meeting with President Bush. Four months ago, we had a very *good* meeting during APEC conference in Shanghai. In today's talk, we reviewed 30 years of Sino-US relations and had in-depth discussions on bilateral relations and the current international situation. We have reached consensus on many *important* issues and achieved positive results in many areas. I wish and believe our meeting will have a positive effect on Sino-US relations.

在处理这种汉语说法时，要考虑英语中是否保留修饰语，如果修饰语过多，容易给人一味溢美的印象，非但不起强调作用，反而偏离原意，则宜略去。

## 【翻译欣赏】

### 1

今天，我们很高兴英国客人到广交会来参观。首先我代表广交会所有工作人员向朋友们表示热烈欢迎。

First of all, on behalf of the staff members of Guangzhou Export Commodities Fair, I'd like to extend a very warm welcome to our friends from Britain, who have come here this morning.

首先我向朋友们简单介绍广交会的情况，然后我们领大家进行参观，参观完后我们还会安排一个 15 分钟的录像节目，向大家全面介绍一下我们广东省近年来的对外贸易发展情况。

I'll give you a short briefing about the Fair and then take you around the

Fair. After that, there will be a 15-minute video show on the recent development of trade and economy of Guangdong Province.

下面我们就先简单介绍一下广交会的情况。广交会的全名是"广州出口商品交易会"。从1957年开始创办,每年春、秋两季举行。

If this plan is all right with you, I'll now begin the brief introduction to the Guangzhou Fair.

The full name of the Fair is Guangzhou Export Commodities Fair. It was inaugurated in 1957 and has since been held twice a year in Guangzhou, regularly in spring and autumn.

广交会展馆场地面积共14万多平方米,馆内配比各种现代化设施。每届到会的客商有4万多人次,来自120多个国家和地区,每年进出口成交总额哒110亿美元以上。展销的产品达5万多种,不仅有各行各业的名、优、特产品,还包括先进的高科技商品。

Modernized as it is now in facility, with a floor space of over 140,000 square meters, the Fair is visited in every session by more than 40,000 business people from over 120 countries and regions of US $11 billion on a yearly basis. The samples on display represent over 50,000 varieties of commodities available for export from the Fair. These export items not only include famous brands and specialties from different parts of China, but also high-tech products as well.

参加广交会的客商越来越多,不仅有来自我国内地和港澳台地区的,还有来自美国、加拿大、日本,以及西欧、东欧、非洲和拉美等国家和地区的客商,大大促进了我国同世界各国和各地区的贸易和合作关系的发展。

More and more people, not only from Hong Kong, Macao, Taiwan and other parts of China, but also from the United States, Canada, Japan and those countries in West Europe, East Europe, Africa and Latin America, are coming to visit the Fair. So it has in this respect greatly promoted our trade relations and cooperations with various countries and regions of the world.

## 2

各位朋友,时间过得太快,短短7天已经过去了。在此,我不得不为大家送行,心中真的有许多眷恋。无奈,天下没有不散的宴席,也没有永远在一起的朋友,但愿我们还有再见的机会。

Ladies and gentlemen, how time flies, and that's almost the end of your short visit to our city. Friends must part, and parting is such sweet sorrow. Now I hate to see you off, but I do believe the old saying, "Friends may meet, but mountains never greet."

承蒙各位朋友的支持,我和王先生感到此次接待工作非常顺利,心情也非常愉快。在此,我代表王先生向大家表示衷心的感谢!但不知大家的心情是否愉快?对我们的工作是否满意?好!如果是这样,我们就更加高兴了!如果我们的服务有不周之处,一方面请大家多多包涵,另一方面还望大家提出来,现在也好,回去写信也好,以便我们不断改进,提高服务质量。

Thanks to your support and cooperation, Mr. Wang and I feel our job has been done smoothly and both of us are very happy. On behalf of him, let me say big thanks to you all. I'm wondering at the moment if you are happy, and satisfied with our job, too. If yes, we'll be even happier. If there is still room for improvement in our service, do let us know in whatever ways, now or back home. We'll do our best to upgrade our service in days to come.

有道是"有缘千里来相会",既然我们是千里相会,就是缘分!所以,在即将分手之际,我们希望大家不要忘记,在这里,有一个你们永远的家——XX旅行社;不要忘记,在这个家里有我和王先生两个与你们有缘而又可以永远信赖的朋友。今后如果再来,或有亲友、同事到来,请提前打声招呼,我们一定热情接待。

When we look back on your days with us, I'm sure they are delightful and memorable. Therefore, before we say good-bye to each other, do remember there is a XXXX Travel Service, your home away from home. In this home, there is a Mr Wang and XX, who are always, always dependable. Next time, when you are planning to come here again, or if your friends and relatives are planning to visit XX again, just feel free to let us know in advance. We'll be ever ready to serve them.

最后,预祝各位朋友在今后的人生旅途中万事顺意,前程无量!

Finally, let us wish you good luck, good health, longevity and prosperity. Bon voyage and Godspeed! Thank you so much!

## 第二节 委婉语的翻译

### 一、汉英委婉语的对比

写作、说话者有时出于忌讳或礼貌等考虑，往往借助于迂回曲折、旁敲侧击式的用语，希望避开直截了当的说法，以免引起读者、听者的怀疑、反感甚至厌恶。这样就出现了委婉语。请看下例：

[例1] 你侬我侬，　　　　Twixt you and me
　　　忒煞多情，　　　　There's too much emotion.
　　　情多处热似火。　　That's the reason why
　　　把一块泥，　　　　There's such a commotion!
　　　捻一个你，　　　　Take a lump of clay,
　　　塑一个我。　　　　Wet it, pat it.
　　　　　　　　　　　　And make an image of me,
　　　　　　　　　　　　And an image of you.

　　　将咱两个，　　　　Then smash them, crash them,
　　　一齐打破，　　　　And add a little water.
　　　用水调和，　　　　Break them and remake them
　　　再捻一个你，　　　Into an image of you,
　　　再塑一个我，　　　And an image of me.
　　　我泥中有你，　　　Then in my clay, there's a little of you.
　　　你泥中有我，　　　And in your clay, there's a little of me.
　　　与你生同一个衾，　And nothing ever shall us sever;
　　　死同一个椁。　　　Living, we shall sleep in the same quilt,
　　　　　　　　　　　　And dead, we'll be buried together.

（管道升《我侬词》林语堂 译）

这一支《我侬词》，千百年来，多少人都把当成了纯情男女的山盟海誓，却忽略了一层"你侬我侬"，温婉甜蜜的面纱之下，其实是一个通过委婉语发出的呼唤甚至警示，成功化解了家庭危机的例子。

从上例中可以看到，委婉语的本质是避免直接提及那些令人感到不快的事物或现象。对这些事物的间接提及或委婉说法便构成了委婉语的灵魂。间接性（也称为含蓄性）是委婉语的最明显的主要特点之一。委婉语同时还具有民族性、地域性、语域性、时代性、模糊性、相关性等特点。

［例2］—I see you not just as a vice president, but a veteran and accomplished public speaker...

—Do I look that old? (*laughter*) Just kidding.

上例的对话中，提问者用的"veteran"一词含蓄委婉，但同时又能使闻者意识到其直接所指的事物与它间接所指的事物之间有着某种相关关系，也就是说，闻者能够通过它所提及的事物联想到它所代表的事物，这就体现了它的含蓄性和相关性。回答者的"Do I look that old? Just kidding."既印证了这种相关性，也表明作为资深政治人物，他意识到了这样的场合不宜为此纠结，反而要以轻松的语言化解之，这就是语域性的体现。同时，从民族性和地域性的角度来看，汉语民族就很少为"veteran"所对应的"老"字困扰。

由此可见，无论汉语还是英语，委婉语都大量存在。由于有着共同的禁忌范畴和共同的委婉手段，汉英语中的委婉语有许多相似之处，甚至还有不少是基本等值的。然而，作为一种文化现象，不同社会之间的文化差异会导致不同语言中的委婉方式的差异。另外，汉英语言本身的差异也使得其委婉语显出不同，甚至造成跨文化交际障碍。由此可见，一篇文章或语言表达方式在某一国家里属于委婉表达，是符合逻辑的，概念表达清楚明了，但由于文化与语言的差异，译成另一种语言时未必是符合逻辑的，这类翻译通常会产生误译或误解。

（一）汉英语言特点的差异

汉英语言本身的差异可能导致跨文化交际障碍。这种差异主要表现在英汉语义特点、构词特点和情态表达等方面。以情态为例，对中方译员而言，情态的把握是一个特别需要留心的问题。一般而言，合同谈妥后，一方会说："请在这儿签字"。译员随翻译为："Please sign here."。该译文套用了汉语的表达结构，使对方觉得讲话口所生硬。若译为"Would you please sign here?"，语气则要婉转、柔和些。再比如，在很多国际场合，中国人常说的"我们双方应该……"，如果直译成"We should..."，往往会让外方觉得过于傲慢或带有威权色彩，如改为"We can..."或者"Let us..."就具有了商洽、邀约的语气，会产生更好的效果。试比较下面两例中译员对情态的处理及其可能产生的效果：

[例 3] Mr. President, we can learn from our people. Chinese and American students and educators, business people, tourists, researchers and scientists, including Chinese Americans who are here today — they work together and make progress together every single day. They know that even as our nations compete in some areas, we can cooperate in so many others, in a spirit of mutual respect, for our mutual benefit.

主席先生，我们可以向我们的人民学习，中国和美国的学生和教育家，企业界人士和游客，研究人员和科学家，包括今天在场的华裔美国人，每天都在并肩合作，共同努力。他们知道：即使我们两国在某些领域彼此竞争，我们还可以在那么多其他领域，本着相互尊敬的精神，为了我们的共同利益而进行合作。

[例 4] 中美伙伴合作应该基于人民广泛参与。中美两国人民相互怀有深厚的友好感情，曾经在决定人类前途命运的重大历史关头并肩战斗。两国人民应该扩大交往、加强友谊，为中美关系发展提供不竭动力。

Our cooperation as partnersshould be based on the extensive involvement of the people. The Chinese and American people cherish deep friendship towards each other, and they fought side by side at defining moments in history when the future and the destiny of mankind were at stake. The two peoples should extend exchanges and enhance friendship. This will offer a inexhaustible driving force for the growth of our relations.

## （二）汉英文化价值的差异

1. 政治方面

政治方面的委婉语主要是以相对柔和的措辞营造出某种程度的礼貌，这既体现了说话者的风度修养，也是一种"斗而不破"的高超政治技巧。

[例 5] 坦率地说，我们对新方案中的两点表示不满。

Frankly speaking, we are not comfortable with two points in your new proposal.

原文也可译为"Frankly speaking, we are not satisfied with two points in your new proposal"，但若在外交场合上则显得不够客气，有点唐突。译文选

用语气较为委婉的"not comfortable with",显得客气,符合外交辞令的要求。

但也有许多政治委婉语的作用不是出于礼貌与修养,而是为了掩饰。比如:在1971年,印度打着"humanitarian intervention(人道主义干预)"的旗号出兵孟加拉,就是为了掩盖其肢解邻国的真实目的。在国际场合,很多发言者将最初的"poor nations"或"backward nations"称为"underdeveloped nations(不发达国家)"、"developing nations(发展中国家)"、"less-developed countries(欠发达国家)"。1980年,美国为营救在德黑兰美国大使馆中的人质,使用直升机对德黑兰进行空袭,造成了重大伤亡,政客称之为"an incomplete success(一次不完全的成功)"。对于战争行为,美国官方用语中充满了 euphemism。比如,用"preemptive action(先发制人的行为)"指"invasion(入侵)";"pacification(安宁)"指"villages were burned and the inhabitants imprisoned(焚烧村庄,囚禁居民)";"ordnance delivery(军械发放)"指"saturation bombing(饱和式轰炸)"; "defoliation(落叶)"指"destroying crops(毁灭庄稼)","friendly fire(友好的炮火)"指猪队友的误伤,等等。

2. 社会生活方面

社会生活中存在的一些习惯认识上的差异可能因 Euphemism 而导致跨文化交际障碍。英语中有关"老""老人"的委婉语特别多,反映了西方人忌讳"老"的社会心态。英美老年人不喜欢 old people,也不喜欢 aged 或 aging 甚至 the elderly 等称呼,较多偏爱 senior citizen(年长、高级的公民)或 golden age(黄金年代的人)、venerable people(由于年龄、德行、职位等而应受到敬重的人)委婉的称呼。老太太则称自己是 mature(成熟的)。

[例6] Social Security and Medicare, together, have lifted entire generations of seniors out of poverty.

与英语不同,汉语中"老"指"年岁"时,不但没有贬义,还常带有尊敬的意思。汉文化素有"尊老爱幼"的传统美德,并不以"老"为禁忌,近年来还将"九九重阳节"定为"老人节",可见中国人对汉语中的"老"字的含义的理解与英语国家的人对"old"词义的理解截然不同。

又比如,英语中有不少关于容貌和身材的委婉语。形容一个人"胖"不说 fat,而是说 plump;形容一个人"瘦"也不说 thin,而是说 slim/slender;如果要形容一个人长得丑,人们也会尽量避免使用 ugly,而是用 plain/homely。

在学校,如果你是教师,千万不要当着家长的面说他的孩子"笨"(stupid),你得小心地说成"他学得慢"(a slow learner),"他尚未发挥潜力"

(under-achiever），因为每个父母都认为自己的孩子是很有潜力的。

对于一些比较底层的职业，人们有时候也会仿造一些高级职业的说法来称呼它们，以此来提升这些职业的"档次"。比如将 hairdresser 称为 beautician，将 plumber 称为 heating engineer，将 mechanic 称为 automobile engineer，sanitary engineer 是 garbage collector 或 dustman（清洁工），packing engineer 是 porter（搬运工），dwelling engineer 是保姆，美容师则称为 appearance engineer，等等。

## 二、委婉语的翻译

翻译委婉语的关键在于听者或读者的反应。采取什么样的语言形式主要取决于读者是否具备识别委婉性质的能力，载体的选择同时也会受到目的语语言习惯的制约，要从语用、句法、语篇和文化等各个角度和层面进行考虑。

译者应考虑到语境因素（语言语境、非语言语境和认知语境），并对源语和目标语进行语言语用对比和社交语用对比，对委婉语的含义进行斟酌推敲，从而达到情感褒贬得当，含蓄程度相应，语体风格相符。

译者还应考虑到文化冲突因素。由于不同语言中的委婉语都与该语言的文化有密不可分的关系，因此不同语言的委婉语在形式、内容、效果上存在的冲突是不可避免的。在冲突发生时，表达效果就会受到影响，而效果与含义、意图有直接的关系。含义、意图越明显，委婉程度越低。通过调整表达手段可以解决形式和内容的冲突，但调整翻译手段，必须以指称义跟原文保持一致为基本原则。换言之，因为源语的词义在目的语中所指的是不同事物，源语的事物概念在目的语中不是同一概念，译员如果坚持代码转译，即将源语按词义转译成目的语的相同词义，就会造成听者所理解的或接收到的信息未必是说话者所特指的。因此，对于委婉语，译员正确的做法是，改采功能翻译法，即在理解源语之后，将源语的功能目的转换到译入语中。

委婉语的翻译方法可以总结如下：

1. 直译或直译加注

尽量将原文中的委婉语译为目标语中的委婉语，如果采取直译的方法可以使委婉语的言外之意在目标语中得到保留，译者就应直译，以保持原文的语言结构形式和风格。有时遇到文化差异较大时，为了将异域文化传达到目标语中，保留形象，可用直译加上脚注或简洁的话，补充说明作者的真正意图。

［例7］There was a heavy silence. "Do your best to limit collateral damage," the caller replied, "but this crisis is severe enough that Professor

Langdon would be an acceptable casualty."

一阵沉重的沉默。"尽你所能减少附带的损失，"打电话的人回答说，"但这次危机已经很严重了，兰登教授的伤亡是可以接受的。"

原文中"collateral damage"就是"伤亡"的委婉说法，译文中直译为"附带的损失"，在上下文语境的呼应下，中文读者也可以理解。

2. 委婉语替换为类似委婉

为了让读者易于理解，用目标语文化中的形象代替源语中的形象；

[例8] He was a tolerant man. After all, he was kind and neighborly to the women with whom he, mom and I shared a bathroom in our small duplex—even after he learned their profession—ladies of the night.

父亲是个宽容大度的人。我家当年和几位女士同住一栋狭小的联式房屋，与她们共用卫生间。即使后来得知这些女士从事"特殊"职业，父亲依然善良和蔼地对待她们。

上例原文出自小布什在父亲老布什葬礼上的悼词。葬礼是一个庄重的场合，悼词中出现 prostitutes 不合适，所以小布什用 ladies of the night 这一委婉语来代替。在译文中也用了具有类似功能的委婉语"'特殊'职业"来表达。

3. 委婉语译为直接语

委婉语的使用者是在特定的交际场合下向特定的交际对象含蓄地传递自己的意图，暗示自己对所谈事物的态度。交际成功与否主要取决于信息接收者在多大程度上能听出言外之意。如果直译使读者迷惑，或目标语中没有相应的委婉语，译者只能舍形求义，将委婉语译为直接语，而不能舍义求形，以形害义。例如：

[例9] Nothing indiscreet. Nothing you'd feel... uncomfortable with. Just tell me what he is up to. But I would prefer for various reasons that my concern go unmentioned. We have what you might call a... difficult relationship.

绝不会侵犯隐私，绝不会让你为难，你只需告诉我他在做些什么。但我希望你对此守口如瓶，因为我和他之间的关系不太融洽。

[例10] Her father is now between jobs.

她父亲现在失业了。

[例11] Mark is a fair-weather friend.

马克这个人只能共欢乐，却无法共患难。

以上三例中，虽然原文的用语明显是字斟句酌、精心挑选的委婉语，但是如果采用直译法，将［例9］中的"go unmentioned"译为"不被提及"，"difficult relationship"译为"困难的关系"，［例10］中的"between jobs"译为"在工作之间"，［例11］中"fair-weather"译为"好天气"，中国读者是很难理解的，所以都转换成了直白的语言。

> ［例12］原来近日水月庵的智能私逃入城，来找秦钟，不意被秦邦业知觉，将智能逐出，将秦钟打了一顿，自己气的老病发了，三五日便呜呼哀哉了……（曹雪芹　高鹗《红楼梦》）
> Now, a few days previously, Chin-neng had stolen away from Water Moon Convent and come to town to look for Chin Chung in his home. She had been caught by his father, who drove her away and gave his son a beating. The old man's rage had brought on an attack of his chronic disorder, and within a few days he was dead. （杨宪益　戴乃迭　译）

上例中"呜呼哀哉"具有很强的文化印记，在英语里没有对应词，所以没有交际背景的支持不可强求形式上的对等。

4. 直接语译为委婉语

如果源语是直接语，而目标语中又有相应的委婉语，可将直接语译为委婉语。

> ［例13］WTO的这些国家已经认识到没有中国参加的WTO是没有代表性的，是忽视了中国这个潜在的最大市场。
> The WTO member states have come to realize that a WTO without China would not be representative enough, or the WTO would have neglected China, the largest potential market in the world.
>
> ［例14］我认为在这个问题上，美国方面的人士犯了两个过低估计的错误。
> I think on this question some people in the United States have made two underestimates.

［例15］中，原文"没有代表性"的说法显得直言不讳，译文用"not representative enough"显得委婉而留有余地，较易为谈判的对方所接受。［例14］译文中把原文的"错误"一词略去不译，也有利于营造一种委婉客气的氛围。

再看下面几个例子：

[例16] 我们之间有太多痛苦的往事。

There is much history between us.

[例17] 他在文章中随意歪曲事实。

In the article he made free with the facts.

[例17] 说到风景，没有一个比得上中国。

Forscenery, there is no country like China.

**【翻译欣赏】**

多少年来，我养成了一个习惯：每天早晨四点在黎明以前起床工作。我不出去跑步或散步，而是一下床就干活儿。因此我对黎明前的北京的了解是在屋子里感觉到的。我从前在什么报上读过一篇文章，讲黎明时分天安门广场上的清洁工人。那情景必然是非常动人的，可惜我从未能见到，只是心向往之而已。

For many years, I have been in the habit of getting up before daybreak to start work at four. Instead of going out for a jog or walk, I'll set about my work as soon as I'm out of bed. As a result, it is from inside my study that I've got the feel of predawn Beijing. Years ago, I hit upon a newspaper article about street cleaner in Tian'anmen Square at daybreak. It must have been a very moving scene, but what a pity I haven't seen it with my own eyes. I can only picture it in my mind longingly.

四十年前，我住在城里在明朝曾经是特务机关的东厂里面。几座深深的大院子，在最里面三个院子里只住着人一个人。朋友们都说这地方阴森可怕，晚上很少有人敢来找我，我则怡然自得。每当夏夜，我起床以后，立刻就闻到院子里那些高大的马缨花树散发出来的阵阵幽香，这些香气破窗而入，我于此时神清气爽，乐不可支，连手中那一枝笨拙的笔也仿佛生了花。

Forty years ago, I lived downtown in Dongchang, a compound which had housed the secret service of the Ming dynasty. There were inside it several deep spacious courtyard one leading into another. I was the sole dweller of the three innermost courtyards. My friends, calling this place too ghastly, seldom dared to come to see me in the evening whereas I myself found it quite agreeable. In summer, the moment I got out of bed before daybreak, I would smell the delicate fragrance of the giant silk trees coming from outside my window. Thereupon, I would feel refreshed and joyful, and the clumsy pen in my hand would seem to have become as agile as it could.

几年以后，我搬到西郊来住，照例四点起床，坐在窗前工作。白天透过窗子能够看到北京展览馆那金光闪闪的高塔的尖顶，此时当然看不到了。但是，我知道，即使我看不见它，它仍然在那里挺然耸入天空，仿佛想带给人以希望，以上进的劲头。我仍然是乐不可支，心也仿佛飞上了高空。

Several years later when I moved to the western suburbs, I kept my habit of rising at four to begin work at the window. The glittering spire atop the tower of the daytime through my window, would no longer be visible now in the early morning haze. Nevertheless I knew that, tough invisible, it remained there intact, towering to the skies to inspire people with hope and the urge for moving ahead. At this, I would be beside myself with joy and feel as if my heart were also flying high up into the skies.

过了十年，我又搬了家。这新居既没有马缨花，也看不到金色的塔顶。但是门前却有一片清碧的荷塘。刚搬来的几年，池塘里还有荷花。夏天早晨四点已经算是黎明时分。在薄暗中透过窗子可以看到接天莲叶，而荷花的香气也幽然袭来，我顾而乐之，大有超出马缨花和金色塔顶之上的意味了。

Ten years after, I moved again. In the new home of mine, I had no silk trees, nor could I get sight of the glittering spire from afar. There was, however, a lotus pond of limpid blue in front of my door. In the first few years after I moved there, lotus flowers continued to blossom on the surface of the pond. In the summertime, when day broke early at four, a vast stretch of lotus leaves looking skywards outside my window came dimly into sight while the quiet fragrance of the lotus flowers assailed my nose. All that delighted me even more than the silk trees and the glittering spire.

难道我欣赏黎明前的北京仅仅由于上述的原因吗？不是的。三十几年以来，我成了一个"开会迷"。说老实话，积三十年之经验，我真有点怕开会了。在白天，一整天说不定什么时候就会接到开会的通知。说一句过火的话，我简直是提心吊胆，心里不得安宁。即使不开会，这种惴惴不安的心情总摆脱不掉。只有在黎明以前，根据我的经验，没有哪里会来找你开会的。因此，我起床往桌子旁边一坐，仿佛有什么近似条件反射的东西立刻就起了作用，我心里安安静静，一下子进入角色，拿起笔来，"文思"（如果也算是文思的话）如泉水喷涌，记忆力也像刚磨过的刀子，锐不可当。当时，我真乐不可支，如果给我机会的话，我简直想手舞足蹈了。

Is it exclusively due to the above-mentioned that I've developed a liking for predawn Beijing? No. for 30 years, I've been bogged down in the mire of meetings. To tell you the truth, with the experience accumulated over the 30 years, I'm now scared of meetings. In the daytime, there is no telling when I may be served a notice for attending a meeting. To exaggerate it a bit, that keeps me in constant suspense and makes me fidgety. Even when no meeting is to take place, I feel restless all the same. However, my experience tells that it is only during the predawn hours that I can be truly havened from any involvement in meetings. As soon as I sit at my desk before dawn, something similar to the conditioned reflex will begin to function within me: Instantly I'll pick up my pen to play my proper part with perfect peace of mind. Then inspiration comes gushing to my mind and my memory becomes as quick as a newly-sharpened knife. I'll feel overjoyed, almost to the point of waving my arms and stamping my feet.

因此，我爱北京，特别爱黎明前的北京。

In short, I love Beijing, especially predawn Beijing.

（季羡林《黎明前的北京》张培基　译）

## 第六章
# 汉英文化对比与翻译

在实务翻译中，翻译往往就是一种交际行为，其策略的选择取决于翻译行为的目的。在目的决定策略的原则下，译者必须超越纯语言层次，消除文化冲突，按照新的交际环境和译文受众的接受程度，消除原文中与译文受众不相宜的因素，更加有效地达到文本的交际目的。

汉、英语言民族文化分属东、西方两种文化，其差异之大是不言而喻的。一个民族的文化取向对于另一个民族的成员来说可能是陌生的、截然不同的，或者是不可接受的。语言表达、风俗习惯、体态表情等是文化差异的外部表现形式。在这种形式的背后隐含着更深层的审美观、价值标准等思维方式的差异以及地理环境、生活习俗等物质方面的差异。鉴于地理环境、生活习俗等乃是实实在在的客观存在，相对容易感知，而且事实上目前已经有了相当多的相关资料，本教程将重点分析较为不容易把握的审美习惯、价值取向的差异上。

# 第一节　汉英价值取向对比与翻译

如果说前一章是基于情景语境的具体场景来考虑翻译的效果，从而在客观上带来译文的调整，带有一定的经验色彩，那么本章则上升到了文化层面，力求系统地梳理改写式翻译的文化视角与增删剪裁的操作路径。

在中国特色社会主义的新阶段，我们的社会主义核心价值观，即富强、民主、文明、和谐，自由、平等、公正、法治，爱国、敬业、诚信、友善，可以说既囊括了中华文明传统价值观的精髓，又容纳了人类现代文明的共同成果。但是，古人言，"非我族类，其心必异"。如果祛除其中的异族偏见成分，这句话确实也反映了各个民族之间在思维方式上还是有着客观存在的差异，翻译人必须要认真对待。对此，在世人思维认知与话语习惯暂难改变的情况下，一个好的翻译员，应该具备"两脚踏中西文化"的心理预期，磨砺自己的文化差异识别能力，扬弃绝对化的误区，以"与其誉尧而非桀也，不如两忘而化其道"为指引，超越价值取向的优劣争议，以促成良好的沟通效果为主要考量，拿捏好"行于所当行，止于所不可不止"的分寸，减少或者避免"You always demand that I learn and follow your culture and not so much my own culture"的抱怨，更好地维护自身切实利益。

## 一、集体与个体

对于汉英翻译工作而言，中西方在集体和个体问题上的观念差异具有举足轻重的影响。

北京奥运会开幕式可谓是中国特色的集体主义价值观的盛典，观众被气势恢宏、波澜壮阔的宏大叙事所震撼，却难以记住表演者的个体特征，因为艺术表演者跟道具一样，宛如大海里的一滴水，都没入了整齐划一的场面巨浪里。相比之下，伦敦奥运会开幕式里，个体的艺术家、表演者，比如说憨豆先生、邦德等，这些人的个体特征非常突出，在表演中起着决定性作用。这两种盛典都是可以互相欣赏的，但是它们体现了两种完全不同的价值取向：中国文化重集体，西方文化重个体。

［例1］Discussing Horton's refusal to stand on the podium next to him, Sun said: "Not everyone likes me. I don't care about it. It is also

OK if you don't respect me personally, but during the victory ceremony, which is the most important event, we all represent our countries, you should stand on the podium, and show your respect to my country China and your country Australia and to the audience."

［例2］Tu's work wasn't published until 1977. As was customary, the authors remained anonymous; in such an egalitarian society the group was considered more important than the individual.

真挚、纯洁、理性而又脚踏实地的集体主义是一种非常高尚的品质，它塑造了中华民族"诚意正心、修齐治平"，"为天地立心，为生民立命"的人文环境，促使社会各阶层将个人价值与集体、社会的发展融为一体，同时清醒识别轻佻浮躁，乃至不讲常识的行为，摒弃看似热血沸腾、实则精致利己的风气，有效推动了经济的持续健康发展和社会的全面进步。

西方人具有突出的个体导向倾向，即认为越靠近自己的就越重要，因而习惯于从最具体、最本地化的视角出发，按小到大的优先顺序进行语言表达与组织。下例摘自哈佛大学某课堂讨论上某同学所做的归纳，颇能说明问题：

［例3］One of the things we've noticed in the three examples is that the people of all chose the most immediate community of which they are a part. The more local one. And I think there is something to be said for that. It's not just random. I mean, there doesn't seem to be a conflict because they know which one is more important. And it's their family over the Ec10 Class, their state over their country, and their family over the commonwealth of Massachusetts. So I think that's the answer to which is more important.

在当代西方社会的一个现象是，个体主义已经走过头了，它天生不全面、顾此失彼，导致了贫富差距扩大、社会分裂、极端主义崛起等严重问题，正陷入种种困境，不时甚至显露出偏执、自私、虚伪、堕落的双重标准嘴脸，合意则罢，不合意就掀桌子，秀下限，视法律和秩序如无物。如何在个人与集体、国家等方面取得平衡，让公平正义免于蒙尘，仍是道阻且长。

诚然，无论是东方人的集体价值倾向，还是西方人的个体价值观念，都不是绝对化的，跨文化交际也因而千姿百态，但是了解并正确处理这两种客观存在的观念差异，对于商务翻译中具有重要的意义。

在西方的体系中，个人主义尽管有种种弊端，但它毕竟是其主流社会价值取向的基石。在中外交往中，有外国人对这种价值差异和缺乏理解做了这样的描述："They will not miss any chance to call you selfish. However, for foreigners this word does not seem so strong and they consider it quite normal to be called selfish—but for Chinese this is not the case."

因此，内外有别是一条重要原则。翻译员尽可以为自己民族的集体精神而自豪，也不认同西方社会强烈的个体意识造就的诸多问题，但在翻译工作中，摈弃轰轰烈烈的形式主义，以事功为考量，酌情控制宏大叙事，使用别人听得懂的语言，接纳一些国际通行的做法，多一些以个人关切为切入点的叙事方式，可能反而会收到"惟其尊重，所以相亲"的效果。这对于中国企业在走出去的过程中，营造出较高的亲和力和可信度，是有裨益的。

另外，中国人偏重综合思维，欧美人偏重分析思维。综合思维是指在思想上将对象的各个部分联成一体，从整体概念角度出发进行思维，即从大到小。分析思维是指在思想上将一个整体的对象分解成各个组成部分，并从部分角度进行思维，即从小到大。这种思维方式可以反映在时间及空间的顺序表达上，其时间和空间排列顺序分别为秒—分—时—日—月—年，和门牌号码—街道—市—省—国家。中国人则恰恰相反，其时间和空间排列顺序分别为年—月—日—时—分—秒，国家—省—市—街道—门牌号码。

[例4] First, I would like to say that it is a great honor for me to stand here to ask you questions. I think I'm so lucky and just appreciate that your speech is so clear that I really do not need such kind of headset. And here comes the question. My name is * * * from Fudan University School of Management. And I would like to ask you the question is that now that someone has asked you something about the Nobel Peace Prize. But I will not ask you in the same aspect. I want to ask you in the other aspect that since it is very hard for you get such kind of an honorable prize, and I would ask you and I wonder and we all wonder how you struggle to get it. What's your college education that brings you to get such kind of prizes? And we are very curious and we would like to invite you to share with us your campus education experience.

[例5] Produced by: Jacobsens Bakery Ltd., Bilanvey 1, 8722 Hendensted, Denmark.

China importer: Ruifuhang Food Trade Co. Ltd., 16/F Yuedu

Hotel, No. 1, Liuliqiao-Beili-Jia, Fengtai Dist., Beijing 100073
原产国：丹麦，由丹麦杰克布森烘焙有限公司制造
中国进口商：瑞富行食品商贸有限公司，北京丰台区六里桥北里甲 1 号悦都大酒店，邮编 100073

基于翻译的具体特点，研究翻译过程中的文化翻译对策，以便更好地传递源语的思想文化内容，而不是仅仅拘泥于两种语言形式的转换，显得尤为重要。这就要求翻译工作者除了具备扎实的语言基本功之外，还要对其文化及思维方式有所了解，否则，翻译只能是徒具文字上的对应，却没有沟通的灵魂，极易结出事与愿违的恶果。

## 二、以我为主与客户导向

一个现实状况是，一些市场行为主体的思维中少了些平等协商，多了些以力服人、以利收买人的色彩，少了些商洽性的同理心、人情味。这在商务文本的创作上，就体现为自说自话地展示企业自身的"硬实力"。因为认识不够，翻译时大多采取字面直译，将这些问题原封不动地搬到了英语世界里，不但亲和力（likability）就此缺失，难以达到增进译文读者的好感、促进消费的翻译目的，甚至还屡有事与愿违的负面效果。这种"自我思维"并非上文所说的个人主义，而是"我们"，是一种以公司形式存在的集体。具体来说，可分为 3 种表现形式：在信息选择上，沉湎于企业自身的历史荣光与发展蓝图，而没有用心去体察读者所关切的实质性信息；在语言形式上，过于看重产品的器物功能，而忽略了柔性的情感氛围；在篇章结构上，又存在着文本过于庞杂，不够简洁明了的问题。

### （一）信息的取舍：自我荣光与客户需求

国内很多商务翻译文本似乎不知道其宗旨乃是增进译文读者的好感，促进消费。相反，这些译文拘泥于源文本的格局，在信息内容的选择上，不是以市场需求为主导，而是带着不合时宜的计划经济时代烙印，浸染浓厚的国有垄断企业的官本位文化，主要立足于吹嘘企业的自我价值，沉湎于展示企业的昔日荣光与宏伟蓝图，不但与消费者的利益关切缺乏必然的、直接的联系，更在自豪中难免透着一丝居高临下的气势，对于消费者（即读者）的感受顾及较少，完全不容于现实的市场经济大环境。其结果是，译文花费大量篇幅着重介绍的内容很有可能让外国消费者觉得不知所云，无异于鸡同鸭讲。在某些极端情况下，甚至会显得目中无人，令人排斥而非亲近，着实难以获得普通消费者的信

任。例如：

[例6]

××Hotel with sheer elegance and peerless grace.

A gorgeous river named Jinjiang is running through the city of Chengdu, the center of western China. Having been standing by Jinjiang River for half a century, the main building of ×× Hotel with its European style is still filled with the generous and degage charm of history and culture, even comparing with thousands of various-styled and abounded skyscrapers around the city nowadays.

The 1958 witnessed the ground-breaking ceremony of ×× Hotel. Marshal Zhu De and Marshal Chen Yi assigned personally "Jinjiang" as the name to the hotel when it was completed. In 1995, ×× Hotel was honored as the first five-star business and tourist hotel in Southwest China, while in 1999, ×× Hotel was conferred the most prestigious Five Star Diamond Award by AAHS. In 2010, ×× Hotel won the top honorable prize in the hospitality of our country, honored as the "Oscar" in hospitality industry in China. In recent years, ×× offered management and supervisor services for decades of star-rated hotels, and got involved in the new eras such like municipal administration, property management, bank service and so on, which led to great achievements and extended the influence of the brand.

Since the founding of the Hotel, fifty years passed and rich culture stayed. The warm and generous, thoughtful and careful unique characteristics of Sichuan people have been played incisively and vividly in ××, which formed a distinctive and prominent service culture. In 2007, ×× people spontaneously took "create touching moment" as corporate core value and published "Moving Declaration: Corporate Culture Brochure of Sichuan ×× Hotel", firstly having "moving culture" nationwide.

Since 2008, with an investment of more than 500 million Yuan, ×× Grand Building has been under construction by the top hotel standards will be completed in two years. Meanwhile, relying on the ×× Station of Chengdu Subway, the second phase project of Jinjiang Hotel, creating a new CBD by the side of Jinjiang River, has been put on the agenda. After that, there will be nearly 900 guestrooms, 1000 pieces of underground parking spaces and nearly 10000m² European-style royal gardens around and the French Michelin Western Restaurant as well as the traditional Japanese Teppanyaki, by virtue of which above, ×× Hotel is going to be one of the largest and the most convenient hotels allover Chengdu with its dignity and distinguished garden style.

In the same year, in order to be in tune with the developing trends of hospitality industry-collectivization, branding, scale extension and specialization, ×× Hotel established "×× International Hotel Co., Ltd". Based on the primary business of hospitality, the brand-new corporation, regarding "Create moving culture to help make ×× the first-class tourism enterprise" as the understanding of development, takes great advantages and benefits of its original brand, management and service and tries to be listed in the next 3 to 5 years with a strategic partner, in order to strive for a further strategic progress in high star-rated hotels and budget hotels and become the leader corporate group of Sichuan tourism.

Entering into domestic national hotel brands of 20 strong and well-known international hotel brands of 200 had already become the development of strategic planning goals of ×× Hotel—a banner of Sichuan tourism, looking for the future, blowing in the wind!

上述译文完全就是对中文进行字面翻译的结果。从实际效果来说，必然导致其对英语世界客户的吸引力大打折扣。比如，该译文完全没有考虑到英文网页所面向的受众，已经不是带有国内政府指令性质的官方协议消费单位，而是竞争性市场经济条件下的英语世界消费者，影响其选择入住酒店的因素，绝非该宾馆的发展历程以及远景规划，而是与其现实利益诉求直接相关的考量。换言之，他们阅读简介是带着很直接的功利性的，主要就是想要以最节约时间的方式，便捷了解酒店的文化定位和交通、旅游、康乐、餐饮等设施的实时状况。

因此，简介的英语译文如果偏离了这个市场需求，转而另搞一套，自说自话地将焦点改为啰唆不堪地大幅介绍自身的发展历程以及远景规划，就是背离了英语世界读者的阅读预期，非但浪费了如同封面一般宝贵的、具有提纲挈领性质的简介版面，对于习惯了被当着上帝供起来的英语读者来说，心里难免觉得酒店缺乏同感心，升起一股对宾馆的服务意识、服务水平的浓黑疑云，觉得继续读下去都是多余，反正"There's plenty of fish in the sea"，转而投向较为符合其品味的其他酒店去了。

与上例相反，对于酒店网页的信息内容，英语世界的酒店网页介绍有着完全不同的取向。上文说过，英语世界的价值观系以个人主义为基石。而在个人主义的世界观中，自我解释的默认单位是个体，一个独立的自我。因此，基本的关系单位是"我－你"，两个独立自主的自我相连接。因此，其话语方式是基于个人主义的"我－你"沟通语体，能够有针对性地展示客户所关切的内容，是以读者（消费者）为出发点，集中展示产品的消费价值或企业与读者（消费者）的利益关系，务求处处让读者感受到酒店交通、旅游、康乐、餐饮等设施的便利与服务的周到，产生"Your home away from home"的好感，诱导出"起而行"的消费欲望。请看下例：

［例7］Kempinski Hotel Hybernska Prague

Whether you are traveling for business or leisure, the wonderful ambience, first-class service and superb facilities of the luxurious Kempinski Hotel Hybernska guarantee you an exceptional stay in Prague.

**Hotel Location**

The Kempinski Hotel Hybernska is perfectly located in the very heart of the Prague City Centre, within a short walking distance of Prague's premiere sightseeing locations, such as the Powder Tower, the Old Town Square with its Astronomical Clock, the Charles Bridge and Wenceslas Square.

The hotel is easily reached by car, taxi or public transport, and the main railway and bus stations are only a 5 minute walk away. The hotel's luxurious BMW limousine will bring you from the airport to the Kempinski Hotel Hybernska in just a 20 minute drive.

The nearest underground station, Náměstí Republiky, is a 100 metre walk away.

**Leisure Facilities**

*Kempinski Gallery*

Visit a unique art exhibition in the hotel's Lobby Lounge and corridors.

Kempinski Gallery shows some of the best artwork of renowned Czech artists, all of which are available for sale.

You can also find some stunning original sculptures displayed in the hotel's beautiful private gardens.

*Fitness &Wellness Treatments*

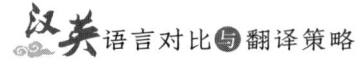

Pamper your body and heal your mind! Get in shape or enjoy a swim in the "World Class Health Academy" that is located just across the road from the hotel. Or relax whilst enjoying a wide range of massage and beauty treatments that can be provided in the privacy of your room or in the Mystic Temple close by the hotel. A team of top professionals will exceed all your expectations!

*Sightseeing & Guided Tours*

The Kempinski Hotel Hybernska cooperates with some of the most experienced tour guides in the city, who will be delighted to take you on a tour of the "Golden City" of Prague on foot, by chauffeur driven vintage car or in a BMW limousine. Tours can be arranged in a number of different languages.

*Hotel Services*

Concierge: Personal attention to our guest's needs

The HotelKempinski Hybernska's experienced concierge team will be delighted to assist you in planning and arranging all of your daytime activities. From reservations for theater performances, sightseeing tours or restaurants, to transfer arrangements, babysitting services and medical assistance, the concierge team will take care of your every need.

For more information, please contact the concierge team on T +420 226 226 126 or e— concierge.prague@kempinski.com

*Kids Care*

Prague is the perfect destination for a family vacation, and the Hotel Kempinski Hybernska will ensure that you can travel easily with your little ones. Cribs, baby carriages, changing tables, baby chairs and bottle warmers are all available for you during your stay. Traveling with teenagers? The hotel can provide a Wii console and DVD's to ensure that they are entertained.

（注：为节约篇幅起见，上例对 Kempinski Hotel Hybernska Prague 的网页相关内容有所删节）

对比以上两个例子，不难发现，前者的译文乃是拘泥于原文内容与思路的字面翻译，完全没有 Kempinski Hotel Hybernska Prague 英文网页介绍的那种吸引力，无疑是很不成功的。这不仅是因为后者处处以消费者（读者）为中心所带来的美好阅读体验，也为凯宾斯基酒店集团全球扩张过程中的成功业绩所佐证。

这种阅读体验与实际业绩的双重差异对于翻译策略的选择有什么影响呢？

从理论上说，前者的缺憾在于，它没有把消费者对译文的可接受性置于首位，背离了广告翻译的宗旨，产生了不符合译入语文化的译文，不但不可能有好的推广效果，而且还会起反作用。现代翻译界广泛认同一种理论，翻译行为受到意识形态（ideology）、赞助人（patronage）、诗学或称文学观念（poetics）等3个因素的操纵（manipulation），实质就是改写（rewriting）。对于具有典型广告属性的酒店官方网页而言，翻译成败的核心，就在于能否注意到消费者（即这里所说的"赞助人"）的关切，按照其习惯的价值观念、审美习惯与话语方式进行改写。至于是否忠实于原文，则并非酒店网页翻译的首要之义。适当情况下，甚至可以"言前人所未言，发前人所未发"。

因此，在目的决定策略的原则下，对于这种文化差异巨大，以市场反应为主要考量的文本，理应恪守等效翻译原则，其正确的翻译策略，当是改写，大幅度的改写，即完全摆脱原文的意识局限，完全以消费者（译文读者）为中心，将与消费者的物质和情感需求无关的部分全部删除，其余部分则基本保留。换言之，在对中文酒店网页进行翻译的时候，译者应考虑译入语国家的文化和价值取向，认真思考信息内容的取舍，将对他们有吸引力的信息作为翻译的重点，而欠缺吸引力的信息则可以少译甚至不译。具体来说，［例6］中Overview部分，除了题头的口号语、第一段、第二段中的两个大奖以外，其余都可删除。在涉及对酒店有着巨大影响力的中国领导人时，如果能够将相关内容的译文从酒店简介部分剥离出来，另外列为一个单独的子项，似乎是一个比较恰当的做法。这样既可以凸显我国领导人有别于他国政治人物的尊崇地位，又可以确保宾馆以普通英语消费者所熟悉的方式，向后者发出明白晓畅的"召唤"。

（二）结构的组织：庞杂长篇与简明子文本

当今社会已经是互联网时代，人们在移动设备上浏览大量的信息，自然会受其影响，并以同样的方式作出反应。一方面，阅读缩略的数字化内容导致了人们的注意力持续时间大大缩短，另一方面，正如英语社交媒体专家GavinHammar所指出的，"Reading short bursts of poorly constructed content from a young age impacts on the learning experience and filters into our everyday lives."这自然也显著影响了人们用英语书写和说话的方式。比如，要在Twitter上让别人懂你的意思，就必须简洁，必须符合那里的140个字符限制的要求，这就深刻地改变了英语这门语言，促使人们越来越多地使用精练的语言，甚至造就了一些新型作家，专门从事一小段一小段的简式语言写作。

有很多中国企业的简介文本喜欢长篇大论，写成了大拼盘式的长篇文本，通篇只有一个"酒店简介"之类的大标题，普遍篇幅较长，内容庞杂，在译成英文时也大致保持了这种长篇大论的格局。上述［例5］中的原文与英语译文都是如此。

仔细阅读［例7］中的文本，就会发现它与［例5］中的译文及其原文在篇章结构上的巨大差距：Kempinski Hotel Hybernska Prague 的文本通过次级小标题和动态链接将整个篇章内容分门别类地组织成各层级的子文本。如在大标题"Kempinski Hotel Hybernska Prague"之下，分有"Hotel Location" "Leisure Facilities" "Hotel Services" 几个二级标题引领的子文本，其下又各自有若干三级标题引领的文本，比如"Leisure Facilities"之下就又分为 *Kempinski Gallery*" "*Fitness & Wellness Treatments*" "*Sightseeing & Guided Tours*" 几项三级标题，显得篇幅简短，脉络清楚，言简意赅，读来一目了然。

相比之下，后者的风格更加符合信息化时代的要求，极大地方便了读者在较短时间内找到自己需要的有用信息。这个对比说明，中文简介译成英文时，最好是牢记KISS原则，采用重组的方法，力求内容简化，层次清楚，重点突出，易于查询。

（三）语言的情理：器物与情感

先来看两个例子：

［例8］

Details and Perfection, Only for Your Most Comfortable Experience

We are providing more than 700 elegant rooms, including 61 Suites. We have various facilities and services:

- King-size and twin beds with extra bed service
- Optional step-out sightseeing balcony, flowers and plants around
- Free Fruits, flowers in room
- Hansgrohe thermostatic sanitary ware
- Flat TV with cable/satellite TV/movie channels
- CD and DVD player
- Administrative staff desk
- Free wireless and wired broadband Internet connection
- International and domestic long-distance call

- Safe deposit box and mini bar
- Independent temperature control
- Non-smoking floor
- Facilities for the disabled
- Executive Floor Privileges
- Butler service
- Rooms for ladies

[例9]

## Rooms & Suites

**Indulge yourself in a pure luxury**

The new and luxurious Kempinski Hotel Hybernska Prague offers a wonderful combination of historical architecture and a contemporary interior. Ensconce yourself in one of the hotel's stunning guestrooms, relax on its private balcony, and admire the beautiful views and sounds of magical Prague.

For further information please contact room reservations on

T +420 226 226 132 or e reservations. prague@kempinski. com

**Rooms**

After a long day of business meetings or an extensive sightseeing tour, relax in the elegance and comfort of the hotel's spacious guest rooms.

Kempinski Hotel Hybernska offers some of the biggest rooms and widest choice of accommodation in the city, whatever the purpose of your stay.

**Suites**

For the traveller that appreciates that extra touch of luxury, the light and airy apartment-style Suites represent the ultimate in comfort. Combined with the exceptional hospitality that the Kempinski Hotels pride themselves on, guests can be sure of a memorable stay.

**Palace Suites**

Imagine watching the sun setting over the towers and spires of Prague and listening to the sound of bells ringing over this magical city. Your vision will come true when you are standing on the beautiful terraces of the hotel's two-bedroom Presidential and Bohemia Suites.

The real "Crème de la Crème".

对比阅读两个例子，不难发现［例5］中的英文产品介绍仍属对于原文的字面直译，显得过于受到原文的局限，交际对象宽泛，语势冰冷疏离，亲和力明显欠缺，难以架起沟通的桥梁与亲近的纽带。而 Kempinski Hotel Hybernska Prague 酒店的产品介绍是软卖型文笔，英语世界的酒店网页产品介绍在关切、体察客户的经济利益的同时，还特别注重客户的人文情感需求，换言之，更加能够有针对性地用有人情味的语言来打动客户，行文多是"You (customer)－Oriented"，通过针对性地选择细节、对话形式、大量适切的祈使句式，再结合美妙宜人的形容词、简洁明快的断句节奏，无形中把潜在客人带入了酒店预设的情境之中，置身于一个美妙遐想的迷人氛围，予人交际对象具体明确、语势温馨亲昵的宜人之感。

这个对比说明，在内容以外，还有一个语言的问题。对于星级酒店网页上的产品介绍，在翻译时要特别注意避免字面翻译所产生的硬卖型广告文本，这不但是因为星级酒店的硬件产品都有着较为一致的国际标准，而且消费者也大都知道这一点，一样一样罗列在译文里实在是多余，还有一个更为重要的普遍性因素：酒店网页产品介绍也是广告文体，其译文必须以广告效果为主要考量，尤其是要想方设法增添用语的人情味，提升亲和力与信任感。参照营销领域的一条广为流行的忠告来说，就是"Don't sell the steak, sell the sizzle（不要卖牛排，要卖牛排的滋滋声）"。因此，高明的译者理应用心体察软卖型广告的核心要义，对硬卖型产品介绍进行针对性的改写，再创一个词汇、句法、修辞都出色，语势温馨宜人的译文，营造出一种醉人氛围，让受众产生想要亲近它、拥有它的渴望。

"人之相识，贵在相知，人之相知，贵在知心"这句话，是中外交流的重要经验。在中文酒店网页的翻译中，理应摆脱那种国有垄断企业式的、"以我为主"的官本位思维与话语方式，超越纯语言层次，尊重交际对象的差异，分析市场经济条件下译文受众的文化习俗与审美习惯，以此为基础，进行有针对性的改写式翻译，从而消除原文中与译文受众不相宜的信息因素，保证译文的简洁与甜美，建立起异域文化下受众对于酒店的亲近感与消费欲，乃是达到酒店网页翻译之目的的必由之路。

往大了说，既要坚定弘扬中国文化的优秀品质，也要兼顾受众的接受程度，要在"行于所当行，止于所不可不止"的原则下，进一步加强和改进国际传播，努力塑造可信、可爱、可敬的中国形象，为我国改革发展稳定营造有利外部舆论环境。"国之交在于民相亲，民相亲在于心相通"，就商务翻译而言，毕竟要以市场推广效能为根本出发点，如果硬要囫囵吞枣般像机器人翻译一样不加甄别地大规模保留源语文化元素，无疑是混淆了商务翻译的角色，过于着意自身的独特性而忽略了一些普遍适用的基本准则，显得与世界格格不入，结果往往是消化不良，造成事与愿违的负面效果。

## 【翻译欣赏】

白天鹅宾馆坐落在广州闹市中的"世外桃源"——榕荫如盖，历史悠久的沙面岛的南边，濒临三江汇集的白鹅潭。宾馆独特的庭园式设计与周围优雅的环境融为一体，一条专用的引桥把宾馆与市中心连接起来，实为商旅人士下榻的最佳之处。

白天鹅宾馆拥有843间精心设计的客房，无论是标准房、豪华套房还是商务楼层，室内装潢及设计都经过深思熟虑，设备齐全，舒适温馨，处处显露出以客为先的服务风范。从客房您更可饱览广州市容和珠江美景。别具特色的中西食府，为您提供中、法、日等精美菜肴。多功能国际会议中心是举办各类大小型会议、中西式酒会、餐舞会的理想场所。另有健康中心、美容发型中心、商务中心、委托代办、票务中心、豪华车队等配套设施。近年来，白天鹅宾馆把经营管理的发展和高科技成果相结合，使宾馆的服务水平紧跟国际酒店发展的潮流。无论您是商务公干，还是旅游度假，在白天鹅宾馆都能感受到居停方便、舒适、自然。

白天鹅宾馆是中国第一家中外合作的五星级宾馆，也是我国第一家由中国人自行设计、施工、管理的大型现代化酒店。1985年被世界一流酒店组织接纳为在中国的首家成员；1990年被国家旅游局评为我国首批三家五星级酒店之一；1996年荣列国家旅游局举办首次全国百优五十佳饭店评选榜首，并连续多年被国际旅游指南和国际著名杂志报纸评为国际商务人士到广州的首选酒店。开业以来，白天鹅宾馆创造了良好的经济效益，共接待了40多个国家的元首和政府首脑，英女王伊丽莎白二世、美国总统布什、尼克松、德国总理科尔及卡斯特罗、基辛格、西哈努克、李光耀等国际名人都曾在此驻足。我国改革开放的总设计师邓小平更是三次莅临"白天鹅"，并亲笔题字，这在国内中外合作的高星级宾馆中是绝无仅有的。

宾馆在实践中把国际先进酒店的管理经验与中国的国情相结合，走出了一条融中西管理模式于一炉的酒店管理之路，不断追求卓越，以严谨、高效的管理和真诚的服务为海内外宾客提供一个温馨的家外之家。

译文 A：

Located on the historical Shamian Island, overlooking the famed Pearl River and facing the White Swan Pool, the White Swan Hotel remains an oasis of tranquility from the hustle and bustle of this busy city. The main building has the height of 34 storeys. The exquisitely beautiful Atrium lobby is an indoor microcosm of the famed landscapes of Southern China. Here waters abound, with a veil-like cascade and a spectacular rockery. Atop the rockery sits an elegant Chinese pavilion, octagon-shaped, with its richly ornate gold top, and a profusion of luxuriant vegetation and flowers.

White Swan Hotel own 843 guest rooms involved standard rooms, deluxe suites and executive floor. Any of them been designed with full consideration to let our customers feel the thoughtful and comfortable during the stay.

Restaurants in White Swan Hotel offering a wonderful variety of Chinese and Western food spread over the public areas from the first floor to the third floor. The Jade River Restaurant, Banquet Hall, Coffee Shop, Grill Room, Provincial Restaurant and Japanese Restaurant serve excellent dishes in an elegant ambience with river view. The International Convention Center is equipped with sound and recording facilities as well as simultaneous translation equipment. This is the ideal venue for international conferences, meetings, receptions and exhibitions. The hotel also offers a chain of hardware and services from laundry to the entertainment.

White Swan Hotel keeps the constant international standard high level service from the very beginning till now, that makes hotel become the first choice for the customers no matter with business or leisure in Canton.

译文 B:

The Only Deluxe Business Hotel in Guangzhou with Resort Facilities

An elegant 28-storey hotel, our White Swan is nestled on historic Shamian Island, overlooking the pearl river. Here, you enjoy far more than bigger rooms, comfortable beds and exceptional service, for we care to provide 1 state-of-the-art convention center and 9 restaurants tempting you with exquisite Chinese and international cuisines. Resort conveniences include 10 tennis courts, 1 health club and spa, squash court, 2 swimming pools, golf driving range and Karaoke club. Shopping and Elizabeth Arden a feature.

## 第二节　汉英审美文化对比与翻译

### 一、模糊与清晰

（一）模糊与清晰之倾向问题

1. 汉语倾向模糊，英语倾向清晰

模糊性存在于英汉两种不同的语言，但若细较起来，其无论内涵与外形，皆可谓大异其趣。模糊感，在英语，它是支流，在汉语，则是主流。

汉语的模糊性呈现了更多普遍存在的个性特征。有学者在对汉语60种修辞格一一进行计量调查之后，发现单从定义和经典例句来看，与模糊修辞密切关联的约占80%。

究其原因，很大程度上在于汉语在字词内部结构与外部形态的特殊性，增强了汉字的表意功能与暗示能力，造成了汉语模糊性的特殊化和普遍性。在印欧语系中，词类和句子成分之间一般有对应关系。要打破对应，往往要通过构词手段或句法手段使词性转化。汉语则不同，每个字都充满独立性，宛如一个封闭的世界，其内在的一笔一画，或象形，或会意，都有其意义，阅读时单个字的内部偏旁部首都可以拆开理解。而且汉字在句法功能上是多功能的，无论是用作动词、形容词、名词、单数、复数、现在时、过去时等使用时，字形上是同一的；专有名词与普通名词之间，也没有通过大小写加以区分。再加上书写时字词之间无需空格，组成词的字与字之间往往既可以合成一个词来理解，也可以拆开成为含义不相干、句法成分也不一样的两个独立成分。种种因素表明，汉语在其发展历程中，并未尽力朝着清晰化的方向发展，而是拥抱了一套完整的模糊机制。比如：

[例1] 某同学背单词迎战四级，终于累倒生病住院，朋友来到病房探望。病床边，朋友握起他的手："你还好吧？医生怎么说？""Doctor."

[例2] 人过大佛寺，寺佛大过人。

[例3] 又一日，塞北送酥一盒至。操自写"一合酥"三字于盒上，置之案头。修入见之，竟取匙与众分食讫。操问其故。修答曰："盒上明书'一人一口酥'，岂敢违丞相之命乎？"

此外，汉语的模糊性见证了专制环境下汉民族"态度"文化的发展历程。对中国文化影响深远的孔子编《春秋》，开启了"春秋笔法"。在恶劣的环境下，他不得不用"曲笔"以讲"微言大义"，很多时候真实性反而居次，形成了尊讳亲隐、迂回转进、寓褒贬于曲折的文笔。比如，《春秋》中有一则，"郑伯克段于鄢"，虽然只是六个字，却记录了这样一件大事：鲁隐公元年，郑国君之弟共叔段，谋划夺取哥哥郑庄公的君位，庄公发现后，巧施心计，采取欲擒故纵的手段，诱使共叔段得寸进尺，愈加骄横，然后在鄢这个地方打败共叔段，使他"出奔"。《左传》对《春秋》这句经文隐含的褒贬用意解释道："书曰：'郑伯克段于鄢。'段不弟，故不言弟。如二君，故曰克。称郑伯，讥失教也。谓之郑志。不言出奔，难之也。"《春秋》中这句话，从表面上看，似乎是纯客观的记录，不流露作者的思想倾向，实际上是有褒有贬的，是以隐晦的方式传递一种态度。

经过"罢黜百家，独尊儒术"之后，这种"曲笔"写法得到了极大的传播推广，以至于汉民族形成了"王顾左右而言他"，讲究弦外之音，委婉、含蓄、藏而不露的民族性格。可以说，千载以来，每个中国人都是运用"春秋笔法"的大师，区别只是在于自觉与不自觉，好与不好的程度上，致使汉语的模糊性特征更为明显。如中学教材《内蒙访古》中，谈到赵长城时，作者写道："不知从什么时候起，在秦始皇面前就站着一个孟姜女，控诉这条举世闻名的万里长城。"在这里，作者用了一句"不知从什么时候起"，扩大了句子的容量，增加了许多附加信息，鲜明表明自己的观点。作为历史学家，坦言自己不知孟姜女何许人也，可见此人纯属子虚乌有。从逻辑上讲，她的控状自然不能成立。作为攻击秦始皇的主要"炮弹"都不能成立，那么对秦始皇就有个重新评价、重新认识的问题。这样后面讴歌赵武灵王就来得自然流畅了。再如，曾国藩初期与太平军交战总是惨败，实在无法向清廷交差，他的幕僚把报告中"臣屡战屡败"改成"臣屡败屡战"，立即从倒霉蛋变成悲情英雄，是典型的"春秋笔法"。

一方面，通过模糊隐晦的曲笔来暗示某种态度或意念是汉语文化的一个重要传统，另一方面，以清楚明晰的语言来传递理性逻辑则是英语文化的精髓。自古希腊始，西方哲学围绕 Logocentrism（逻各斯中心主义，即理性语言中心论）展开，致力于 "ultimate truth（终极真理）" 的求索，强调理性与语言间的对应统一。理性认知精神被归结为语言对现实本质的概括阐释，注重语言运用的逻辑与规范，相信语言逻辑与事物逻辑相吻合，使语言服从现实理性支配，而非像汉语那样服从于意念，受人情、感觉的支配。近代以来，自然科学的成就,科技理论的发达,使理性认知传统进一步加强,认识论成为西方哲学的基本视野,清晰的逻辑化语言被认为是表达真理唯一可靠的工具。

从语言本身来说,英语带有较强的综合语特征,即有形态变化,有大小写,有词性变化,重形合衔接,这些都使得英语单词句法功能固定、明确,含义清楚、确切,天然有着精确性的倾向,从而导致英语行文讲究简洁明快、逻辑严谨、文风质朴。

[例4] On one of those sober and rather melancholy days, in the later part of Autumn, when the shadows of morning and evening almost mingle together, and throw a gloom over the decline of the year, I passed several hours in rambling about Westminster Abbey. There was something congenial to the season in the mournful magnificence of the old pile; and, as I passed its threshold, seemed like stepping back into the regions of antiquity, and losing myself among the shades of former age.

时方晚秋,气象肃穆,晨昏莫辨,略带忧郁。我就在这么一个岁将云暮、昏昏沉沉的时节,到西敏大寺去散步了几个钟头。古寺巍巍,森森然似有鬼气,和阴沉沉的气候正好调和;我跨进大门,恍如置身远古,相忘于古人的鬼影之中。

[例5] When the light has become a little stronger, you have one of the fairest and softest pictures imaginable. You have the intense green of the massed and crowded foliage nearby; you see it paling shade by shade in front of you; upon the next projecting cape, a mile off or more, the tint has lightened to the tender young green of spring; the cape beyond that one has almost lost colour, and the furthest one, miles away under the horizon, sleeps upon the water a mere dim vapour, and hardly separable from the sky above it and about it. And all this stretch of river is a mirror, and you have shadowy reflections of the leafage and the curving shores and the receding capes pictured in it. Well, this is all beautiful; and when the sun get well up, and distributes a pink flush here and a powder of gold yonder and a purple haze where it will yield the best effect, you grant that you have something that is worth remembering.

等到昕昀烁夜,展现在眼前的便是一幅至柔至美的画卷:身前身后的树木枝繁叶茂、堆绿叠翠，浓黛浅消。放眼望去，一英里开外有一个河岬，河岬上的树木淡妆轻抹，仿佛春天般的娇嫩；远处的河岬则树色隐隐，微茫难辨；地平线尽头的河岬似乎枕在水面上，像一团迷蒙蒸腾的雾，融入浩渺的水天之中。广阔的河面好似一面巨大的镜子，淡淡地映照着丛集的枝叶、曲折的河岸和渐行渐远的河岬，勾勒出一幅生动的画面，轻柔婉转，超逸绵邈。太阳慢慢爬上天空，或浅红横突，或金粉竖抹，或紫霭漫洒，奇异曼妙，难以言传。这一切，能不令人怀想？

英语原文的结构严谨，用词简明、朴实，跟汉语译文结构简约，词意模糊适成对照，却又相映生辉。

相对而言，英语对模糊美感的追求则从未成为主流，乃是带有较强功利色彩的刻意为之，比如运用抽象词汇，以示学养深厚；利用词汇的转义，追求表达之形象；运用各色辞格，以求委婉；运用歧义，获得幽默，等等。但无论如何，它绝不类于汉语的模糊美感，不是那种自然而然的、信手拈来的产物。

2. 模糊美的普适性

汉语重模糊，英语重确切，这只是相对而言的一个概念。事实上，每种语言都是既有模糊性，又有精确性。鉴于模糊性更难把握，本节就主要分析一下英汉语在模糊性方面的差异。

在某些方面，语言趋向模糊，可令表达平添一种含蓄慰藉的委婉，具有一种磨语锋、藏峥嵘的圆融之美，符合语用学的"礼貌原则"，是社会文明进步的必然。这可以从以下一些层面反映出来。

（1）求委婉。

[例6] I used to think I was poor. Then they told me I wasn't poor; I was needy. Then they said it was self-defeating to think of myself as needy, that I was culturally deprived. Then they told me deprived was a bad image, that I was underprivileged. Then they told me that underprivileged was overused, that I was disadvantaged. I still don't have a dime. But I have a great vocabulary.

我以前总认为自己很穷，后来他们告诉我说我并非"穷"，而是"匮乏的"；而后他们说认为自己"匮乏"未免自我坍台，还是说"被剥夺文化教育权利的"；而后他们又说"被剥夺"三字形象不佳，应该说，"享有较少权益的"；而后他们又说这个说法已经用腻了，现在该说"缺乏有利条件的"。到头来我还是一文不名，可词儿却有了一大堆。

在上例中，poor → needy → culturally → deprived → underprivileged → disadvantaged 五个形容词一字排开，从明晰到模糊，从简单到复杂。最后，"poor"这个再简单不过的意思，居然用"disadvantaged（缺乏有利条件的）"这样一个云遮雾罩的词来表示。

（2）求文采。

文采往往意味着不能太直白，因为直白那会压缩读者的想象空间。相反，遣词浅显、句义空泛的文笔，往往能够营造出意境模糊的美好氛围。

[例7] The true artist lets himself go. He is natural. He swims easily in the stream of his own temperament... He becomes all men in himself. ... The function of the artist is to disturb... He makes uneasy the static, the set and the still... He is an agitator, a disturber of the peace, quick, impatient, positive, restless and disquieting. (Norman Bethune *The True Artist*)

真正的艺术家是狂放不羁的。他自由自在，悠然自得畅游于自己个性的川流中。……他成了所有人的化身。……艺术家的职责就是要惊世骇俗……他令平静、凝滞、死寂的一切苏活……他又是擅长鼓动、乐于打破平静的活动家。他机智敏锐，自信乐观，热烈急切，不满现状，激人奋发。

由以上例子可以看出，喜好含蓄并非中国文化所独有，相反，性格比较外向的西方民族并不排斥模糊与含蓄。可以说，鉴于其内涵较之精确语言具有更多的暗示性、蕴含性、妥帖性、独创性、简洁性、音乐性等特点，模糊性是自然语言的共性，具有更高的审美价值。古今中外，都有着对模糊表达的追求，但是其发展程度或有先后，侧重方面或有异同，在翻译实务中构成重大的语际转换障碍。

（二）英汉语模糊性的常见形式

1. 汉语模糊表达常见形式

（1）叠音词。

汉语的叠音词，不仅音美，而且意美，意美就美在模糊，美在让读者心领神会，却难以逻辑与分析使之精确化。比如写女孩，用"楚楚"，用"婷婷"，写杨柳，用"依依"，写远山，用"苍苍莽莽"，等等，其形如何，其状为甚，纵有丹青妙笔，也难以捕捉，偏又似乎人人都能感触某种玄妙灵动的丰姿。

[例8] 念天地之悠悠，独怅然而涕下。

Heaven and earth would forever last;
In loneliness I shed tears from my heart.

[例9] 那晚月儿已瘦削了两三分。她晚妆才罢，盈盈的上了柳梢头。天是蓝得可爱，仿佛一汪水似的；月儿便更出落得精神了。岸上原有三株两株的垂杨树，淡淡的影在水里摇曳着。它们那柔细的枝条浴着月光，就像一支支美人的臂膊，交互的缠着，挽着；又像是月儿披着的发。（朱自清：《桨声灯影里的秦淮河》）

That night the moon was a little slimmer. Having made up herself, she gracefully rose up on the tip of a willow, unveiling a more spiritual look in the lovely sky as azure as a bowl of water. On the bank were those couples of poplar trees swaying their translucent shadows in the river. Their branches twisted and coiled up like arms of nymph showered in the moonlight, as if the hairs of the moon.

以上各例，"悠悠""盈盈""淡淡"，读之，可放缓速度，淡雅而从容，诵之，可产生意象，朦胧而迷离，从音美到形美，从形美到意美，美轮美奂，充满了妙不可言的神韵。如此享受，英译文实难补偿。

再看下例：

[例10] It was a day as fresh as grass growing up and clouds going over and butterflies coming down can make it. It was a day compounded from silences of bee and flower and ocean and land, which were not silences at all, but motions, stirs, flutters, risings, fallings, each in its own time and matchless rhythm.

绿草萋萋，白云冉冉，彩蝶翩翩，这日子是如此清新可爱；蜜蜂无言，春花不语，海波声歇，大地音寂，这日子是如此安静。然而并非安静，因为万物各以其特有的节奏，或动，或摇，或震，或起，或伏。

"绿草萋萋，白云冉冉，彩蝶翩翩"，这里的叠音词，以汉语为母语者，能讲出、能析出其具体含义者，也许并不多。不能讲出，无法析出，主要原因在于其模糊。这种模糊，并非语义层面的模糊。当这些叠音词描写的是一种感受、一种意境，以神驭形，情景交融的时候，那是不可能讲得清、道得明的，同时也是没有必要去讲清楚道明白的。

（2）赋比兴。

赋就是铺陈，是将一连串内容紧密关联的景观物象、事态现象、人物形象和性格行为，按照一定的顺序铺排，组成结构基本相同、语气基本一致的句群，既可以淋漓尽致地细腻铺写，又可以一气贯注、加强语势，还可以渲染某种环境、气氛和情绪，如：

［例 11］七月流火，九月授衣。（《诗经·国风·豳风·七月》）

在富丽华美的汉赋和诗词作品中，赋法被广泛地采用，与四六骈体等排偶结构结合，特别措意于音律的和谐。《乐记》谈到音乐的由来，说："凡音之起，由人心生也。人心之动，物使之然也。感于物而动，故形于声"。"韵协则言顺，言顺则声易入"，当赋法叠加排偶，自易产生"骈四俪六，锦心绣口"的效果，更添一番韵味，在浓郁的对称美和节奏感中，透着一种整体意境上的模糊美。虽然经不起严格的逻辑推敲，但并不影响中国人对它们的大致意象或整体感悟，因为在中国人的文化里，特别注重"悟性"，能够从整体上去把握这种凝练而又铺陈的骈偶结构，捕捉住那一丝难以言说的玄妙之美。

［例 12］我不能忘记那一天

夕阳在山，清风微漾。（梁宗岱《途遇》）

How can I forget that evening:

The sun setting on the mountains,

the air rippling with a gentle breeze. （庞秉钧　闵福德　高尔登译）

"The sun setting on the mountains, the air rippling with a gentle breeze"与"夕阳在山，清风微漾"字面上基本对应，其意境之美，则差之远矣。再来看下例英译汉中通过四六骈体营造出来的美感：

［例 13］The shows of day, the dewy morning, the rainbow, mountains, orchards in blossom, stars, moonlight, shadows in still water, and the like, if too eagerly hunted, become shows merely, and mock us with their unreality. （Ralph Waldo Emerson *Beauty*）

一天阴晴的变化，多露的早晨，彩虹与星星，青山一抹，桃李满园，明月清辉，碧潭疏影等等美景，假如求之过切，反而成了皮相之美，美景犹如幻境，看者未免扫兴。（夏济安　译）

比就是类比，是以彼物比此物。用来作比的事物往往比本体事物更加生动具体、鲜明浅近，便于人们联想和想象。比如：

［例 14］手如柔荑，肤如凝脂，领如蝤蛴，齿如瓠犀，螓首蛾眉，巧笑倩

兮，美目盼兮。(《诗经·卫风·硕人》)

兴是有感，是先言他物以激发读者的联想，即依据事物微妙处来寄托意义，引起情感，产生形象鲜明、意蕴悠长的艺术效果。正如刘勰在《文心雕龙·明诗》中说，"人禀七情，应物斯感，感物吟志，莫非自然"。比如：

[例15] 长亭外，古道边，
　　　　芳草碧连天。
　　　　晚风拂柳笛声残，
　　　　夕阳山外山。
　　　　天之涯，地之角，
　　　　知交半零落。
　　　　一壶浊酒尽余欢，
　　　　今宵别梦寒。(李叔同《送别》)

赋比兴三者中，比、兴二者尤为重要，相对而言，比显而兴隐，所以运用的方式略有不同。但都不外乎情景交融，意在言外，其作用是要从骨子里去体会的。龙榆生先生在《词学十讲·论比兴》中指出，"比兴手法，总不外乎情和景，外景和内心的恰相融会，或后先激射，或神光离合，要以言近旨远、含蕴无尽为最富于感染力"，而使作者内蕴的深厚情感，成为"言有尽而意无穷"的弦外之音。

这种言在此而意在彼的内蕴，也就是古诗词先贤大家所说的"寄托"。刘熙载在《诗概》中说："'昔我往矣，杨柳依依。今我来思，雨雪霏霏。'(《诗经·小雅·鹿鸣之什·采薇》)雅人深致，正在借景言情。"他又在《词曲概》中说："词深于兴，则觉事异而情同，事浅而情深。故没要紧语正是极要紧语，乱道语正是极不乱道语……"

诚如王国维所言，"无我之境，以物观物，故不知何者为我，何者为物。""雾失楼台，月迷津渡""寒波澹澹起，白鸟悠悠下"，比兴手法就是这样，淡淡著笔，寓情于景，而读之似有似无，"剪不断，理还乱"，袅袅余音不断萦绕于灵魂深处。

再看下例：

[例16] 缺月挂疏桐，漏断人初静。
　　　　谁见幽人独往来，
　　　　缥缈孤鸿影。
　　　　惊起却回头，有恨无人省。
　　　　拣尽寒枝不肯栖，

寂寞沙洲冷。(苏轼《卜算子》)

纵有无限感伤，也只是用寻常景语烘托出来，寄情于物，"骚情雅意，哀怨无端，读者亦不自知何以心醉，何以泪堕？"

(3) 模糊附加词。

汉语和英语都有模糊附加词。但是，相对而言，汉语的模糊附加词不仅数量众多，而且，其模糊度也更大一些。仅以"然"字为例，在汉语中，以"然"字为后缀的词语，简直不计其数。不仅有"A+然"的结构，而且还有"A+A+然"的结构。这个后缀"然"字一添加，清晰便演绎成模糊，言传幻化成了意会。比如，"邯郸旧梦，对此惘然"中的"惘然"，能与 at a loss 画等号吗？所谓"惘然"，兼有"模糊不清、怅然若失"等只宜意会难以言说之感，又岂是 at a loss 所能概括的？

再看以下各例：

[例 17] 古之真人，不知说生，不知恶死。其出不欣，其入不距。翛然而往，翛然而来而已矣。(《庄子·内篇·大宗师》)

The true man of old did not know what it was to love life or to hate death. They did not rejoice in birth, nor strive to put off dissolution. Unconcerned they came and unconcerned they went. That was all. (林语堂 译)

[例 16] 是之谓不以心捐道，不以人助天。凄然似秋，暖然似春，喜怒通四时，与物有宜而莫知其极。《庄子·内篇·大宗师》

This is what is called not to lead the heart astray from Tao, and not to supplement the natural by human means. Sometimes disconsolate like autumn, and sometimes warm like spring, their joys and sorrows are in direct touch with the four seasons, in harmony with all creation, and none know the limit thereof. (林语堂 译)

(4) 高度省略。

行文省略，即语义留白。留白是中国艺术追求的一种空灵境界。中国画、中国戏剧、中国诗文，皆有"留白"之说。留白，即营造模糊的主要艺术手段之一，不仅符合艺术创作的规律，而且能给受众留下遐想和创造的空间，乃是一种"似有还无"之感，可谓"此时无声胜有声"。

[例 17] 青青子佩，

悠悠我思，

纵我不往，

子宁不来。(《诗经·国风·郑风·子衿》)

O you with the blue (strings to your) girdle-gems,

Long, long do I think of you.

Although I do not go (to you),

Why do you not come (to me)? (James Legge 译)

上例中留白部分通过比较英译一目了然，只是英译中没了留白之后，神韵也便荡然无存。

汉语的用词组句，偏重心理，略于形式。它没有单复数、没有分词、没有大小写，没有动词、名词、形容词、副词的形态变化，重意合而非形合，主语、连接词都可以省略，古代汉语甚至连标点符号都没有，因此汉语的语句繁简自如，虚实相间，弹性很大。它强调体验与感悟，重视个性与创造，常呈现多义性、模糊性特征。如李白的《静夜思》："床前明月光，疑是地上霜。举头望明月，低头思故乡。"诗中的人称和时态都不加限制，思念的主体即句子的主语被省略，可以是诗人，可以是他人，也可以是读者自己，动词的时态可以由读者自己去补充，使得诗歌意境深远，令人回味不已。

[例18] 床前明月光，　　Abed, I see a silver light,

疑是地上霜。　　I wonder if it's frost aground.

举头望明月，　　Looking up, I find the moon bright;

低头思故乡。　　Bowing, in homesickness I'm drowned.

(李白《静夜思》许渊冲　译)

需要指出的是，囿于其对严谨语法结构的刚性要求，英语对留白的使用远不如汉语频繁，这在诗歌中表现得尤其明显，较之中国古诗词的浓烈，英文诗歌平淡得多，可以说是弗如远甚。很多汉语古诗词在翻译成英文后，加上了完整的主谓结构、连接词以及时态等形态变化，便如同一杯清香浓郁的春茶混入了一桶自来水，立时清香尽去，淡而无味了。这也从一个侧面说明，留白能够创造出令人回味无穷的凝练朦胧的美，在其长期熏陶下，中国人早已习惯了浓浓的汉诗唐韵，而英语诗歌虽有其深沉内敛之特色，但在中国人读来，往往觉得不过瘾，"不像诗"。汉诗英译自不消说，就更容易让国人失落了。

如果说上例还是古诗词，那么下面《阿Q正传》中的一句话则说明，现代白话汉语的高度省略也是屡见不鲜的：

[例19] 阿Q没有家，住在本社的土谷祠里；没有固定的职业，只给人家做短工，割麦便割麦，舂米便舂米，撑船便撑船。(鲁迅《阿Q

正传》）

假如把省略部分补充出来，就应该是：

阿Q没有家，（他）住在本社的土谷祠里；没有固定的职业，只给人家做短工，（人家叫他）割麦（他）便割麦，（人家叫他）舂米（他）便舂米，（人家叫他）撑船（他）便撑船。

再来看看它的英语译文：

Ah Q had no family but lived in the Tutelary God's Temple at Weizhuang. He had no regular work either, being simply an odd-job man for others: When there was wheat to be cut he would cut *it*; when there was rice to be hulled he would hull *it*; when there was a boat to be punted he would punt *it*. （杨宪益　戴乃迭　译）

括号内的词语，汉语可以省略，英语却省略不得，反过来英语中用的替换手法，汉语却又大多用了重复字词。由是可见，汉语表达重在以意统形，辞约义丰，体现出一种线性的流动，既充满重复，又有着大量的省略，语言组织松散脱落却又生动活泼。

2. 英语模糊表达常见形式

（1）抽象词汇。

英语中有许多词汇，意义抽象，在汉语中缺乏对等的表达，如 size, dimension, credit, identify, privacy, community, shelter 等等。在英语中，这些寻常词汇，其语义内涵却具有相当的模糊性。换言之，以汉语为母语者，很难充分理解到利用此类词汇的模糊语义。比如，"distraction" 的基本含义是"分散注意力"。但它还有别的一些含义，具有明显的模糊色彩，如：

［例20］ Distraction is his usual strategy.
　　　　他特别爱搞声东击西。

［例21］ She sought the distraction of distance.
　　　　她想要远走高飞，免得心烦。

（2）词的转义。

英语词典之所以厚，部分原因在于，一个单词除了其本义之外，往往还有几个、十几个，甚至几十个的转义、引申义、比喻义。请看下例英译文中"home"与"west"的引申义所带来的朦胧美感：

［例22］归巢的鸟儿，　　　　　　The homing bird,
　　　　尽管是倦了，　　　　　　Though tired,
　　　　还是托着斜阳回去。　　　Still carries back the westering sun.

| | |
|---|---|
| 双翅一翻， | Flaps his wings, |
| 把斜阳掉在江上， | Drops the sun on the river; |
| 头白的芦苇， | And the white-haired reeds |
| 也妆成一瞬的红颜了。 | Wear an instant of rouge. |

（刘大白《秋晚的江上》庞秉钧　闵福德　高尔登　译）

(3) 修辞手法。

与许多人的印象相反，作为一种较为成熟、理性的现代语言，英语是很注意说话的分寸感的，很多时候甚至反而不像当代的某些缺少文化传承的国人那样唐突、直接。

在众多英语修辞格中，委婉语、暗指、低调陈述都是运用间接、温和的语言形式来追求语义的模糊、淡化，产生清晰化为模糊，开门见山化为云遮雾障的效果，其中尤以低调陈述最为突出。所谓低调陈述，乃是用一种弱化的或有节制的词语替代一种较直接的、唐突的言辞。低调陈述常常用于日常生活、社会交际或政治生活中，大都具有平和动听的作用，借以达到避免刺激、缓和气氛、掩饰窘态、表示谦虚、讲究礼节的目的，是一种用善意的话语把事实掩盖起来的修辞手段，体现了较为成熟的同理心。请看下例：

[例 23] An Englishman will say "I have a little house in the country". When he invites you to stay with him, you will discover that the little house is a place with three hundred bedrooms. If you are a world tennis champion, say "I don't play too badly". If you have crossed the Atlantic alone in a small boat, say "I do a little sailing".

一个英国人会说，"我在乡下有个小屋。"可是当他邀你与他同住时，你会发现，"小屋"竟是包括了 300 间卧室的豪宅。如果你是网球世界冠军，要说"是的，我的网球打得不算太糟"。如果你有孤舟横渡大西洋之壮举，也只是说"我会点航海"。

（三）清晰与模糊的翻译

1. 翻译转换中模糊美感尤易磨蚀

作为典型的意合语言，汉语较少使用连词、介词、关系代词等逻辑标志，又常省略主语；作为分析型语言，它较少语法限制，没有单复数、时态、形容词词缀、副词词缀等形态变化，其结果既造成了汉语字词组合巧妙多变，能用较少的语言表达丰富的含义,也造成了句子成分之间缺乏明确的语义关系,歧义结构特别多。例如:"我和他的老师""热爱学校的教授""找到了孩子的妈妈",等等。汉语中很多句子,一旦摆脱语境就既可以做这样理解,也可以那样理解,各种语义关系难以精确界定,于是汉语中的话语形式经常表现出一定的模糊性。正如洪堡所言:"在汉语的句子里,每个词摆在那儿,要你斟酌,要你从各种不同的关系去考察,然后才能往下读。由于思想的联系是由这些关系产生的,因此,这一纯粹的默想就代替了一部分语法。"

汉语在语法上的这个特点使汉语虽不太适宜精密地描写对象与表达思想,但它立足于读者的悟性,整体的悟性,自有其句法流散、自由、模糊的独特气质。而由于英语是以语法规范为首要之义,以逻辑明晰为主流美学,主语是主语,谓语是谓语,宾语是宾语,连词、介词、冠词、代词、冠词,"一个也不能少"。请看下例:

[例24] The young girls laugh as they drive the geese over the rocks; they laugh as they climb the low stone walls with their baskets; they laugh as they call off the wild dogs that threaten to devour the stranger; they laugh most of all, so I am told, on evenings at dance time when the men are home from overseas and the fiddles twitter over the hills of Achill like birds under an eave.

A:当年轻的姑娘们把鹅赶过乱石滩时,她们大笑;当她们背着竹篮越过石垒矮墙时,她们大笑;当她们驱赶走威胁吞噬陌生人的野狗时,她们大笑;当男人们从海外归来后,在晚间的舞会时间,她们笑得最厉害了,那时候小提琴在阿基尔岛的山野间回荡,就像鸟儿在屋檐下鸣叫。

B:年轻的姑娘们欢笑着把鹅赶过乱石滩;她们欢笑着身背竹篮,越过石垒矮墙;她们欢笑着赶跑吓坏陌生人的吠狗。她们笑得最快乐的时候,莫过于在男人们从海外归来后举办的晚间舞会上,那时候小提琴在阿基尔岛的山野间回荡,就像鸟儿在屋檐下婉转啁啾。

在译文 A 中,按照英语的习惯,语法完整了,时间关系词等衔接清晰明了,但流散、自由结构滋养的默想、咀嚼、感悟,也都没有了,让位于清晰直白,美感自然磨蚀,甚至拘谨以至于啰嗦,效果远远不如做了做了模糊化处理、句法关系、字词含义相对不那么清晰的译文 B。

除了上述的语法差异因素,汉语重意境、讲究铺陈、写意、妍美,英语注重逻辑分析、讲究写实的巨大文化差异,也会导致模糊美感在翻译中虽说偶或挽留,但却多有磨蚀,使得模糊与清晰的翻译转换成为一个十分棘手的问题。

2. 模糊与清晰的转换模式

如前所述,英语是以语法规范为首要之义,以逻辑明晰为主流美学,模糊感在英语中是支流,在汉语中则是主流。因此,汉英两种不同的主流美学之间,呈现出颇为复杂的转换模式。大致说来,模糊与清晰的转换,有下面几种情况:

(1) 清晰→清晰。

[例25]　今夜,复自弹这一曲调　　Tonight, I pluck this tune once more
　　　　悲凉如冰刀　　　　　　　Mournful as an icy knife

　　　　缺憾的是年龄的半边　　　Half my age is disappointment
　　　　岁月交驰于额　　　　　　The years race across my brow
　　　　交齿于额　　　　　　　　Bite into each other on my forehead

　　　　悬崖落马处　　　　　　　On the cliff, where the horse falls
　　　　必将有一轮斜月孤明　　　Must shine a solitary, waning moon
　　　　冷冷为我奠祭　　　　　　Pouring me a cold, cold libation
　　　　(洪素丽《今夜》庞秉钧　闵福德　高尔登　译)

译文中对原文里各种形象化的语言进行了基本对应的文本转换,较好地再现了原诗的风格,令人印象深刻。

(2) 清晰→模糊。

[例26] 花园里面是人生的乐园,有吃不完的大米白面,穿不完的绫罗绸缎和用不完的金银财宝。

　　A：The garden was the paradise of life, with more rice and flour than could be eaten, more silk and satin than could be used for clothes, and more gold, silver and other treasuries than could be spent.

　　B：The garden was the paradise on earth, with more food and clothes than could be consumed and more money than could be spent.

相对于"rice and flour""silk and satin""gold, silver and other treasuries","food""clothes""money"较为笼统模糊,读来更加流畅自然。

（3）模糊→清晰。

［例 27］Many men have recognized the similarity of plants to the behavior of animals, and have dreamed wistfully, but forlornly, upon some method or source of rejuvenation such as Ponce de Leon sought in the Fountain of Youth several centuries ago.

A：许多人已经认识到植物的行为与动物的行为有相似之处，于是就梦想着有某种方法或来源能使人返老还小，就像几个世纪前庞塞·德·莱昂在青春泉中寻找的那样，结果难免失意。

B：许多人认为，植物的习性与动物相似，于是梦寐以求地去探索什么"返老还童"的"灵丹妙药"，就像数百年前彭斯·德·利昂在青春泉祈求仙水一样，结果只能是竹篮打水一场空。

模糊虚泛的"method or source"译文 A 字面直译为"方法"，译文 B 改为"灵丹妙药"，"forlornly"译文 A 字面直译为"失意"，效果也是一般，译文 B 改为清晰明了的"竹篮打水一场空"，立显生动形象。

（4）模糊→模糊。

［例 28］Aside from damaging the island's international image, Liao said the skimpily clad women caused car accidents and spurred juvenile crime. He said they attracted the attention of teenagers who got into fights, even though sex isn't generally on offer.

A：除了有损此岛的国际形象之外，廖说，这些穿"三点式"服装的女子常诱发小轿车的交通事故，导致少年犯罪。他说，这些女子对十几岁的青少年颇具诱惑力，而常引起斗殴，即使这些女子通常不出卖其肉体。

B：除了有损此岛的国际形象之外，廖说，这些女子穿着太过"清凉"，常诱发交通事故，引发青少年犯罪。他说，这些女子对十几岁的青少年颇具诱惑力，而常引起斗殴，尽管这些女子通常不从事色情交易。

上例中的 skimpily clad 值得咀嚼。其字面意思就是"很吝啬地用一丁点布料蔽体的"，含着一种幽默味儿。译文 a 将其处理为"穿'三点式'服装的女子"，实属引申过分，明晰过度，失却了模糊处理可以获得的朦胧美。同样，"car accidents"译为"小轿车的交通事故"也是典型的貌似精确，其实大谬；"even though sex isn't generally on offer"译为赤裸裸的"即使这些女子通常不出卖其肉体"更是让人反感。

如斯可见,朦胧的译文,有时能获得表达的贴切和优雅。

## 二、写意与写实

### (一)汉语的写意倾向与英语的写实倾向

言之无文,行而不远。世界上所有的说话者都会尽量营造出语言的美感,而各个民族内部由于长期的共同交流,形成了有别于其他民族的语言美感。

踏遍青山不是山。中国人非常熟悉空灵朦胧的写意,惯于从整体上去找感觉,去体会意境;而西方人则相反,他们会把描写当作清楚明白的写实,会对每一个字都条分缕析地较真解析。

翻翻中国绘画史,就会知道,中国士大夫偏好带有"禅意"的泼墨山水画,近看枝节一团乱麻,远望整体空灵飘逸。中国古代文人讲究"雅",诗、书、画、文须得样样精通,其美学艺术与其文学艺术自然互相影响,在长期的潜移默化之下,形成了汉语重悟性(而非逻辑)、重主体意识(而非个体意识)、重整体意境(而非结构解析)的独特语言心理。一言以蔽之,汉语有这么一个显著特征:"迷离中传递语义,朦胧中孕育意境",迷离最好,朦胧最美!

如果说汉语是迷离之中找感觉,英语就是清晰之中求写实。相对而言,虽然英语也有朦胧、模糊的时候,但并不突出。相反,英语突出的特点是:逻辑与分析携手、语义清朗、结构清楚、表述明晰。

### (二)写意的基础

朦胧空灵的意境是怎样营造出来的呢?

1. 虚实相生

从写作素材上说,乃是意与境谐,虚实相生。王国维有言:"境非独谓景物也。喜怒哀乐,亦人心中之一境界。故能写真景物、真感情者,谓之有境界。否则谓之无境界。""境"虽说偏于物,但在这里更侧重于情的注入。也就是说,境界之成,乃情景交融,物我合一,如:

[例1] 坐潭上,四面竹树环合,寂寥无人,凄神寒骨,悄怆幽邃。(柳宗元《小石潭记》)

虽只21个汉字,却是既有"情感"("凄""寒""寂寥""悄怆"),又有"景物"("潭上""竹树环合""神""骨"),而且虚实交叉相配("凄"与

"神","寒"与"骨","悄怆"与"幽邃"),虽只寥寥几句,却已情景交融,形神兼备,虚又似为实,实又似为虚,交织缠绕,莫可分别。

2. 凝练

从字词组合上来说,乃是凝练。通过上句我们还可以看到,汉字简直就是一个个各具灵气的小精灵,只要排列出奇,组合凝练,三言两语,就能出景、出情,意境深远。如:

[例2] 清风徐来,水波不兴。举酒属客,诵明月之诗,歌窈窕之章。少焉,月出于东山之上,徘徊于斗牛之间。白露横江,水光接天。纵一苇之所如,凌万顷之茫然。浩浩乎如冯虚御风,而不知其所止;飘飘乎如遗世独立,羽化而登仙。(苏轼《前赤壁赋》)

"清风徐来,水波不兴","白露横江,水光接天","纵一苇之所如,凌万顷之茫然"意境可谓深幽!"浩浩乎如冯虚御风,而不知其所止;飘飘乎如遗世独立,羽化而登仙"文笔又何其写意!这样的字词组合,关键就在凝练二字。凝练出美。唯其凝练,才能给读者留下朦胧迷离的空间,引导读者去品味那余音绕梁的含蓄美。

3. 骈偶

从句式上说,多采用"四言""八字",多对仗、排比、对偶,行文妍美、铺陈、节奏优美。(当然,从坏的方面说,反映出一种求和求同、尚慕虚华、堆砌重复的审美心理。)如:

[例3] 暧暧远人村,依依墟里烟。
狗吠深巷中,鸡鸣桑树颠。(陶渊明《归园田居》)

这一段文字,对偶铺陈妍美,收放自如,再加上优美的叠音词,音美、形美、意美如行云流水,空灵写意,真乃众妙毕集,给读者以绝美的视听享受,不啻欣赏了一曲高山流水,余音缭绕,回味悠长。

其可能的英语译文:

The villages afar located under the warm sun,

The village-market's smoke curling can be seen.

The dogs are barking in the inner passing lane,

In the mulberry, cocks call once again.

囿于英语本身的特点所限,译文无法完整再现原文的完美骈偶,其意境幽美,回味无穷的感觉,所余无几矣。

## （三）写意与写实的翻译转换

### 1. 写意汉语→写实英语

鉴于两种语言文化的巨大审美习惯差异，特别是由于英语世界较难领会朦胧写意的语言，因此，在汉翻英的时候，为了求得译文的"达"，有时必须在朦胧与明晰之间做出转换——往往还是痛苦的取舍。

（1）以实代虚。

以实代虚，可作退而求其次的选项。请看下例：

[例4] 余冬日往视，但见衰柳寒烟，一水茫茫而已。（沈复《浮生六记》）

> I went there, however, on a winter day and saw only a stretch of cold water against some sparse willow trees and a frosty sky. （林语堂 译）

原文既有"意"（"衰""寒""茫茫"），又有"境"（"冬日""柳""烟""水"），而且虚实交叉相配（"衰"与"柳"，"烟"与"寒"，"水"与"茫茫"），景随情动。情迁景移，典型的虚实相生写法，真可谓情景交融，深邃悠远。译文中，从"衰柳寒烟→some sparse willow trees and a frosty sky""一水茫茫而已→only a stretch of cold water"的转换中可以看到，原本空灵的"衰""烟"二字，皆由"虚"转"实"，被分别译成了 sparse 和 frosty，原本朦胧的"茫茫"也失去朦胧，被译成了 a stretch of。虽然原文的意境折损大半，但由于英语中缺乏相应的"虚"的词眼，译者也只能退而求其次，以实代虚，止步于描绘客观图景，表现思想感情了。

再看下例：

[例5] 寓居去江无十步，风涛烟雨，晓夕百变。江南诸山在几席，此幸未始有也。（苏轼《临皋闲题》）

> A: My house is only about a dozen steps from the bank of the river. The beautiful mountains of the South lie spread around my "desk" of mist over the river with all the winds and clouds while the view changes a hundred times a day. I have never had such luck before.
>
> B: My house is only about a dozen steps from the bank of the river. The beautiful mountains of the South lie spread before my window, and with the high winds and changing clouds and misty weather, the view changes a hundred times a day. I have

never had such luck before.

上例中，译文 A 的处理更好地保留了原文的美妙形象，但对于"desk"这个 metaphor，即使在书面语中也要加上引号以帮助读者理解。如果是在口头翻译场合，为了避免听众一头雾水，就只有像译文 B 般便宜从事，以实代虚了。

（2）凝练。

在确保文法正确的前提下，尽量做到凝练。

［例6］ 而或长烟一空，皓月千里，浮光跃金，静影沉璧，渔歌互答，此乐何极！登斯楼也，则有心旷神怡，宠辱皆忘，把酒临风，其喜洋洋者矣。（范仲淹《岳阳楼记》）

A：Or when dusk falls over this vast expanse and bright moon casts its light a thousand li, when the rolling waves glitter like gold and silent shadows in the water glimmer like jade, and the fishermen sing to each other for sheer joy, then men coming up to this pavilion may feel complete freedom of heart and ease of spirit, forgetting every worldly gain or setback, to hold their winecups in the breeze in absolute elation, delighted with life.

B：When dusk falls upon this vast expanse, and the moon shines over a thousand li; or when the gold waves roll past glimmering shades, and the fishermen sing to each other for sheer joy, men coming up here may, rejoicing in winecups amid breezes, feel complete ease of mind with all worldly gains and losses gone.

"浮光跃金""静影沉璧""渔歌互答""把酒临风"，这样凝练写意的文笔，在古汉语中运用极广。它们以单音节字词为基础进行组合，最能营造出朦胧迷离，令人心驰神往的意境。如果一字不漏地转换成英语，再加上英语对形合衔接和各种"主＋谓"语法结构的刚性要求，就成了处处做加法，原本富有韵味的凝练用语，就如同一杯馥郁香浓的龙井里掺了一大桶水，饮之无味了，译文 A 就是一个典型的例子。而译文 B 则按"有增有减、总体平衡"的原则，尽量朝着"等效凝练"的方向操作，比如，把与"浮光跃金"字面上对等的"rolling waves glitter like gold"简化为"gold waves"，与"静影沉璧"字面上对等的"silent shadows in the water glimmer like jade"也用同样的思路简化为"glimmering shades"。这就意味着在迁就英语的形合等刚性要求而增加字词的同时，作了大量的精简处理，尤其是删掉了很多汉语中很凝练（单音节），英语中则啰唆重复的形容词，效果显而易见：译文 B 的流畅度和韵味远胜译文 A。

然而，上例也告诉我们，英语到底是形合语言，要真说起凝练来，虽可奋力以求，但终究是没法跟汉语相比的。再看下面两例：

［例7］东坡居士酒醉饭饱，倚于几上，白云左绕，青江右回，重门洞开，林峦岔入。当是时，若有思而无所思，以受万物之备。惭愧，惭愧。（苏轼《临皋闲题》）

After a drink and a good meal, the Recluse of Eastern Slope leans over his desk, with white clouds on his left and the clear river on his right. Both the outer and the inner doors are wide open, giving a direct view of the hills and the peaks. At such a time I sit as if I were thinking of something and again as if I were thinking of nothing at all. In such a state of mind I receive so freely the bounty of nature spread before me, that I feel almost ashamed.（林语堂 译）

（3）简化铺排。

对一些行云流水般铺陈的对仗、排比，对音韵节奏，英译时无须强求。

［例8］有的人如游客，不急不慌，走走停停，看花开花落，看云卷云舒，有时也在风中走，雨里行，心却像张开的网，放过了焦躁烦恼。

A: Others travel leisurely like tourists. They would take time off now and then for a look at blooming flowers or fallen petals. They would stop to admire clouds gathering and dispersing. Even when they go against the wind or are caught in the rain, they never get annoyed, for worries slip off their mind as from an open net.

B: Others are like tourists, traveling leisurely. They take time off now and then, rejoicing in a look at blooming flowers, gathering clouds, and setting suns. Even when caught in wind and rain, they never get annoyed, for worries slip off their mind as from an open net.

上例中，译文 A 力图再现原文铺排华美、行云流水般的骈偶结构，但忽视了英语本身并不适合这样的结构，导致译文显得啰唆累赘。译文 B 放弃了铺排的骈偶结构,确保了基本的流畅度。

(4) 重组。

打破原文重复堆砌的铺陈,以明晰的条理进行结构重组。

[例9] 满树金花,芳香四溢的金桂;花白如雪,香气扑鼻的银桂;红里透黄,花多味浓的紫砂桂;花色似银,季季有花的四季桂;竞相开放,争妍媲美。进入桂花公园,阵阵桂香扑鼻而来。

The Park of Sweet Osmanthus is noted for its profusion of osmanthus trees. Flowers from these trees in different colors are in full bloom, pervading the whole park with pleasant fragrance.

上例原文,可谓以神驭形的汉语典范。词意重复,辞藻堆砌,在很大程度上是出于行文工整对仗的需要。一些文字意义模糊,且有些花名很难找到相应的英译。亦步亦趋的英译只会使译文读者莫名其妙,因此必须打破原文重复堆砌的铺陈,以明晰的条理进行结构重组,以精确译模糊,尽量使原文的含义摆脱朦胧,走进明朗。

若将英语译文"回译"为汉语,可以是:

桂花公园以其众多的桂花而著称,园内桂树上色彩各异的桂花盛开,使公园满溢着沁人心脾的芳香。

汉语,就是这样,铺陈渲染,文笔细腻,表意朦胧;英语,就是这样,干净利落,句意豁然,逻辑明晰。再比较下例中的译文 A 与译文 B:

[例10] 峡内重峦叠嶂,连绵不尽,奇峰异岭,高插入云,云雾弥漫,迷幻莫测。

A: On both sides of the gorges there are ranges upon ranges of rolling mountains. Everywhere you can see cliffs of unique shapes and peaks of fantastic aspects towering into the clouds. The mist and the low-lying clouds add an aura of mystery to the raw natural beauty.

B: Along the gorges are rolling mountains with piercing peaks and precipitous cliffs enveloped by magic clouds.

(5) 省略。

在渲染整体感觉时,写意语言局部地方可能会有夸张,个别细节甚至是矛盾的,不合情理的。对此,要细加甄别,可略去原文中不合情理的部分。

[例11] 一双丹凤三角眼,两弯柳叶吊梢眉,身量苗条,体格风骚,粉面含春威不露,丹唇未启笑先闻。(曹雪芹《红楼梦》)

She had the almond-shaped eyes of a phoenix, slanting eyebrows as long and drooping as willow leaves. Her figure was slender and her manner vivacious. The springtime charm of her powdered face gave no hint of her latent formidability. And before her crimson lips parted, her laughter rang out. （杨宪益　戴乃迭 译）

"三角眼"明明是市井刁民之眼，电视剧《地下交通站》里的贾贵便是"光辉"代表，与"丹凤眼"完全矛盾，何美之有？有人认为，"丹凤眼"写的是王大美人的外表，"三角眼"是内在心灵。无论懂与不懂，中国人大都习惯了这种出于心灵视点的写意手法。但老外却往往会单纯地从物理的具象视角来看，因而感到困惑不已。鉴于此，译者将"三角眼"译成了"almond-shaped eyes（杏仁眼）"。又如：

[例12] 临皋亭下十数步，便是大江，其半是峨眉雪水。吾饮食沐浴皆取焉，何必归乡哉？江水风月本无常主，闲者便是主人。闻范子丰新第园地，与此孰胜？所以不如君者，无两税及助役钱尔。（苏轼《临皋闲题》）

The Great River lies only a few dozen steps below me and half of its water comes from the Omei Mountain, so that it is almost as good as seeing our hometown. The hills and the river, the wind the moon, have no owner; they belong to anybody who has the leisure to enjoy them. How would your new garden compare with mine? I suppose you have the advantage of paying the summer and autumn taxes on it, and the draft exemption besides, while I don't. （林语堂　译）

2. 写实英语→写意汉语

以上分析多针对汉语写意倾向的英译。相对而言，汉语世界对于英语写实倾向的接受就要容易多了。因此，写实倾向的英语汉译时一般可照搬原文的写实风格，难度自然要小一些。但在某些文学材料中，译者仍可以挑战一下自己，尝试一下虚实相生、字词凝练、铺排妍美的技法，将相对写实的英语译成空灵写意的汉语。试比较下例的译文 A 和译文 B：

[例13] When I was as young as you are now, towering in confidence of twenty-one, little did I suspect that I should be at forty-nine, what I now am.

A：我像你这么年轻的时候，洋溢着二十一岁的冲天豪情，就没怎么想过会变成今天这个四十九岁的样子。

B：我在你这个年纪的时候，二十出头，小荷尖尖，意气风发，哪里会想到四十九岁今天的我呢？

［例 14］ It was a typical summer evening in June, the atmosphere being in such delicate equilibrium and so transmissive that inanimate objects seemed endowed with two or three senses, if not five. There was no distinction between the near and the far, and an auditor felt close to everything within the horizon. The soundlessness impressed her as a positive entity rather than as the mere negation of noise. It was broken by the strumming of strings.

A：那是一个典型的六月黄昏。大气的平衡如此精微，传导力如此敏锐，就连冥顽的无生物也有了知觉——如果不是五种知觉的话，也有两三种。远和近已经失去了差异，地平线以内的声音都仿佛近在咫尺。这一片寂静在她耳朵里并非是消极的默无声息，而仿佛是一种积极的实际存在。而这种声音却被拨弄琴弦的声音打破了。

B：这是六月里特有的夏日黄昏。暮色格外柔和静美且极富感染力，连那些冥顽之物都仿佛平添了几分灵性，有了各种知觉。远近一切，难分彼此；天际间任何一丝声息，听来都恍如近在耳畔。她觉得这静寂并非单纯的悄无声息，而是一种实实在在的感受。不想这静寂却被瑟瑟的琴声打破了。

［例 15］ Some fishing boats were becalmed just in front of us. Their shadow slept, or almost slept, upon that water, a gentle quivering alone showing that it was not complete sleep, or if sleep, that it was sleep with dreams.

A：一些渔船停泊在我们眼前。他们的影子在水面上睡着了，或者说是几乎睡着了。单单一个轻微的颤动就显示，它没有完全睡着，或者说，假如睡着了，那么，那也是一边睡着了，一边还在做梦。

B：渔舟三五，横泊眼前，樯影倒映水面，仿佛睡去，偶或微颤，似又未尝深眠，恍若惊梦。

当然，对于写实英语转换为写意汉语，一般以文学作品为宜。否则，就容易陷入浮夸的泥淖，甚或授人以柄，落人口实。试比较下例的译文 A 和译文 B：

[例 16] These were truly exceptional Games!

And now, in accordance with tradition, I declare the Games of the XXIX Olympiad closed, and I call upon the youth of the world to assemble four years from now in London to celebrate the Games of the XXX Olympiad.

A：这是一届真正的无与伦比的奥运会，现在，遵照惯例，我宣布第 29 届奥林匹克运动会闭幕，并号召全世界青年四年后在伦敦举办的第 30 届奥林匹克运动会上相聚。

B：这是一届非凡的奥运会，现在，遵照惯例，我宣布第 29 届奥林匹克运动会闭幕，并邀请全世界青年四年后在伦敦举办的第 30 届奥林匹克运动会上相聚。

上例真切地说明，写意思维如果不加控制，恣意蔓延，是有可能带来负面影响的。哲学家庞朴曾经提出一分为三的观点。他认为，在拥护与打倒之间，在歌颂与批判之间，在圣人和败类之间，在英明和昏乱之间，都应该允许有大规模的中间地带。自媒体时代的舆论和言说，却时常意气用事，在两极之间飘摇不定；公众的情绪，不断被气势汹汹的责骂和不假思索的感动所"引导"。食品没有添加剂，或一个人不偷东西，无非是做人、经营企业底线而已，如果达到了，就夸奖说是最美、最好、最感动，反过来，只要是不合自己意愿的，就是最雷人、最丑恶、最无耻，仿佛这世界，不是天堂就是地狱。语出惊人才能吸引眼球，回归常识却无人喝彩。这样的舆论生态，难免对人们的认知产生影响。于是，表态先于判断，判断先于思考。许多的观点，表达者追求的是转发、评论，而不是全面、理性的中肯；许多的争论，辩论者想要获得的是支持，是认同，而不是真相。换言之，很多人所追求的，实在于观点是否标新立异、耸人听闻，而不在于这些观点是不是真正经过深思熟虑，有没有稳定的价值判断，以及缜密的逻辑框架。其思维与文章，非黑即白，固执偏颇，轰动极端之余，面对淡定平实的论述，徒有一副呐喊者的强硬外壳，其实脆弱不堪一击。在翻译中如不细加甄别，极易陷入窘境。

## 三、华美与简洁

### (一) 汉语的华美倾向与英语的简洁倾向

从纯语言的角度来说,由于汉语句内讲究凝练朦胧,如果只有很单薄的一句,总觉意犹未尽,甚至不甚明了。反之,如果有了多个含义相近、凝练朦胧的压缩结构反复铺排渲染,则可化短为长,意蕴深远,畅快华美。

但英语则不然,因为有着句内结构必须严谨规整的硬性语法要求,所以英语每一个句子都是结构完整、含义清晰的。在这种情况下,如果硬要把句内凝练压缩、句际铺排渲染,整体讲究华美写意的朦胧汉语一句一句都勉强翻译成英语,不但得反复增补主语、人称代词、冠词、逻辑关系词等,而且句子之间含义也多有重叠,结果就会不可避免地走向臃肿累赘甚至啰唆,毫无美感可言。针对凝练、压缩的汉语句式,在译成英语时,必须是因应英语严谨规整的语法要求,补充主语、情态、冠词等成分,但对于铺排渲染的重复成分,则往往需要删去。

从内容的角度来说,汉语文章也喜欢长篇大论。以高校网页中的学校简介为例,有很多国内高校网页中的学校简介写成了大拼盘式的长篇文本,通篇只有一个"学校简介"之类的大标题,普遍篇幅较长,内容庞杂。如:

[例1] ××简介

××大学创办于1898年,初名××大学堂,是中国第一所国立综合性大学,也是当时中国最高教育行政机关。辛亥革命后,于1912年改为现名。

作为新文化运动的中心和五四运动的策源地,作为中国最早传播马克思主义和民主科学思想的发祥地,作为中国共产党最早的活动基地,××大学为民族的振兴和解放、国家的建设和发展、社会的文明和进步做出了不可替代的贡献,在中国走向现代化的进程中起到了重要的先锋作用。爱国、进步、民主、科学的传统精神和勤奋、严谨、求实、创新的学风在这里生生不息、代代相传。

1917年,著名教育家蔡元培出任××大学校长,他"循思想自由原则,取兼容并包主义",对××大学进行了卓有成效的改革,促进了思想解放和学术繁荣。陈独秀、李大钊、毛泽东以及鲁迅、胡适等一批杰出人才都曾在××大学任职或任教。

1937年卢沟桥事变后,××大学与××大学、××大学南迁长沙,共同组成长沙临时大学。不久,临时大学又迁到昆明,改称国立西南联合大学。抗日战争胜利后，××大学于1946年10月在北平复学。

中华人民共和国成立后，全国高校于1952年进行院系调整，××大学成为一所以文理基础教学和研究为主的综合性大学，为国家培养了大批人才。据不完全统计，××大学的校友和教师有400多位两院院士，中国人文社科界有影响的人士相当多也出自××大学。

改革开放以来，××大学进入了一个前所未有的大发展、大建设的新时期，并成为国家"211工程"重点建设的两所大学之一。

1998年5月4日，××大学百年校庆之际，国家主席江泽民在庆祝××大学建校一百周年大会上发表讲话，发出了"为了实现现代化，我国要有若干所具有世界先进水平的一流大学"的号召。在国家的支持下，××大学适时启动"创建世界一流大学计划"，从此，××大学的历史翻开了新的一页。

2000年4月3日，××大学与原××医科大学合并，组建了新的××大学。原××医科大学的前身是国立××医学专门学校，创建于1912年10月26日。20世纪三、四十年代，学校一度名为××大学医学院，并于1946年7月并入××大学。1952年在全国高校院系调整中，××大学医学院脱离××大学，独立为××医学院。1985年更名为××医科大学，1996年成为国家首批"211工程"重点支持的医科大学。两校合并进一步拓宽了××大学的学科结构，为促进医学与人文社会科学及理科的结合，改革医学教育奠定了基础。

近年来，在"211工程"和"985工程"的支持下，××大学进入了一个新的历史发展阶段，在学科建设、人才培养、师资队伍建设、教学科研等各方面都取得了显著成绩，为将××大学建设成为世界一流大学奠定了坚实的基础。今天的××大学已经成为国家培养高素质、创造性人才的摇篮、科学研究的前沿和知识创新的重要基地和国际交流的重要桥梁和窗口。

与之不同的是，国外一些著名高校网页的学校简介部分，大多是通过次级小标题和动态链接将整个篇章内容分门别类地组织成各层级的子文本。如"President's Welcome" "History" "Documents" "Factsheet"等，每一个子文本篇幅简短，言简意赅，甚至多有以表格形式代替语段文本的，读来一目了然。如：

［例2］**Harvard at a Glance**

**Established**

1636

**Faculty**

About 2,100 faculty members and more than 10,000 academic

appointments in affiliated teaching hospitals.

**Students**

Harvard College-About 6,700

Graduate and professional students-About 14,500

Total-About 21,000

**Living Alumni**

More than 323,000, over 271,000 in the U. S., nearly 52,000 in some 201 other countries. See the alumni website for more information.

**Nobel Laureates**

44 current and former faculty members

**Motto**

Veritas (Latin for "truth")

**Real Estate Holdings**

5,076 acres

**Library Collection**

About 17 million volumes

**Faculties, Schools, and an Institute**

Harvard University is made up of 11 principal academic units-ten faculties and the Radcliffe Institute for Advanced Study. The ten faculties oversee schools and divisions that offer courses and award academic degrees.

UNDERGRADUATE COST AND FINANCIAL AID

Families with students on scholarship pay an average of $11,500 annually toward the cost of a Harvard education. More than 60 percent of Harvard College students receive scholarship aid, and the average grant this year is $40,000.

Since 2007, Harvard's investment in financial aid has climbed by more than 70 percent, from $96.6 million to $166 million per year.

During the 2012—2013 academic year, students from families with incomes below $65,000, and with assets typical for that income level, will generally pay nothing toward the cost of attending Harvard College. Families with incomes between $65,000 and $150,000 will contribute from 0 to 10 percent of income, depending on individual circumstances. Significant financial aid also is available for families above those income ranges.

Harvard College launched a "net price calculator" into which applicants and their families can enter their financial data to estimate the net price they will be expected to pay for a year at Harvard. Please use the calculator to estimate the net cost of attendance.

The total 2011－2012 cost of attending Harvard College without financial aid is $36,305 for tuition and $52,652 for tuition, room, board and fees combined.

**University Professors**

22 "individuals of distinction"

**Harvard University President**

Drew Gilpin Faust

**University Income (Fiscal Year 2010)**

$3.7 billion

**University Expenses (Fiscal Year 2010)**

$3.7 billion

**Endowment (Fiscal Year 2011)**

$32 billion

**Naming**

The name Harvard comes from the college's first benefactor, the young minister John Harvard of Charlestown. Upon his death in 1638, he left his library and half his estate to the institution established in 1636 by vote of the Great and General Court of the Massachusetts Bay Colony.

[例3] **Yale University in brief**

| | |
|---|---|
| Undergraduate students * | 5,322 |
| Graduate and professional students * | 6,526 |
| International students * | 2,072 |
| Faculty * | 3,953 |
| Staff * | 9,183 |

| Undergraduate students * | 5,322 |
| --- | --- |
| International scholars * | 2,239 |
| Living alumni | 168,987 |
| Library holdings | 12.99 million volumes |
| Varsity athletic teams | 35 |
| Total number of buildings | 439 |
| Endowment (market value) | $19.2 billion |
| Operating budget * | $2.68 billion |

相比之下,后者的风格更加符合信息化时代的要求,能够使读者在较短时间内找到自己需要的有用信息。中文简介译成英文时,最好是采用省略与重组的方法,力求内容简化,重点突出。请看下例:

[例4]

南京,她有层出不穷的风流人物和彪炳千秋的不朽业绩。大都会特有的凝聚力,吸引了无数风云人物、仁人志士在这里角逐称雄,一逞豪彦。从孙权、谢安到洪秀全、孙中山,从祖冲之、葛洪到李时珍、郑和,从刘勰、萧统到曹雪芹、吴敬梓,从王羲之、顾恺之到徐悲鸿、傅抱石,还有陶行知、杨廷宝等等,中国历史上一批杰出的政治家、军事家、科学家、文学家、艺术家、教育家、建筑家等荟萃于此,在这块钟灵毓秀的土地上一园他们的辉煌之梦。他们是中华民族的优秀儿女。巍巍钟山、滚滚长江养育了他们,为他们提供了施展抱负的舞台,他们也以自己的雄才大略、聪明智慧为中华民族的灿烂文明增添了流光溢彩的新篇章。

Nanjing has witnessed the continuous emergence of many distinguished talents and noble heartswith their monumental achievements that shone through the ages. Attracted by her special appeal, a great number of powerful figures have stayed in or frequented this metropolis to give play to their genius and virtues. Among them are:

Statesmensuch as Sun Quan, Xie An, Hong Xiuquan and Dr. Sun Yat-sen;

*Scientists* like Zu Chongzhi, Ge Hong, Li Shizhen and Zheng He;

*Men of letters* such as Liu Xie, Xiao Tong, Cao Xueqin and Wu Jingzi;

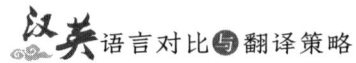

*Artists* like Wang Xizhi, Gu Kaizhi, Xu Beihong and Fu Baoshi;
*Educators* such as Tao Xingzhi;
*Architects* like Yang Tingbao
…

All these renowned historical figures used to settle on this blessed land to have their splendid dreams fulfilled. The towering Purple Mountains and billowing Yangtze River nurtured them and provided them with arenas to realize their aspirations in. By virtue of their genius, vision, and sagacity, these best and brightest sons and daughters of the nation made spectacular contributions to the resplendent Chinese civilization.

【翻译欣赏】

### 1

One cannot see too many summer sunrises on the Mississippi. They are enchanting. First, there is the eloquence of silence; for a sleep hush broods everywhere. Next, there is the haunting sense of loneliness, isolation, remoteness from the worry and bustle of the World. The dawn creeps in stealthily; the solid walls of the black forest soften to gray, and the vast stretches of the river open up and reveal themselves; the water is glass-smooth, gives off spectral little wreaths of white-mist, there is not the faintest breath of wind, not stir of leaf; the tranquility is profound and infinitely satisfying.

密西西比河夏天的日出真是百看不厌，让人神往。起先，万籁俱寂，静谧笼罩一切；接着，寂寞、孤独，还有远离尘嚣之感萦绕于怀，挥之不去。晨曦微露，郁郁葱葱，色泽深暗的树林渐渐呈现灰色，宽广的密西西比河撩起了面纱，端容渐露。江面上，水波不兴，白雾袅袅，萦纡迷离，风静而枝闲，恬谧深沉，令人心旷神怡。

### 2

峨眉山位于中国西南部的四川省，距成都156公里，走高速公路需1.5小时。主峰金顶绝壁凌空高插云霄，巍然屹立。登临其间，可西眺皑皑雪峰，东瞰莽莽平川，气势雄而景观奇，有云海、日出、佛光、圣灯四大奇观。中部群山峰峦叠嶂，含烟凝翠，飞瀑流泉，鸟语花香，草木茂而风光秀。它是我国著名的游览圣地，1996年被联合国教科文组织列入"世界自然与文化遗产"。

A: 156 kilometers (*1.5－hour drive*) away from *Sichuan's capital city Chengdu* in southwest China, stands Mt. Emei, with its summit Jingding (the Golden Top) *towering above ranges of snow-capped* mountains westward and *overlooking vast expanse of fertile prairie* eastward. The land of wonder boasts of its mountainous spectacles of clouds sea, sunrise, and *the marvellous natural phenomena* of "Buddha's Halo" and "Holy Lamp", *which are breathtaking*, as well as *enchanting* landscapes of *flowers, woods, streams, waterfalls*... As one of the best known tourist attractions, Mt Emei has been listed as a World Natural and Cultural Heritage Site by the United Nations Educational, Scientific and Cultural Organization (UNESCO).

B: 156 kilometers (1.5－hour drive) away from the Chengdu City in the Sichuan basin, southwest of China, stands the Mt. Emei with its summit Jingding (the Golden Top) towering above range upon range of rolling mountains stretching westward, all covered with snow, and in an eastward distance lying a wide expanse of flat land. It boasts of its mountainous spectacles of clouds sea, sunrise, and the marvellous natural phenomena of "Buddha's Halo" and "Holy Lamp", as well as its natural landscapes of large-green-woods, exuberant vegetation, flowers, streams, waterfalls etc. As one of the best known tourist attractions, Mt Emei has been listed as a World Natural and Cultural Heritage Site by the United Nations Educational, Scientific and Cultural Organization (UNESCO).

# 参考文献

Bassnett, M S. & Lefevere, A. Translation, History and Culture: A Source Book [M]. London: Routledge, 1992.

Cao, Xueqin & Gao E. A Dream of Red Mansions [M]. Trans. Yang Hsienyi & Gladys Yang, 1978.

Cao, Xueqin & Gao E. The Story of the Stone [M]. Trans. D. Hawkes, 1986.

Catford J C. A Linguistic Theory of Translation [M]. London: Oxford University Press, 1965.

Catford J C. Translation Shifts [A]. In A. Chesterman (ed.), Readings in Translation Theory. Finland: Oy Finn Lectura Ab, 1989.

Even-Zohar I. The Position of Translated Literature within the LiteraryPolysystem [A]. In J. S. Holmes, J. Lambert, R. van den Broeck (ed.) Literature and Translation. Leuven: ACCO, 1978.

Halliday M A K. An Introduction to Functional Grammar [M]. London: Edward Arnold Ltd, 1985.

Kelly J & Mao N K (trans.). Fortress Besieged [Z]. Beijing: Foreign Languages Teaching & Research Press, 2003

Leech G N. Style in Fiction [M]. New York: Longman, 1983.

Lefevere A. Chinese and Western Thinking on Translation [A]. In S. Bassnet. & A. Lefevere (ed.), Constructing Cultures: Essays on Literary Translation. Clevedon/ Philadelphia/ Toronto/ Sydney/ Hohannesburg: Multilingual Matters Ltd, 1998.

Newmark P. A Textbook of Translation [M]. London: Prentice Hall International (UK) Ltd, 1988.

Nida E A. Language Culture, and Translating [M]. Shanghai: Shanghai

Foreign Language Education Press,1993.

Nida E A. Science of Translation [A], in A. Chesterman (ed.), Readings in Translation Theory. Finland: Oy Finn Lectura Ab,1989.

Nord C Text Analysis in Translation [M]. Beijing: Foreign Language Teaching and Research Press,2006.

Nord C Translating as a Purposeful Activity: Functionalist Approaches Explained [M]. Manchester: St. Jerome,1997.

Simon S. Gender in Translation: Cultural Identity and the Politics of Transmission [M]. Manchester: St. Jerome,1996.

Snell-Hornby M. Translation Studies: An Integrated Approach [M]. Amsterdam: John Benjamins,1988.

Toury G. Descriptive Translation Studies and Beyond [M]. Amsterdam: John Benjamins,1995.

Venuti L. The Translator's Invisibility: A History of Translation [M]. London & New York: Routledge,1995.

Vermeer H J. Skopos and Commission in Translational Action [A]. In A. Chesterman (ed.), Readings in Translation Theory [C]. Finland: Oy Finn Lectura Ab,1989.

Wartenberg, Thomas E. 什么是艺术 [M]. 李凤栖 张云胥全文 吴瑜 译. 重庆: 重庆大学出版社,2011.2.

奥斯特(Auster. P.). 巫和雄,译. 美国短篇故事125篇 [C]. 南京:译林出版社,2004.

大卫·J. 贡克尔(David J. Gunkel). 李凤栖,等,译. 机器人权利 [M]. 北京:清华大学出版社,2020.

蔡基刚. 英汉汉英段落翻译与实践 [M]. 上海:复旦大学出版社,2001.

蔡志忠. 六祖坛经 Wisdom of the Zen Masters [M]. B Bruya,译. 北京:现代出版社,2005.

曹雪芹,高鹗. 红楼梦 [M]. 长沙:岳麓出版社,1987.

陈丹青. 纽约琐记 [M]. 桂林:广西师范大学出版社,2007.

陈宏薇. 汉英翻译基础 [M]. 上海:上海外语教育出版社,2000.

陈恕. 爱尔兰文学名篇选注 [C]. 北京:外语教学与研究出版社,2004.5.

陈文伯. 译艺:英汉汉英双向笔译 [M]. 北京:世界知识出版社,2004.

程镇球. 翻译问题探索 [M]. 北京:商务印书馆,1980.

褚东伟. 翻译家林语堂［M］. 上海：上海外语教育出版社，2012.

崔永禄. 文学翻译佳作对比赏析［M］. 天津：南开大学出版社，2001.

大卫·J. 贡克尔. 机器人权利［M］. 李凤栖，等，译. 北京：清华大学出版社，2020.

邓小平. 邓小平文选［M］. 北京：人民文学出版社，1993.

邓炎昌，刘润清. 语言与文化——英汉语言文化对比［M］. 北京：外语教学与研究出版社，1989.

董洪川. 翻译教学与研究. 第二辑［C］. 重庆：重庆出版社，2017.11.

范家材. 英文修辞［M］. 上海：复旦大学出版社，2017.

方梦之，毛忠明. 英汉-汉英应用翻译综合教程［M］. 上海：上海外语教育出版社. 2008.

傅莹. 如果西方能够倾听中国 If the West Could Listen Attentively to China. ［EB/OL］. http://m.kdnet.net/share-2191787.html.

耿静先. 商务英语翻译教程·笔译［M］. 北京：中国水利水电出版社，2010.

古今明. 英汉翻译基础［M］. 上海：上海外语教育出版社，1997.

黄杲炘. 英语青春诗选：英汉对照［M］. 武汉：湖北教育出版社，2011.6.

黄杲炘. 英语趣诗选：英汉对照［M］. 武汉：湖北教育出版社，2011.6.

胡开宝，郭鸿杰. 英汉语言对比与翻译［M］. 大连：大连理工大学出版社，2007.

胡缨. 翻译的传说：中国新女性的形成［M］. 龙瑜宬，彭珊珊，译. 南京：江苏人民出版社，2009.

贾文波. 汉英时文翻译高级教程［M］. 北京：中国对外翻译出版有限公司，2012.

姜秋霞. 实用外事英语翻译［M］. 北京：商务印书馆，2011.

江曾培. 世界华文微型小说精选. 中国卷上册［M］. 祁寿华，译. 上海：上海外语教育出版社，2007.

江曾培. 世界华文微型小说精选. 中国卷. 下册［M］. 祁寿华，译. 上海：上海外语教育出版社，2007.

金隄. 等效翻译探索［M］. 北京：中国对外翻译出版公司，1989.

金惠康. 跨文化交际翻译［M］. 北京：中国对外翻译出版有限公司，2003.

金惠康. 跨文化交际翻译续编［M］. 北京：中国对外翻译出版有限公司，2004.

金莉. 翻译特训（英语八级专业考试）［M］. 北京：机械工业出版社，2007.

贾文波. 汉英时文翻译高级教程［M］. 北京：中国对外翻译出版有限公司，2012.

拉宾德拉纳特·泰戈尔. 园丁集［M］. 冰心，译. 南京：译林出版社，2009.

李建军. 英汉应用文互译［M］. 上海：上海交通大学，2008.

李克兴. 广告翻译理论与实践［M］. 北京：北京大学出版社，2010.

李运兴. 汉英翻译教程［M］. 北京：新华出版社，2006..

连淑能. 英汉对比研究［M］. 北京：高等教育出版社，1993.

连淑能. 英汉对比研究（增订本）［M］. 北京：高等教育出版社，2010.

林茨. 中国绘画艺术［Z］. 阎新建，倪严硕，译. 北京：五洲传播出版社，2006.

林语堂. 吾国与吾民（英汉对照）［M］. 越裔汉，译. 西安：陕西师范大学出版社，2008.

林语堂. 生活的艺术（英汉对照）［M］. 越裔汉，译. 西安：陕西师范大学出版社，2008.

林语堂. 古文小品译英［M］. 北京：外语教学与研究出版社，2009.

柳岸之居士. 《背影》两译，比读有益 http://blog.sina.com.cn/s/blog_4ccc25d30100cw44.html.

刘敬国. 翻译通论［M］. 北京：外语教学与研究出版社，2011.

刘宓庆. 翻译与语言哲学［M］. 北京：中国对外翻译出版公司，2007.

刘宓庆. 新编汉英对比与翻译［M］. 北京：中国对外翻译出版公司，2006.

刘润清. 西方语言学流派［M］. 北京：外语教学与研究出版社，1995.

刘士聪. 英汉·汉英美文翻译与鉴赏：新编版［C］. 南京：译林出版社，2007.

刘英凯. 英汉语音修辞［M］. 广州：广东高等教育出版社，1998.

刘重德. 英汉语比较与翻译［M］. 青岛：青岛出版社，1998.

龙榆生. 词学十讲［M］. 南京：江苏人民出版社. 2019.7.

卢信朝. 英汉口译技能教程：口译［M］. 北京：旅游教育出版社，2009.

鲁迅. 鲁迅杂文选：英汉对照［M］. 杨宪益，戴乃迭，译. 南京：译林出版社，2009.

鲁迅. 鲁迅杂文小说选［M］. 杨宪益，戴乃迭，译. 北京：外文出版社，1956.

鲁迅. 呐喊［M］. 杨宪益，戴乃迭，译. 北京：外文出版社，2000.

吕和发，任林静，等. 全球化商务翻译［M］. 北京：外文出版社，2011.

吕和发，任林静，等. 文化创意产业翻译［M］. 北京：外文出版社，2011.

吕煦. 实用英语修辞［M］. 北京：清华大学出版社，2004.

马会娟，苗菊. 当代西方翻译理论选读［M］. 北京：外语教学与研究出版社，2009.

马爱英. 中英文化翻译：当代中国文本译释个案研究［M］. 北京：科学出版社，2006.

毛荣贵. 翻译美学［M］. 上海：上海交通大学出版社，2005.

毛荣贵. 美学翻译——指导翻译实践的一盏明灯［A］//胡庚申，主编. 翻译与跨文化交流：转向与拓展. 上海：上海外语教育出版社，2007.

毛荣贵，廖晟. 译朝译夕［M］. 北京：中国对外翻译出版公司，2005.

梅德明. 英语口译实务·三级［M］. 北京：外文出版社，2009.

繆崇群. 花床［J］. 高巍，刘士聪，译. 中国翻译，2004，(5)：93—95.

庞秉钧，闵福德，高尔登. 中国现代诗选：汉英对照［C］. 北京：中国对外翻译出版公司，2008.

培根（Bacon F.）. Of Studies 谈读书［A］//王佐良，译. 朱明炬，谢少华，吴万伟 编著. 英汉名篇名译. 南京：译林出版社，2007.

倪家耀. 恍悟于比较阅读之时——从 parataxis 到 hypotaxis［J］. 科技英语学习，2001（4）.

钱冠连. 美学语言学［M］. 深圳：海天出版社，1993.

钱钟书. 围城［M］. 北京：人民文学出版社，2001.

乔丹（Jordan, S. B.）. That Lean and Hungry Look 瘦人瘦相［A］//刘士聪 马会娟，译. 刘士聪. 英汉·汉英美文翻译与鉴赏：新编版. 南京：译林出版社，2007.

乔龙宝. 英语散文佳作赏析与翻译［M］. 上海：上海社会科学院出版社，2006.

裘小龙. "轻松英语"唐宋诗词 100 首［M］. 上海：华东师范大学出版社，2005.

任月花. 商务翻译概论［M］. 广州：暨南大学出版社，2010.

邵志洪. 汉英对比翻译导论［M］. 上海：华东理工大学出版社，2005.

沈从文. 湘西散记：英汉对照［M］. 杨宪益，戴乃迭，译. 南京：译林出版社，2009.

沈少华. 英汉趣味修辞格［M］. 北京：语文出版社，1999.

申小龙. 汉语与中国文化［M］. 上海：复旦大学出版社，2003.

史忠义，辜正坤. 国际翻译学新探［M］. 天津：百花文艺出版社，2006.

思果. 译道探微［M］. 北京：中国对外翻译出版公司，2001.

司显柱，曾剑平. 汉译英教程［M］. 上海：东华大学出版社，2006.

隋荣谊. 汉英翻译新教程［M］. 北京：中国电力出版社，2004.

孙致礼. 中国的文学翻译：从归化趋向异化［J］. 中国翻译，2000，（1）：40-44.

谭载喜. 西方翻译简史：增订版［M］. 北京：商务印书馆，2004.

王秉钦. 20世纪中国翻译思想史［M］. 天津：南开大学出版社，2004.

王国维. 人间词话图解祥析［M］//鸿恩，主编. 北京：北京联合出版公司，2014.10（2017.4重印）

王宏. 翻译研究新视角［M］. 上海：上海外语教育出版社，2011.

王辉. 英文合同解读：语用、条款及文本范例［M］. 北京：法律出版社，2007.10.

王希杰. 修辞学导论［M］. 杭州：浙江教育出版社，2000.

王雪. 红楼梦两种译文之比较赏析［A］//崔永禄，主编. 文学翻译佳作对比赏析. 南开大学出版社，2001.

王燕. 英语口译实务·二级［M］. 北京：外文出版社，2009.

王佐良. 翻译：思考与试笔［M］. 北京：外语教学与研究出版社，1989.

王佐良，丁往道. 英语文体学引论［M］. 北京：外语教学与研究出版社，1990.

翁显良. 意态由来画不成？［M］. 北京：中国对外翻译出版公司，1983.

吴云编著. 英语会展口译［M］. 上海：华东理工大学出版社，2008.1.

肖人夫，舒天楚. 中文译著的喜与忧［A］//光明网-《光明日报》，2021-10-24.

谢天振. 当代外国翻译理论导读［M］. 天津：南开大学出版社，2008.

徐莉娜. 委婉语翻译的语用和语篇策略［J］. 中国翻译，2003，（6）：15-19.

徐小贞，赵敏懿，刘建珠. 商务现场口译［Z］. 北京：外语教学与研究出版社，2006.

徐小贞，赵敏懿，刘建珠. 商务现场口译：教师用书［Z］. 北京：外语教学与研究出版社，2007.

徐燕谋，等. 现代英国名家文选［C］. 上海：复旦大学出版社，2006.

许渊冲. 中国学派的文学翻译理论［A］//胡庚申，主编. 翻译与跨文化交流：转向与拓展. 上海：上海外语教育出版社，2007.

许渊冲. 精选宋词与宋画［M］. 北京：五洲传播出版社，2005.

许渊冲. 道德经与神仙画［M］. 北京：五洲传播出版社，2005.

许渊冲. 精选诗经与诗意画［M］. 北京：五洲传播出版社，2005.

尹燕. 英文导游词的创作与讲解［M］. 北京：中国旅游出版社，2007.

余光中. 余光中谈翻译［M］. 北京：中国对外翻译出版公司，2000.

约翰逊（Johnson S.）. Samuel Johnson to Lord Chesterfield 约翰逊致切斯菲尔德伯爵书［A］//黄继忠，译. 朱明炬，谢少华，吴万伟. 英汉名篇名译. 南京：译林出版社，2007.

张梦井. 比较翻译概论［M］. 武汉：湖北教育出版社，2007.

张南峰. 中西译学批评［M］. 北京：清华大学出版社，2004.10.

张培基. 英译中国现代散文选：汉、英对照［M］. 上海：上海外语教育出版社，1999.

张培基. 英译中国现代散文选. 第2辑［M］. 上海：上海外语教育出版社，2003.

张培基. 英译中国现代散文选（三）［M］. 上海：上海外语教育出版社，2007.

张云. 英汉翻译基础［M］. 成都：四川大学出版社，2019.

赵军峰. 商务口译［M］. 北京：外语教学与研究出版社，2009.

《中国翻译》编辑部. "韩素音青年翻译奖"竞赛作品与评析：英汉对照［M］. 柯平，译. 南京：译林出版社，2008.

赵丽宏. 英译中国当代美文选［M］. 徐英才，译. 上海：上海外语教育出版社，2013.

仲伟合. 英语口语教程·上［M］. 北京：高等教育出版社，2006.

仲伟合. 英语口语教程·下［M］. 北京：高等教育出版社，2006.

朱纯深. 从文体学和话语分析看《荷塘月色》的美学意义［M］. 名作欣赏，1994，（4）：77-82.

朱纯深. 翻译探微：语言·文本·诗学［M］. 南京：译林出版社，2008.

朱纯深. 古意新声：品赏本［M］. 武汉：湖北教育出版社，2002.

朱巧莲. 接待与洽谈口译［M］. 北京：人民教育出版社，2009.

朱曼华. 中国历代诗词翻译集锦：英汉对照［M］. 北京：商务印书馆国际有限公司，2013.

朱梅萍. 商务英语口译［M］. 北京：外语教学与研究出版社，2009.

朱明炬，谢少华，吴万伟. 英汉名篇名译［Z］. 南京：译林出版社，2007.